# Lewd Ghosts

By the same author:

*The Secrets of Aleister Crowley*
*The Riddles of Aleister Crowley*
*The Wrath of Aleister Crowley*

Published by Diamond Books

# Lewd Ghosts

## Magic, Sex and Horror

by

**Amado Crowley**

*Diamond Books*

Published by Diamond Books, the imprint of Transym
Computer Services Ltd, Morrison Stoneham, Prudential
Buildings, Epsom Road, Guildford

First edition 1994

Any and all correspondence intended for the author
should be directed to: BM-Box 77, London, WC1N 3XX,
without the author's name. Please include an
International Reply Paid Coupon, but please note
that the publisher cannot guarantee a reply.

Printed and bound in Great Britain by
Butler & Tanner Ltd, Frome and London

To Manu, a fallen sparrow, with love.

I'll be there soon, my lad, and we'll
open a circus in Heaven's High Street.

# Contents

# Foreword

*A Sadist is a person who strips you naked,*
*shackles you to the bed, oils his whip, and*
*then settles down to football on the telly.*

This is not a nice book! I have to admit that parts of it get quite nasty. I don't apologise because I have my reasons.

For one thing: people often resemble those very old houses, with attics that are locked, and cellars that have been boarded up. It can be quite a jolt when someone opens a door or a window, and lets in some light and fresh air. It takes a shock like that to realise that there are corners which have never been swept. There is a darkness in those corners. And in the darkness ... something moves...

For another thing: there are the matters of sex and magic. Both of these are very interesting. Most people are secretly fascinated by them. Yet both – together or separately – are very touchy topics in Britain. Indeed, they are so extremely controversial, you might say they are almost taboo.

If ever we do talk about these subjects – horror, sex and magic – we do it in damp, dusty, distant voices as if we were paddling in the sewers. God forbid that you should lick your lips or let your eyes twinkle. You are not supposed to have any interest! Why is that, I wonder? Horror is a product of our own mind. Sex is something we all do. And magic? Well, even the ordination of women is magic, though I don't know if it's good or bad.

Oh, while I remember: please do excuse the language that I use from time to time. If it seems crude or vulgar, that's because of the characters I am writing about – and the subject matter. I mean to say, this is not a book about icing cakes! And I do know all about these things. As my own father told me: breeding still counts.

I get tons of letters. You wouldn't believe it. A person from Japan asked "Please to send one virility for savage competing in Korea". That was weird enough. But then a group of Christians in the USA said "We are praying for your death and cordially invite you to join the good work"! I wrote back and said I was praying for theirs. But I also get some sad, wild and pathetic messages too. Like the boy aged fifteen who used the Enochian alphabet of Doctor John Dee – in order to say nothing in particular. It was the alphabet that thrilled him. He wanted to become a code.

Before you begin, I want to tell you that every single story is based on a real event. Some may be funny. Others may be appalling. But either I was involved with them or else I witnessed them. To be sure, I do alter names, and I switch locations. I also take a little bit of artistic license. But I have only varied the tone. I have simply made them suitable for a book. I twang the strings that you might have missed.

Science once included alchemy and astrology. Today it denies that magic exists. But to be fair, the occult world is just as daft at times – just as deaf and narrow-minded when it suits its purpose. There is nastiness all around us. Have you noticed? While we play games and win our quarrels, that nastiness is gaining ground. But the strange thing is that state agencies and government departments use magic, just as they have used murder, sex and scandal.

Can you guess which countries conduct research into the strategic value of magic? Dare you mention a number? Not one of them would waste a penny if it wasn't worth it – and the budgets run into millions. Oh you will pooh-pooh my words. "Just a story-teller," you'll say. But no, I'm not. I'm also a magician. Check out my name again.

There are two faces to magic. They are called Black and White, and they both work, but in different ways. So as not to tempt you into making foolish experiments, none of the magical recipes in this book are either accurate or complete. I hope you will enjoy reading it – although, perhaps, enjoy is not quite the right word. Let's say that I wish you find something of value. If you like it, write and tell me. I can always write more.

Amado Crowley,
Geneva, 21st July 1994

# Punch and Judy

*Whoever would become as a child*
*Must overcome his youth too.*

Nietzsche

*1.*

Men in showers do behave strangely!

I'm not talking about the weather in England in April. I'm talking about that method of washing one's body when you stand under a spray of warm water that comes out of a perforated head made of metal. If you're English it's base metal. If you are a Sheik it's pure gold. If you live in the Vatican it's made of ivory and shaped like an angel's trumpet. That's another of those little jokes by Michaelangelo, who took a bath with anybody!

With so much therapy based on crystals and magnets, I'm surprised that no one sells copper sprays which give small electric shocks. Before you leap for your blow-lamp, let me add that I have given the idea to a friend who has already patented it. The secret of such an apparatus is: how not to parboil your clients! One wouldn't want too many of them going early to their Maker.

Let us return to men. Under the showers, you'd think they'd be quite blasé. No one has anything the others have not got. Have you ever seen one with two, if you follow my drift? Nevertheless, this is where the great error creeps in. My point is that the things they have got are actually rather curious.

As you have probably noticed, these things are external

and, like a dart-board, they have been put very close to the bulls-eye. Moreover, they are not "as like as two peas in a pod". Far from being clones, or spitting images of each other, they differ a great deal. I am thinking of such physical facts as length, girth, and the small sack of spare parts that is slung underneath. We may all have minds as pure as driven snow. But one can't help noticing – especially at the Olympics – that when male athletes stop, parts of them keep moving. They also bring down the cross-bar of the pole-vault. I mean to say: it's as if Father Christmas had a reindeer between his legs with a lit-up, blinking red-nose. No matter what you find in your Christmas stocking, these doodads are sure to draw the eye.

Women, I'm told, are not all that taken by the sight of a man's penis. It puts them in mind of stuff they'd find in a kitchen, like squid or sardines. Their creative impulse is probably to sprinkle it with grated cheese. But then, in a sexual sense, women have much further to go before they come, if I may so put it. Hence, they are much less interested in the way that the pump works, than in the octane level of the petrol.

But men themselves are highly intrigued by their own, and anyone else's penis. Don't forget that they have been holding on to it for dear life, ever since they were very small boys. They all remember what happens to party balloons when you let go of the rubbery neck. It is a perpetual nightmare that it, with the rest of their body following, might take off like a demented zeppelin and go zooming over the rainbow.

It also looks rather like the strap for a passenger standing in a bus or an underground train. They then get it confused with the notice attached to a different handle nearby which explains what the penalty will be for pulling it without appropriate reason. For these, and many other reasons, men are quite nervous and sensitive about their penis. Some of them try never to look at it – especially when they pee.

"Why the hell should we?" they might ask. "We know where it is!" And, in all honesty, one has to admit that one's trouser flies can be opened without the need for a bar-code or a credit card! Nevertheless, the fact remains that there are two types of men: those who stare at it, and those who wet their shoes.

But neither kind seems very much to like what he sees. It is normally viewed from above ... unless one is in the habit of doing handstands ... and it has crossed every man's mind at one time or another that the blessed thing does seem to be possessed of a perverse intelligence all its own. It rarely does what you want it to do – until it's too late and you've stopped wanting it to do it. Then, at the precise moment when it would be a disaster, it winks at you and does it.

If you've had a couple of pints, it may even turn its head round as if searching for something to hiss at. That is quite unnerving!

We may not care to admit it, least of all to ourselves, but these things do indeed attract our attention ... other men's cocks, that is. We don't let on, of course, and we do it as casually as a butterfly collector. But when the opportunity presents itself, we do tend to cast quick, furtive glances in the other chap's direction.

2.

This may not be denied. Scholars have filmed these things as part of their research. Each of us reacts very strongly indeed. Even if we ignore it, we do so only by using colossal will-power. If we pretend that there are no sails on the horizon and we refuse to glance south-south-east – then we are more aware of the wind direction than most.

Men's penises send out signals, rather like those one-clawed crabs that wave at each other on tropical beaches. How we react depends on the strength of that signal, how well we interpret it, and the state of our own receptors. It is no good plugging yourself in to the back of a television set. You might get Big Ben. All that's required is a casual glance in a public lavatory, or a careless towel-flick after a rugby game. When men watch an obscene film, they inspect the studs and not just the girls.

In fact, we do this so often that one or two of us begin to get worried that we might just be, er, turning pink around the edges. It is one of those neuroses that nibbles at your mind when you're about the age of sixteen. But no, it's not that. We have no longing to touch one or play with one. We're having quite enough trouble with our own! The explanation is that each of us wants to know whether he is par for the course. Are the others like us? Are we like them?

I hope it's clear that I do not go along with the opinions so dear to the gay liberation movement, that every man and woman is a latent homosexual at heart. That's not what Aleister Crowley meant when he proclaimed that every man and woman was a star. Neither would he allow the feminist movement to state that God is a woman.

Since this sort of statement cannot be proved, it follows that it cannot be disproved either. Therefore, the argument is won by the side which shouts the loudest. Votes are gained purely by propaganda, which is very cunning when you think about it. But let me put the record straight. In the history of mankind, there have been far more female gods than male ones – not that it made a great deal of difference to anything. Neither does what we say, or what we force a church to declare, change the Divine Nature one whit.

It was all to do with the way we gained our food, our main source of life. While it was arable crops, then God was a Mother of Fertility. When it was herds of food animals, then God was a Golden Bull. When it was slavery, then God expressed the Triumph of War and the Glory of the Nation. In this industrial age, where food comes in tins, boxes and aluminium trays, God has become a bottle of tomato sauce. But it does nothing to help the cosmic plan to argue whether He, She or It has a screw-top or a cork.

Another point: as far as one can judge, there has been the same percentage of deviance in the population throughout history. They do not reproduce themselves, you know! But whatever causes such a percentage to exist, it seems to be a fairly constant rule or a natural law. There are notably fewer (per thousand men) in the country than in towns. There are fewer still among primitive tribes than in sprawling suburbs. What can be the secret factor then? Well, not hormones, I'm afraid. We can change the level of hormones ourselves! No, the one thing that does differ between all these possible locations is the level of stress. Mental and emotional stress, plus all the ills that follow on from that.

Now I agree that when you have an 'itch', it's nice if someone will scratch it for you. But it does not therefore follow that all your itches have always to be scratched by the same person, or the same sex. Remember when you had chicken pox? Try not to scratch, they said. You'll spread the germs, they said, and you'll blemish your face. Myself, I was curious about what caused the itch, and was scratching the only relief? My dad said that any fool could scratch. "But who has the talent to find a cure?"

Oh yes, a man's love can be a tender and heroic thing. And a man's body can ward off fear when the night is dark, cold and full of shadows. There is even a form of magical love between men, but it has nothing to do with preference, lack of choice, or fear of the other sex. Pardon me, my brothers and sisters who are gay. I do not hate you. I think you're all enchanted.

So to come back to the penis, if you'll pardon the pun.

### 3.

A penis is rather a strange object, when you think about it. Put yourself in the shoes of a visitor from another planet and imagine that you are exploring the city for the first time. If you stumbled on a penis in the street – dropped by a careless football rowdy one Saturday night – you'd have a hard time guessing what its purpose might be. Your first thought might be that it was a sort of deformed nose. Then you ask if it isn't a baby hedgehog, still blind and without pricks. After that you wonder if it might be poison put down to exterminate rats.

If you will just apply your minds to the problem, the way it works is not immediately obvious to the eye. God knows, it takes the owner himself about twelve years to find out what it's for. Even then, he is never sure that he got it right.

I know one lad who made love upside down. He couldn't remember why or how it began. Then I found out he was a fan of the Tarot cards, and was heavily impressed by Number Twelve, otherwise known as 'The Hanging Man'! He was also out of work a lot of the time, because he kept on dislocating his shoulder. I told him to try his luck in Hamburg, where they have some very inventive cabaret shows. One of his problems was that the male penis is not an extremely aesthetic thing. This is a foolish state of affairs, with one or two quite lunatic issues running off at a tangent.

In fact, women took little delight in having his feet in their face, especially as he rarely cut his toe-nails.

"He walked all over me," is how they actually put it.

With all the anguish and heartache that causes, and is caused by, homosexual love, you'd imagine straight love would be easy as falling off a log. But it isn't. Not at all. About half the couples in the world are not at all happy with each other, and the other half are blithely ignorant of what it is they are missing. I do not include you, of course. Anyone who reads this book must be different, and I am quite willing to accept that life, for you, is total, one hundred per cent ecstasy. Except ...

I shall keep my first story short. I will tell it as briefly as the notes I made when I was consulted. I think you'll find it of some interest. Besides which, it will help to get you used to some of the worse language that I shall have to use later on.

A girl called Alice was worried about men's bodies. That is precisely the way that she put it. Then of course she tried to explain that she didn't quite mean the whole of his body. His head was all right. So were his feet, as a matter of fact. But there were other parts midway which made her convulse with yowls.

In my line of work, psychology, one has to get used to 'indirect references'. When people said they had something wrong "round the back", it was no good looking in their dustbin. They probably had piles. You must be alert to the fact that certain words are taboo for the English. When they have to refer to their genitals or urinary tract, they make allusion to "the water works". Don't reach for your monkey wrench. In France it's even worse. They call the penis either "a pipe" or "a tap", and refer to the testicles as "the family jewels". It makes for a very interesting life on the buses during the morning rush-hour.

But even in English, there are many euphemisms – that is to say, there are nicer, less ominous ways of naming names without actually giving tongue to them. For instance, that part of a man which attests that he is not a woman! We have a wide selection of terms: John Thomas, Chapel hat-peg, Willy, Old Man, Cock, Chopper, Hampton and even Thingy. But Alice couldn't bring herself to use any of them. She avoided all reference to it, as if the mere thought were enough to turn her stomach. But considering what she suffered from, one could not dodge the topic for ever.

She rejected outright the plain technical term, penis. It was just the same as regards tool, instrument, or even private parts. Finally, I got her to agree on "organ". Even this is quite ambiguous! With a sense of humour like mine, you imagine something in a cathedral and dear, old Handel thrashing out "See, the conquering Hero comes"! But my hands were tied, so to speak. She came to me for therapy and I was obliged to humour her.


## 4.


It was out of the question that I should quarrel with her on the weakness of her vocabulary.

"The world," she asserted vehemently, "is full of them!"

I have to admit that this did indeed sound like a line from one of those older science fiction films: 'The Invaders' maybe, or 'It Came from Outer Space'. Thinking that this could be of some relevance, I opened my mouth to ask her if she had ever seen one. But before I could speak, she took in a deep, quavering breath.

"Every man has got one, you know." And she shuddered.

This came as no great news to me. As a matter of fact, I felt like expanding on her point. Any person who lacked one would not have been a man. But then, I recalled the case of a farmer who slid off the seat of his combine harvester! Had the fools but thought of looking for it, something might have been done. But it had taken them twenty minutes to stop laughing!

Alice started to tremble. Having now mentioned men's things, she was no doubt picturing them, in regiments, marching across Europe in serried ranks, and all looking for her. She broke out in a cold sweat. So did I. She was getting very close to panic. So I changed tack. I begged her pardon for even being a man. At the same time I pointed out carefully that while working in the clinic, I wasn't a man at all.

"Oh," she said with faultless logic, "but you've got a long white coat on."

Which indeed I had, though I didn't quite see how this

could possibly neuter me. My confusion must have shown on my face. "There, there," she soothed, patting my hand in a motherly manner. "Just don't take it off, that's all."

I swear that I saw a flash of murder in her eyes.

I didn't quite know how to take this. I wasn't sure why, but my dignity seemed to fall. Should I be offended that she did not see me as other men? Or should I be insulted by the fact that, without my white coat, I too represented the same, general type of fearful menace? I'd had enough of this tiptoeing around.

"Would you prefer it if all penises were covered up?" I asked rather sharply.

"I'd like it much better if they were all chopped off!" she hissed viciously.

I was so stunned that my hand jerked. My pencil made a zigzag electric symbol all across my notes. I had the strong suspicion that perhaps I should have frisked her for manicure scissors.

"Can I have cocaine?" I said as I tried to lighten the mood.

I could tell by the way she stared at me that she had no sense of humour. "You'll have to grin and bear it," she snarled. "You'll have to take it like a man."

A touch of humour is often the best instrument in a doctor's bag. "I think I'll keep it," I quipped. "I've grown attached to it over the years."

5.

"Tell me, Alice: have you ever been in love?"

She swallowed as her eyes went misty and wistful. "There are boys that I've liked."

Good. That meant she was probably not a Lesbian. "Were these boys effeminate?" I pursued.

"Not at all!"

"Then what did they have in common?"

"They were nice."

"But what was it that made them nice?"

Her eyes wandered. She thought back. "They were so gentle."

"They made love to you gently?"

"Oh no!" she was outraged. "They never made love to me. None of them. They were all – so shy."

I nodded kindly to lend her a bit of support. "Not really men at all," I said with sympathy.

She wept a great deal during our sessions. I didn't let that distract me. My attitude is that if there is weeping to be done then we are getting close to the source of the pain.

What are we doing with all this talk anyway? We're really asking the same question over and over again: does this hurt, does that hurt, is this painful, and so on. She'd be healthy and happy if she could. She doesn't want to be sick. She has only come to you because she can't find a way of handling it alone.

Then why does she weep? These are tears she bottled up a long time ago. This is an anguish she has hidden in a cold, dark room like a pantry. We are piercing balloons. We are opening cages. We are letting out pent-up emotions to wing away free. So she weeps out of anxiety. She weeps because she feels as if her back is up against a solid, brick wall.

"I don't want them touching me," she moaned.

"A stylist for your hair?" I said.

"I cut my own hair," she snapped. It looked like it too. It was the most obvious thing about her. Her tangled locks looked like a sheep that has been worried to death by dogs.

"But could you love a boy who is handsome?" I asked.

"Handsome is as handsome does", she flung out, parrot fashion. Ah, I thought, catching a hint of her code.

"Would you like him to be a eunuch – a male who cannot 'do'?"

She shuddered. "That's loathsome."

"Then you'd love a handsome boy who could – but does not try – to do?"

"I want to be loved," she sobbed.

"And isn't sex the language of love?"

Her face looked harrowed and her eyes filled with horror. "No," she groaned. "That's using. That's being a sandbag while they practice killing." She banged the chair arms and twisted her head from side to side violently. "And I can't do it. I can't do it. I've tried, oh God I've tried, but it's no use ... I can't do it."

She buried her face in her hands and shook with great

sobs that burst like bubbles rising from the depths of her being. "Can't you understand?" she howled.

I understood perfectly. She was 'frigid'.

This is a badly understood term. People bandy it about with no thought, and they have their own, inaccurate, idea of what it signifies. Let's put it this way, frigidity is to a woman, what impotence is to a man! Ply him with sodium pentothal, and the average man will admit that there have been moments when things have gone off the boil without warning. We sit in a darkened cinema and yearn for sex, but nothing much will happen if the projector won't project. Well, in just the same way, a woman's love and yearning to be embraced can be blocked by hidden fears. She runs away.

In a very severe case, she may suffer from vaginismus. This is so terrifying that men are helpless and can therefore only joke about it to relieve their own anguish. The woman's vagina closes tight – very tight. So much so that the tissues become as hard as iron and no man could penetrate her.

And the agony is that this is not how she herself wishes to behave. She can adore someone, worship the ground they walk on, and yearn to surrender herself in love to him. But before any intimacy can occur, she hears a silent alarm. The tissues of her body lose their softness and change into armour.

I have seen husbands lose their reason. I have seen women hack at themselves with knives and knitting needles. And the cause is almost always the same kind of disgust at oneself.

## 6.

Her story was fairly typical when at last she decided to tell it. Her father had made frequent sexual use of her since an early age. Worse still, he had wickedly urged her three brothers to do the same. It had stopped when she grew up and ran away from home. The police brought her back, of course, and everyone had acted as if they were one, big, loving family.

No, they didn't touch her after that but she had needed to talk, to work things out. If she asked, they pretended not to remember anything at all about it. Her brothers knew nothing. Her father knew nothing. There was a conspiracy of silence throughout the entire house and no one ever mentioned those things again. It was as if they had all forgotten.

She tried to talk to her mother, but her mother didn't want to hear. She seemed terrified of her words. When she lost control and screamed things at her, her mother said it was all a tainted dream that touched girls of her age. Then the poor woman would lock herself in the lavatory and come out a quarter of an hour later with eyes like bleeding rubies.

No one in the family could face up to the truth. Not even she. She wore mannish gear or things she bought at a market. She never used any make-up at all and went about life looking like a scarecrow. She talked like a man and used a hostile tone of voice. She was prickly too, dangerous, like a no-man's land threaded with barbed wire, scattered with booby traps and littered with decaying, severed hands.

At college, the others took her for some sort of radical or an extremist who was trying to air her political views. That amused her and she laughed at them. She laughed too at the comrades who came her way. She squeezed a drop of revenge out of them by humbling them in the extreme. She did not realise that she was also slaying their lives, their manhood, and their chances of ever being happy.

It is easily done, you know – destroying a chap's manhood. Lots of girls do it out of pure bad temper. They pay for it though, later. We all pay for the harm we do.

During my military service, when I was nineteen, I remember how the lads in the barracks were in a state of perpetual rut. Not far away was the special building for the WAAFs, as they were called then, the women who joined the Royal Air Force. The randiest lad in the whole barracks did everything he could to try and spy on them. He rigged up periscopes, telescopes and a hundred other gadgets and was forever clawing at his crotch.

One evening, just for a raucous joke, some other lads trussed him up naked and deposited him in the entrance lobby of the girls' barracks. They thought this was an hilarious escapade, and one that might make his wildest dreams come true. When they let him come back before reveille, he was sullen and hostile. At midday he hanged himself in one of aeroplane hangars. Nobody in the WAAF contingent ever smiled again. There were haunted looks in our barracks too.

The average person is so abysmally ignorant about these things. I don't just mean the study of the mind. In some respects, the world might be a better place if psychology had never been invented. No, I'm talking about a basic understanding of the essentials of 'being' and 'happiness'. I doubt if one in a hundred people has any insight. Yet each of them believes that he – only he – is the expert.

"It's my mind," they'll say. "They're my emotions!"

They don't have that attitude when it comes to cancer. They don't demand the right to perform their own kidney transplant. But it's the biggest bar to spiritual peace and earthly happiness in modern society. The pride and the reluctance. The joy and the shame. The conflict between Nature (as God made it) and a supreme control of self (as God's servants preach it).

It was Alice's problem too. If she went to a priest and confessed all, he would tell her to forgive her father and brothers ... which would be right. But he'd tell her to pray, trust in God, and be remade a virgin all over again. I can see how that might give her temporary peace. But it is not a way that actually heals and makes whole again. How could absolution make her the woman that she needed to be? She was not a criminal but the victim of crime. She needed no pardon, but a miracle.

I found her that miracle. His name was Ralph.

7.

He was a perfectly ordinary person. He was not very tall. He was very thin. If he'd been an athlete, he was the kind who never heard the starting gun. He was a bachelor, and that little bit scruffy that gives the show away. As with other lads caught in the same trap, he had gradually developed some interests which were of a solitary kind. He was a keen rambler, for example, and he liked nothing better than trekking across vast, forsaken spaces and being alone with nature. He was very keen on ancient monuments and the sites of historic events. He also read books, listened to records and – very common this – he worked abnormal hours, making a go of the small firm that he owned.

It is always a very telling point when boys, seemingly happy, avoid the company of other people. You have to look for it because, as you can guess, they will do their best to hide it. Tell them you're an expert on behaviour and see how quickly they develop measles or 'flu as they scatter to all points of the compass.

Whilst being quite normal, Ralph's sexuality was not very high on his list of life's priorities. This is another key symptom. Unless he's lost a testicle, or they have never descended, it is quite unnatural for a healthy man not to have a keen interest in sex. Even when a man is a seminarist – i.e., studying to be a priest – he may well take a vow of chastity, but he ought to be a normal man.

Did you know this was once regarded as a vital matter to the Catholic church? So much so, they had a special chair, with a hole cut in the seat. When a pope was chosen, he had to sit in a stoic posture while someone 'checked his trim'. It is still part of Canon Law that a eunuch may not become Supreme Pontiff, nor a bastard become a cardinal.

Ralph was not a Catholic though, and so he had no ambitions ever to become a pope or a cardinal. It was just that, for him, sex did not loom very large. There are people like that. They are quite rare. When there's no one to love or be loved by, they don't deflect their energies into lust. He just wasn't all that worried.

I put it to him that Alice was a pretty girl. I pointed out that she seemed not to have any suitor. I also hinted, without actually lying, that it seemed to me she looked in his direction quite often. I said exactly the same things to her as regards Ralph, and I left the stew to simmer for a couple of weeks.

Nature being the way that Nature is, and me knowing as much as I do about magic, they did actually fall in love. But they came to me, this time as a couple, to discuss "their problem". I was quite pleased at the new development. The fact that is was now "their" problem, rather then "hers", showed a radical change in her basic attitude. At least, with Ralph, she was not wreaking revenge.

As far as Alice was concerned though, matters were now a hundred times worse. She was in love with this lad – but still she couldn't have sex with him.

"I play with him," she sighed.

"She plays with me," he whined.

"I can even bring him off," she added.

"Yes, she brings me off."

But.." she finished lamely.

"You know!" he limped.

The time for delicacy and discretion was gone. "Do you want him to enter you?" I asked her bluntly. "Do you long for insertion?"

She shivered as she answered, "Oh, yes."

"And you?" I asked, turning to Ralph, "What does it feel like when you're up against this wall of steel?"

"Like she's rejecting me," he whispered.

They held each other and both of them cried. I heard the gods telling me what to do.

First, I prepared a bottle of magic oil. Second, I wrote something down on a piece of paper. "Here I said," giving him the bottle. "Once every night you must massage her gently with this oil." I turned to Alice and I gave her the piece of paper. "This is the ancient design that you must draw."

Ralph looked at the paper and went pale. It was a face. But it had to be painted on the head of his penis. The tiny opening of his urethra became a smiling mouth, the corona of his gland became a kind of curly wig, and there were grinning eyes and a clownish nose.

"I hope to God you're not suggesting that she buys a tattoo outfit," he gasped.

"Just theatrical make-up or a small kit you can buy at a toy-shop. When it's finished," I said to her, "you must tie a ribbon round its neck and make a big, floppy bow. It will be your magical dolly."

I doubt if anyone has gone on their honeymoon in quite this frame of mind.

8.

They didn't come back for two months. I began to wonder if I hadn't been a bit too inventive and sickened their young hearts. But no. It was Ralph who called round first.

"It worked," he said simply. "She played with it, cuddled

it, and kissed it, you know, a long, long time. I tried like hell not to let it happen but she was determined. She swallowed it all and licked it clean."

He suspected that the memory was arousing him again because he got that certain look in his eyes. "And...?" I encouraged.

"The oil is working too. She's relaxing. She's much softer." He blushed slightly and grinned. "I can even get my finger in."

I asked him to send Alice round and she was a changed girl. She was... serene.

"Are you still a wee bit frightened of it?" I asked.

"No," she smiled generously. "I'm getting very fond of it."

"You must make him happier still, my dear. It's all very well to have a tea-party on the lawn – but isn't it time that you invited him in to dinner?"

I called Ralph back into the room. While she watched and he clenched his teeth, I sketched a face on the head of his penis, using a felt-tip pen. I spoke a magic formula and made a few mystic passes over it. She was quite fascinated by this charm. He was more irked about it being indelible ink.

But they were not aware that I was performing an ancient ritual which, in French, has become corrupted, via Latin, into the word 'sortilege'. Today, that can be roughly translated as 'throwing lots' or 'divining the future'. But a long time ago, it used to mean 'going out of your own free will'. But what's in a name? What does the title matter? All I really did was call on The Guardians of Gateways and ask them for a favour.

It was done by Moses on the shores of the Red Sea, it is said. It was also done by Ali Baba to open a cave of treasure. "Open sesame," is what he is supposed to have said. Quite probably, every English child knows this magic phrase very well indeed. It features in so many books of fairy tales or other children's stories. But very few people indeed have ever realised that this small phrase is a survival from former times. What is actually being said is: "Oh Ptah, Seth, Amon!", which is the start of a prayer that was once used in Ancient Egypt to open the first door to the Underworld.

Well, my little bit of magic did the trick. It touched the spot. Or, if you like, it hit the nail right on the head. Science

15

must see it as pure chance or else the result must be ascribed to something else. But I was not doing an experiment. I wasn't trying to prove anything to anybody. I simply wanted to help two young people find their happiness. In that sense then, I felt like shouting my mother's favourite cry of triumph: "Bingo!"

Their troubles have been blown away a long time ago now. They are happily married. They have a growing family. They quarrel every Monday, and spend the other six days of the week making up. They are normal. They are natural. They are what they should be.

They gave me back the rest of the oil and the piece of ribbon. But they have always kept that quiet, golden glow in their hearts because – it is theirs. What I mean to say is: they made that.

---

*We were, fair queen,*
*Two lads that thought there was no more behind*
*But such a day tomorrow as today,*
*And to be boy eternal.*

Two Gentlemen of Verona

# Refugee

*Ex opere operato: this is a term used in Roman Catholic theology and it expresses the belief that all sacraments work if the proper conditions are met. God's grace does not depend on anyone's attitudes or opinions.*

## 1.

The boy was sixteen years old. He had fawn-like eyes that looked at her so gently. She thought he was daring her. Enticing her. Boys of that age can behave like winsome girls at times. You wonder whether they are quite as innocent as they seem, or if they know something. Not that it makes any difference. You believe what you want to believe. He is as pure as a lamb. He is as wanton as a billy goat. When they are as young as that, you play whichever game you want.

She put her hand on his knees. She could not be sure but the corners of his mouth may have twitched with a faint smile ... or was he biting back his horror? "Do you like that?" she asked, sliding her hand up and down the full length of the muscle.

"I don't mind," he answered flatly.

She could have dug her nails into his flesh and raked him into bleeding mush. It made her angry if they began to play with her. But there was no other sign of his being difficult. She was being too sensitive again. She was often like that, especially when she had found a young one.

"Would you like it," she murmured in a low voice, "if I did rather more?"

"I can't tell until you do it, can I?"

Either he fenced clever, this one, or else he was really

17

ignorant of these things. Anything was possible. Sixteen in the town is not the same as sixteen in the country. Those American films, for one thing. Those dance halls. The word 'boy' meant a different thing every ten kilometres. He was far too nice to be cunning. No, not this one. Like a tight oyster, and she urgently needed to gulp him down.

She was sliding her hand higher and higher at every stroke. Her gentle rubbing of the cloth of his ragged trousers made a strange kind of hard warmth. His leg couldn't possibly be that hot. It was just her, getting excited again.

"I think you want me to seduce you," she teased, whispering into his ear. "I think you'd like me to be very naughty with you, and go all the way."

He said nothing. He didn't move. She might have been speaking Greek. She licked the lobe of his ear with her tongue and let her hand fall inside his thigh. He shivered, like someone who is taking cold.

"Have you ever been loved by a woman?" she asked. She wanted so much to be the first. She would have given two years off her life if she could just be the first.

"My mother loves me. And my sisters."

"Stop playing games," she snapped, a little too harshly. She nibbled on his ear in apology. "You know very well what I mean."

He drew his head back slightly and looked at her in silent and total puzzlement. "No, I don't," he muttered in surprise. "Won't you please tell me, so that I may know?"

2.

Was it possible? In this day and age? In this war-torn land? They're not made like that any more. Boys sell themselves at street corners. Their mothers make them do it for food or for money. You could get a strapping youth for a head of cabbage. There used to be twins in the town that you could have for two apples – or just one apple if it was close to midnight. She knew these things. She knew what a virgin of sixteen was worth – a thousand times more to her than to anyone else.

There were girls too, of course. Almost twice as many girls as boys. Male needs were more urgent, she knew.

They'd take the boys only if they were cheaper, or if they preferred them anyway. She had never dared. Well, not in broad daylight. Not where anyone might see her, remember her face. Neighbours are never nice. None of us are nice. We talk. We interpret. We grow scandal in a pot on the window-sill. No, if you had shameful desires it was better to keep them secret.

Her left hand slipped behind his neck and fingered the long, wavy hair. Her right hand swooped down between his legs and gave him a long, slow caress. His eyes never left hers. He was watching, or so she guessed, for the least sign of laughter, mockery or ridicule. He could just about take it. If he clenched his teeth together hard, he could just about bear it. But she had to be sincere. There had to be some slight semblance of love.

"If you make a fool of me, I will die." That is what his eyes were telling her. He regarded her with that calm, marble beauty as she fondled him right there and then. His crotch grew hot and the smell of a man in a state of arousal began to seep into his sweat. She kissed his forehead and tasted the salt.

"How big you are," she said in a hoarse whisper. "So very big for a boy of sixteen."

She let her lips hover down the length of his nose and patter against his mouth. When she kissed him, deeply, she could taste the herbs which he'd probably been eating along the way. She forced her tongue deep into his mouth and she knew straight away that he really was a virgin. No one had ever kissed him that way before. He was part revolted, like boys of that age are when you try to make them eat something from your own plate. And he was part mesmerised by the strange sensations that her kissing awoke in him.

There is always that knowledge, or that special kind of complicity that grows between men. But kissing a young boy makes a woman feel like a bumble-bee sipping its first nectar. All her life those rough, crude brutes have been crazed by her fragility! Now it's her turn to be strong and to rip the silk, tear the lace, and trample muddy feet across dainty flowers.

## 3.

As she kissed him, so he kissed her. She was like a teacher enthused by a vision, while he was like a child fired by her burning zeal. Whatever she showed him, he did it himself at once. His tongue lapped like a cat and slithered pinkly round hers. When she insinuated her fingers across his back, his own plucked at the neck of her dress.

"I want to undress you," she murmured in the deepest notes of an organ fugue.

He did not hesitate. His amazing eyes looked at her as he lay back meekly. It was an offer or an invitation, like a dog exposing its belly to your touch. It is a gesture as ancient as time. "Do with me as you wish", it seems to say. "Take me, for I am thine."

Her fingers fumbled with his belt buckle. It was much too big for his childlike waist. Then she unhooked the metal tongue that held the top of his flies together, and worked at the buttons one by one. The cheap cloth parted like a wound in his abdomen. Coaxingly, she let her fingers settle on his genital bulge with all the delicacy of a butterfly. She stroked him slowly and then gave it a tender squeeze.

She unbuttoned his shirt and opened that, flinging aside the two halves like Hedda Gabbler in Ibsen's gloomy play, letting the sunlight in. "Oh God," she thought. It was all she could think of, just that: Oh God! His chest and belly were beautiful beyond words. She leaned over him like Pope Joan and licked the altar. He moaned sweetly and squirmed.

With the tip of her tongue, she gently drew a trail down the length of his body. She lingered on his navel and toyed with it for a while. She went lower, marvelling at the delicate, near invisible gold hairs that lay on his flesh. Just above the band of his dated, country underpants – the loose kind that fastened to his braces by loops of cotton tape – the hairs grew thicker and his flies gaped slightly. She could see the root of his cock. It resembled a small branch pushing out from a bigger trunk. A certain aroma rose from his flesh – the male odour. It was the scent of stalwart gravy or a virility smell that makes the mouth water.

She let her tongue slide playfully under the waistband for a moment but then, as if changing her mind, she went down over the surface of the cotton material. My god, he was hard. It felt like a stick of sweating dynamite and she nibbled on it through the flimsy cloth. When she twisted her head to explore underneath, he raised his knees in exquisite pleasure and opened wide his legs. It was like guards at the frontier lifting the barrier – access was being given.

She looked at him again. His eyes were heavy with desire. "Just a gesture," she begged. "You take them off for me." She leaned in close. She wanted to drink it all in. She licked her lips with gusto.

### 4.

I dare say that her story would disgust you ... she, a married woman, a mother, more than forty years old. But her husband had been sent to the fighting. Oh, no, you needn't feel too sorry for him. He went freely. He stepped forward and put his hand up. He was what they call a 'patriot', you see. Men love patriots, don't they? Give them medals, bury them with flags and trumpets, and console the mothers and widows with fine words and, sometimes, a pension.

Every 'patriot' is a traitor to his mistress, his wife, his mother and his children. What right has he to offer his life when he already owes it to others? How dare he squander his blood or spill his seed? When he takes his oath of loyalty, he breaks his marriage vows! When he strides off to drum and colours, he's already shot the priest who married them and the organist who played her splendid bridal march. That is why she made her decision. It was as easy as tearing that precious dress into shreds. She did not belong to him any more. She was a woman who had renounced her man.

Her children were taken to the west for safety. She was supposed to stay in her house and look after her garden so that there'd be fresh food if the army retreated. What fools! What blind fools! If the enemy came, she'd give it all to them. She'd give herself to them. Women are not traitors, they help the race survive. There are greater loyalties than coloured patches on a map!

He had been gone for several months and she needed him. They had taken her children away and she also needed them. Is this why she felt so terribly attracted by childlike men? She did not feel any need to apologise. There was no shame in her soul. All she could do was feel, not think. It meant nothing that she was in her middle years, falling in love with an unfilled drawing of a man.

Before he came, while she was still alone, her dreams had already started to turn towards these half-men, these teenagers. They were softer, not so much hair everywhere, and more like dolls than road-drills. Being made love to by them was that much farther away from being raped. There was less muscle and more sweetness, fewer moments of violent pain and more of those floating caresses. It was like making love to a man who's had his fangs and claws torn out. She didn't want a gorilla on her pillow but an athlete with no hips and tousled hair.

There are no neighbours any more. They have all gone. They took what they could and the rest has somehow vanished. Even the wood is being torn off their walls and the windows have been stripped. Along this forgotten road, her house is so obvious. The only one not over-grown with weeds. The only one with walls and windows intact. What's more, the only one with lights at night and the smell of cooking during the day.

No, there is no one to peep through curtains and go tut-tut. No one to pass in the street and be ignored by. No pinched noses. No heads tossed in censure. No outrage or disgust. They'd had money. That is why the others were able to go as soon as the signs of war grew serious. They had been gone for months, and their husbands with them, long before anyone could order them into the army. What did they know about men and women when they had tiptoed through life like trembling field-mice?

They would not have understood. They would not have pardoned, even though it wasn't in their gift to pardon anyone. It would not have been possible ever to tell them. She could never have tried to explain. When they told me this story, at first I could not believe. So I do sympathise – and smile.

5.

She remembered suddenly the first time, when she was fourteen. It had been the tall German boy, thin but not really thin. More like a long stalk of maize. She remembered above

22

all else the small of his back. His small, tight buttocks worked like hammers, and the small of his back wept with raindrops of sweat. She didn't play with him much. She learned later that when they are that age, so young, there isn't much time for play. His thing had twitched like a divining-rod, and he had plunged it in with a hissing kind of murmured "Oh my God". She had just lain there – half dreaming – feeling like the virgin land in which a future forest has been planted.

She remember fingering his arse. It was like trying to sharpen a pencil on a moving train. And when he came, his body went into a wild paroxysm. His sphincter muscles all but bit her finger off. Then his warm custard pulsed into her with the rhythm of a machine that waters a lawn.

It had been his first time with a girl. He was dazed. She played with him a long time after he was spent. His eyes never left hers. Whatever she did, however she did it, his eyes were glued on hers like a television camera fixed on an Olympic skating champion. He wanted to know if she had liked it. He needed urgently to understand if the earth had trembled for her the same way it had for him. It was then that she first understood men. She sank back with a whimper, and in pure sympathy she whimpered again and then groaned.

"Was it good?" he had gasped with zeal.

She didn't lie. She didn't tell the truth. She just went "... Ohh!..." And he had wept. They lay there, side by side, his head turned into her neck, her hand holding his flaccid cock, and he cried.

That was when she first felt like a goddess.

She felt herself seized by power. It felt like a cramp at first. It began in her stomach and spread outward. It was like an electric shock, but slowed down a thousand times. Her whole body writhed as her hands ... he had screeched like an owl. Pain or ecstasy? She can't tell you. She was lying there in full triumph, his sperm inside her, and his torn-off genitals held high with the blood dripping down on them.

He had screamed but – he probably understood.

It was a long time ago, when she was a girl. He and she, they had both been virgins.

There had been so many since. So many tender, untouched boys. It is quite essential that they be untouched. That's how she likes them: as tender as baby frogs and as green as lamb's lettuce. She wants to be the first, you understand. That is necessary. No other woman's hand may have touched them since their mother stopped bathing them in the sink. As she was very fond of saying: they are best when they are tender.

There was some mystery behind those words, without doubt, but who can say what it was? Does it help if I tell you that she couldn't tolerate any dirt in her house? Are you any further forward in knowing that she washed her hands a hundred times a day? Mental medicine no doubt has a name for these things. But a name is a very long way from understanding.

I wish Christian ladies with blue hair had the brain to perceive that burning at the stake does not cure anything. Do they forget why Christ died? And was he crucified only for them? Why do ex-sinners behave so badly to those not yet fully redeemed? And what did they themselves do to deserve it?

### 6.

This one now. This boy who had knocked on the door and asked for a glass of water. She hadn't asked where he had come from nor even where he was going. There were so many people passing by her door these days. Somewhere, somewhere far to the East, that was where they said the war was raging. She watched them sometimes, plodding past, not talking, just the uneasy creak from the wheels of a child's pram stacked with blankets.

She'd had a notice made and put next to the lane. "I have nothing else left," it said. "Intruders will be shot."

It had been hard to put it up. Hard to see the children dragged by but looking at her windows. They didn't believe the first phrase. They dare not ignore the second. So they just flowed by, a constant trickle like a silent brook. Big eyes. Dead eyes. Just driven on by bombs and guns that sounded like distant thunder.

There had been a knock at the door. The first unexpected sound in three and a half months. She had felt afraid. There was no postman. There was no post. Had the new militia

arrived after all? She had gone to the door almost ready to vomit. It was only him. A tall, slender stripling of a man, whose clothes did not fit, and whose face expected a rifle-butt to bruise him back down the path. There had been a tear – no, not that – his eyes had simply been moist. He held the door-post with grimy hands whose nails were cracked and filthy.

"I beg your pardon," he gasped as he fell down at her threshold.

She managed to catch him. He looked light but he weighed even less than she had imagined. She had more flesh on her own body, and she felt her first twinge of shame. It wasn't difficult to pull him to the sofa with its coloured wool cover she had crocheted herself. She pulled his feet up and took his shoes off. She stared at him a long time, knowing what she ought to do, but unable to go and do it.

She was stroking him all the time he was senseless. She was still stroking him when he woke up. He had stared at her too, trying to interpret the action of her hands, and understand the burning bright expression on her face.

"I am so hungry," he murmured. "Please, anything – anything at all."

"I have a turnip," she said, still stroking him. "If I search in the garden, we may find a couple of carrots and a potato." Hands still wandering up and down his body. "It's two days since I inspected the traps so we may even have a rat, or at least a small mouse."

"Am I in heaven?" he smiled before swooning again.

She stopped stroking him and prepared the magic soup that was cooked up from practically nothing. She ate none of it herself. She had other hungers, more pressing, and it was crucial to give this boy some strength back.

7.

She didn't know why she felt this blinding urge to explore his body. We all have it. Perhaps it is due to memories of long ago, when nappies were changed, bottoms were wiped, and one was bundled in a great, fleecy blanket after the bath. Is that what it is: souvenirs of comfort? It's irrelevant

26

anyway. It was beside the point. All she knew was, she wanted to play with him.

He was moaning now, moaning and crooning, and his young cock was hard and twanging with tension inside the threadbare underpants.

"You take them off for me," she said again. "Do it as a kind of gesture."

No expression at all on his face. He hooked his thumbs in the waistband and slid them down. Out it sprang, in full tumescence – a flagpole rearing for a National Salute, or a ship's mast ready to let out the billowing sails. Its two eyes glittered like lazy drops of gold.

She didn't react at once. She didn't think she believed it. She could feel the heat radiating from his groin. She could smell the male-sweat perfume of his curling pubic hair. And she was mesmerised by the sight of his long, hard, majestic member – except that it had eyes. He had balls, yes. They hung like golden plums, except that they pulsed. Yes, they were beating faintly, like twin dissected frog's hearts.

He moaned and his mouth sagged open. His great, sweet, boy's eyes looked at her with desire. She ran her hands over him. It was like stroking a new-born babe, or a pink, hairless pup. So soft his skin was. Like wild silk. She gazed with deep yearning at his penis. With an index finger, the nail still flecked with ruby varnish, she lightly stroked the lips of its tiny mouth.

She was not at all surprised when it sucked at her finger. It was like a lamb dabbing its blind head at a teat. She was delighted when he somehow took her whole finger in. How heavenly! What a strangely rapturous thing to happen.

She heard the boards creak on the verandah outside the house. But she did not worry. It was like entering into a state of orgasm but – please understand me – not suddenly, which is what they mean by the expression 'coming'. It was more like crossing a field and making for a shadowy forest. It was a slow process, as if she were learning to swim again and moving toward the deeper end.

His penis had swallowed the whole of her hand now. It felt marvellous. A gentle suction that went along with the slow, pulsing massage of her flesh. Again she smiled at her whimsy that it was much more the case that he was raping her. He was eating her. Swallowing her. This sublime male

27

tool was but the opening of a tunnel, leading to the lower kingdom, and he was digesting her whole.

## 8.

Out of the corner of her eye she saw faces at the window of the room. Such pale people. Such hollow cheeks and grimy skin. They watched with blank eyes, no emotion, as if they were too old or too ill to savour what she was doing. Well what did she care! All right, so she might be older than this glorious youth – old enough even to be his mother. But he was taking her. That's what mattered. He was accepting her. And she didn't give a damn if it was the wrong way round ... she was being made love to.

She could feel it already: the approach of ecstasy, like a bath that is steadily filling up with water. He was much slower than he would normally have been. You have only to wink at lads of his age and they wet their vests. Too eager, too quick, most unlovely for a woman to see. But lack of food and physical weariness had slowed him down. His climax was going to coincide with hers.

Her spread fingers seemed to touch something that was plucking at the wool cover she had made for the settee. It was chitinous. It crackled, like one of those plastic packs for biscuits, no longer to be found there. She lifted her hand back quickly. Something that had wandered in from the blasted fields. Some poor hungry creature, no doubt. She couldn't bother her head about that, not now, not with this luscious-man thing lying beneath her like a living sacrifice.

It didn't matter that he wasn't inserting it into her body. She was content to see it, to be against him, to feel that she possessed him. He was, so to speak, the ultimate one of her flock. She was in love with every part of him, even though that masculine proboscis was the highlight of it all.

It was becoming monstrous in size. But instead of being fearful or reacting with panic, she laughed and laughed, and tried to rub it with her free hand. But it was so thick, she could no longer get her fingers round it. The lips, around her elbow, seemed to dribble and she touched them to wipe away a kind of mucid spittle. They sucked at her finger too. Both hands were in.

28

Her own private parts were over the young teenager's face and he was licking her like an expert gigolo. Oh he knew quite well what he was about. She had been quite right about that. He wasn't as innocent as he had seemed. He gave a heave beneath her. Music by Mahler plunged through her body, whilst he writhed as if he were a conger eel. His penis had swallowed her up to both shoulders. His mouth had somehow taken in her legs and feet.

He was fat now. He was fat and sleek and golden. He looked like the pupa of a moonlit moth. He resembled the queen of a termite colony, a thousand times larger than anyone else. She was riding him now, lying on his distorted belly, her face against his groin and her cunt beneath his nose. "You look like Hitler," she screamed, and she went in up to her navel.

She realised then that something was going to go wrong. Being sucked by both ends of a beautiful boy was close to ecstasy. But he was too fat to bend, whereas she had always kept her figure fragile. Can you imagine? She wore corsets even in this day and age. She had a waist as slender as the last Queen of Hungary. But ...

The tongue of his penis wrapped itself around her head and pulled it into its gaping mouth. So pink he was. So wet with saliva. He was having an orgasm at both ends. His fluids frothed around her neck and around her belly. He gave one last, titanic heave, and she was covered totally by his viscid, nacreous cream. And she snapped in two at the narrowest point of her hour-glass figure. Her last words, which nobody heard, were "I'm going!"

9.

He lay there like a bloated, drowned walrus, the flesh of his body the colour of coral, and his limbs swollen like inflated, plastic tubes. His penis was small now, like a snail that has run away from home, and which shelters at the foot of a rounded, hairy mountain.

They came in now, his people. Through the door, through the windows and through the cracks in the walls. The whole of his village was there – twelve legs apiece and each one flat, black, crackling. "Come," he said, for they waited on

29

his word, and all of them attached themselves to any space on his body. He writhed in an ecstasy all his own now, as if he were pierced by a hundred needles each sucking, each thrusting, and each nuzzling him toward the brink of eternity.

They guzzled on a silver fluid that oozed from his flesh. He felt like the main beam of a Gothic cathedral being gnawed away by worms. They fattened. He thinned. They grew chubby as he became a boy again. One by one the carbon hued insects fell off him and panted on the floor. One by one they scuttled outside again and changed into refugees. They were still pale-faced and haggard because they hid their exultant grins. The rags and sacks concealed their chicken-like plumpness. He came out of the house and they picked up their things and rejoined the river of misery flowing away from the war. A girl slid forward from a group of Rumanians and tried to make it look like a casual encounter. There was also a man in Bulgarian dress who leered at him. The boy gave a nod of the head toward both of them. He had the refined air of a lord.

"Do you like company?" asked the girl making sheep's eyes at him.

"I like anything," he said calmly, looking at the man.

When they got to the border, five days later, there were eight people less for the train. No one noticed. If anyone missed a relative or friend, they just thought he was further back in the line, or had somehow wandered ahead. Officials from the Red Cross counted as they boarded the emergency trains. When they reached the terminus, there were fewer once again. Nobody cared. As long as there were was no one extra trying to sneak through.

Somehow or other, the entire village had managed to stick together. When the Red Cross agents realised this, they decided to relocate them as one big bunch. Being with family and friends would help them to settle in. They sent them to a southern part of Germany, close to the Swiss border, to land that was sparsely populated. They gave all the necessary papers to the former postman travelling in the group. There was a local mayor, but the 'village' was scattered over the sides of a remote valley.

It took one more day to reach their journey's end. The mayor of the remote village looked at the papers warily. "Are they all here?" he asked.

"Oh yes," breathed the fussy, little postman who seemed no worse off for the long trek up the steep valley. "We had a head-count when we set out, and we repeated it at every stage of the journey." He smiled proudly. "That's how we've managed to stay together."

"Has there been a count since you got off the train?" demanded the mayor.

"But of course," beamed the jolly, fat postman. "We had a count all the time. We never did anything without a count." He looked at his people and they all nodded with a small, pleasant smile.

With the postman's help, the mayor allocated houses and chalets to different groups and they didn't seem worried that they were so widely spread out. "We are used to wandering. We will fit in quietly. You will get no citizens complaining about us."

The mayor thought this a promising attitude and shook the postman's hand warmly. "Perhaps you would like to be my deputy," he suggested. "You could represent your people."

"Our people," smiled the postman. "We are all one, now."

"Of course," said the mayor. "Quite so." He wondered how it was that this man, and the others, spoke such good German.

"We have a good teacher," said the postman oddly.

"That's what counts," agreed the mayor uneasily.

"No doubt he will drop in to see you."

"That would be a pleasure."

The postman bowed politely. "An even greater one for him."

---

*VAMPIRE*: In south Slavonic folklore, the spirit of a dead person, or a corpse revived by an evil spirit. It leaves its grave by night to suck the blood of sleeping prey.

*INCUBUS*: Latin "he who lies on top". A male demon who forces sleeping women to have sex. In ancient Rome and modern Italy, it is also called an "Alp" or an "Alb".

*LAMIA*: "she who swallows up". In Ancient Greece, a spirit which abducted young children and sucked people's blood.

*LEMURES, LARVAE*: In Ancient Rome, spirits of the dead who wander the streets searching for those they have known. On feast days, householders threw them black beans, but kept their heads averted.

*MAHR, MORA, MORAVA*: A Slav demon, the soul of a living person which quits the sleeping body as a moth, a hair or a wisp of straw, to suck the blood of others. N.B. Moravia = the land of the Morava.

*SOUL*: An imprecise word meaning "live essence". In some tongues it also means "shadow" which is seen as part of the soul. Evil can more easily devour the soul or shadow by means of a sexual approach. When a person is 'covered', their shadow is captured. Semen is a shadow of life, and life essence can be squeezed or expressed from the body in the form of a silvery liquid.

# Chocolate Finger

## *1.*

It was standing at the edge of the pavement – one of those small sandwich boards designed to catch your eye. Restaurants often have them. So do young girls, and not so young girls, who offer their services as 'models'. You also get them outside cinemas, saying 'Queue Here' or 'House Full'. I've even seen them outside hair-dressing salons, when they often say 'Special Offer: OAPs Half-Price'.

One way or another, they are meant to attract your interest and entice more customers. Do they work, really? I suppose that depends on the level of your appetite. If you had missed lunch and felt famished, then a sign outside a restaurant might just pull you in. I dare say the prospect of a 'model' might make you tramp up three flights of stairs ... if you had a folding tripod and a large roll of film.

The cinema though ... the word is out, and it's either a good film or it's not. As for the hair-dressers ... who wants an OAP at half-price? But this one was different – the sandwich-board that I mentioned at the beginning. It was just a simple declaration, written in felt-tip pen with black ink. All it said was:

> I can tell you
> WHEN AND WHERE
> YOU SHALL DIE.

I'd always wondered what it meant when someone said "Ooo, it gave me quite a turn." Now I knew. For a moment, I felt a distinct jolt in my stomach, as if the sweet and sour chicken I'd just eaten was trying to get out and run. It was all so unlikely ... and weird. Other people didn't take any notice. There weren't all that many of them about. Even so, you'd have thought that one or two of them would be struck by it. They didn't even slow down to read it. It did cross my mind that maybe not everyone could see it. Know what I mean?

It could have been the strong breeze that was slowly changing into a wind. Have you noticed? Hats are nowhere near as popular as they used to be, but during a wind, people still dip their heads down. It must be a reflex. Or perhaps it has more to do with shielding your eyes from rain, and the risk of being hit by something. I saw a young farmer once. Walking in the field, he was, head down and hair streaming out behind him. Went straight into the thresher. I remember how the cloud of chaff turned red.

I don't know why all these thoughts went through my head just then. In any case, they all flashed by in a fraction of a second. I don't think I actually stopped. It was more like a hesitation. I just faltered ever so slightly – and the door of the shop opened with the tinkle of a little bell.

I was still closer to the pavement edge, nearer to the curb than the shop door. But I had the feeling that it had been opened just for me. I struggled with my innate sense of politeness. I do that a lot, you know – have a big fight with my conscience. I have to cross the road to avoid beggars, because I can't bear to refuse them. When there are hordes of them, like the city centre, I have to turn back, or else get on a bus. And I'm sure that they know. There's something in the way they look at me ... with that smirk.

I couldn't just go on walking away. I think perhaps someone inside must have known what my character was like. Maybe they can do that – maybe the showmen in showrooms can pick out the one who is most likely to buy a car. When a lion attacks a herd of wildebeest, they say he has already chosen the one he's going to bring down. In the speed of events you get a false impression. It all looks so random and haphazard. But it isn't. Not at all. That is how the predator stays alive – and the prey doesn't.

34

I found myself walking across the paving stones in a sort of diagonal fashion – as if I were skirting back to the newspaper shop to take another glance at the headlines. But I stared into the open door, and then I studied the window. There was a sort of shallow shelf, and a backing of yellowing newspaper. There was nothing at all on display. Nothing to say what the trade might be. Against my better judgement, and in spite of the timidity which told me to run away, I strolled airily into the shop.

## 2.

"Hello!" I called very quietly. "Anyone on duty?"

The place wasn't very big. Against one wall there stood a kind display case, with a series of glass doors. I could imagine it filled with socks, knickers, vests and other sorts of drapery. There was a round table, and two easy chairs. That put me in mind of a doctor's waiting room. The funny thing was, I couldn't see a counter. I couldn't even make out where a counter might have stood. I wondered how the establishment had carried out its business.

"We did not sell goods, but our services." A man was sitting in one of the armchairs. "The point was to put our clients at ease and to chat to them in a kindly manner about their requirements."

It took me a moment to regain my nerve. He had taken me by surprise. "Who ..." I asked in a voice pitched too high, "Who were your clients?"

"The bereaved, of course."

"The bereaved?"

"Yes. We were one of the longest established companies of true family Undertakers, who plied their profession in London."

"Profession?" I managed to stammer. Then, just to show I wasn't nervous, I became cheeky. "I thought that term applied only to the Law, to Medicine and to the Church?"

"Those are 'the learned professions'," he corrected, "and in any case, we had to know about all three! According to Kipling, the most ancient profession in the world is that of the Harlot." He looked at me sardonically. "What do you call them today – Tarts or Prostitutes?"

I knew I'd go red, and I did. I felt it spreading across my face like strawberry jam. "I don't call them anything," I said in a slightly offended voice, wishing like that my blushing would stop.

"No," he sighed. "I don't suppose you would. I was speaking generally – I used the pronoun 'you' in an impersonal way. I should have said 'one'. Nowadays 'one' has become rather old-hat but, as you have just seen – it still has its uses." He smiled at me slightly. It was a true undertaker's smile in that it meant whatever you wished it to mean. One could translate it in so many different ways: Your stomach will calm down soon; He is resting in the arms of Jesus; or even – Guess how much this is going to set you back!

"You wish to ask me about the Notice?" He caught me on the hop. He saw the confusion in my eyes. "I'm rather proud of it, you know. I find the wording so – so inoffensive, and yet, at the same time, so – enigmatic. Don't you?"

"What's the catch?" I asked suspiciously.

"Oh, you young people!" He threw his hands up. "You are all so cynical today. You believe in nothing."

"Then, what is the fee?"

"The fee?" He seemed really outraged. "One asks a fee for – for cutting your toe-nails – for mending your roof – or for spying on your wife." He stopped suddenly. "By the way, do you have a wife?" I shook my head. "But one does not," he went on, "ask a fee for carrying out a sacred duty – for performing a service to one's God." He gave me another sharp glance. "Do you believe in God?" This time I nodded, but not too enthusiastically.

"Ah!" he said gravely. "Not God, qua God, but God qua 'something other' or 'something higher'? Is that it? Is that a bit closer to the mark?"

I nodded. "I'm not an atheist."

"Absolutely not! But my dear chap, who is? Who is? Hmm?" He smiled the smile of a wily old man. "You pay me if I'm right," he said softly. "If I'm wrong ... then I pay you."

"Right? Wrong?" I shook my head in bewilderment. "What are you talking about?"

He seemed rather surprised. His eyebrows shot up. "Why

– the time and place of your death, of course!" He leaned forward. "Did you think I wasn't serious?"

## 3.

I had thought he might be mad. The simple idea of it made me quite uneasy. But the shop door was open, just behind me. I could feel the slight push of air when a bus went past. I could hear the noise of footsteps and the murmur of voices. He might be eccentric but I doubted if he was mad.

"Thank you," he said. I raised my eyebrows again. "For taking me as an eccentric, and not as an out and out maniac." He smiled his obsequious smile and almost rubbed his hands. "Yes," he went on, reading my thoughts, "I can read thoughts. But there are rules, as you may know. I am only allowed to read them if I have your tacit consent."

"I didn't say."

"Exactly. Tacit comes from Tacitus – it's Latin for dumb. But you gave me your consent silently, just by coming in here and sitting down. Don't be alarmed. I shall not say a thing." He laughed and patted his own chest. "Who'd believe me anyway? There is no evidence."

"Of course," he said, picking up my train of thought. "It is very entertaining indeed – especially at my age." He chuckled wickedly. "I'm not exactly 'Action Man', you know!" I must have blushed because he smiled. It was much more a chess player's smile by this time.

I strove very hard to steer my mind off in safe directions. "Do you get many clients?" I asked. I tried to sound casual, as if I were just passing the time of day.

"Not as many as I hoped – but more than you imagine."

"You have your hands full then?"

"Mine ... and those of my assistant."

There was a strange note in his voice – a semi-tone too sharp.

"Why do you need an assistant?"

"For the night-shift, you know." He nodded at a small, fading notice. "At people's service, night and day. They don't just die during commercial hours, when it would be most convenient. They're not like bank managers, or civil servants – knocking off at a set time. That is more or less implicit in my little announcement, out there: we can choose neither the where nor the when."

"You mean that you still do ... undertaking?"

He licked his lips, as if they were the nib of a pen. "Er, not as such, no."

"Then ..."

"Would you like to meet my child – that is to say, my priceless assistant?"

"A young man or a young woman?"

"Whichever you prefer."

Somehow or other, his question didn't throw me, though I realized later how odd and out of place it had been. "I have no preference," I lied.

"How very modern and shocking!"

"You don't understand. I mean, I have no preference about which of your children does the night shift."

"But I have only the one ... Mr ... er? Ah yes," he smiled as my name flashed through my head. "Foster ... Donald Foster. You will find my daughter very beautiful – just like the girl of your dreams."

And she was. Oh my God, she certainly was. She came into the room – but not really. I imagined she came in. I imagined everything. It was like being slightly drunk, at the cinema, or at the night club ... it all seems to be happening, but part of you doesn't actually believe it. The old man was making her in my thoughts, and he was enjoying my reactions. It felt ... glorious, and it also felt ... obscene.

"Let yourself go," he murmured, as my head swam. "Give yourself to the experience."

And I did too. It was better – oh a hundred times better than any dream I'd ever had. We made love, but how frail and inadequate words are. Made? No. Love? Not at all. In no way do they do justice to the way we drowned together in an ocean of perfumed body fluids. She did all the things I had ever visualized being done to me, and more – far more. She smiled with frenzy as she made me do them back to her. It was like leaping out of an aeroplane, groping our way through caves – everything I was frightened of and longed for.

When at last I shuddered into orgasm, it was like being in Japan when an earthquake hits. My whole body went into a tetanoid spasm, and my penis belched out scalding sperm that had long passed its sell-by date. When the terror subsided, I drew in some breath with a hiss, and opened my eyes. We were alone. Just the old man and me. His face was gleaming with sweat and I was dimly aware of a warm wetness in my groin.

"Excellent," he hissed feebly. "Who would ever think, to look at you, that you had such energy in you?"

"Who would have thought the old man had so much blood in him," I murmured.

"Macbeth!" He chuckled and gave a show of silent applause. "Oh I was correct about you," he muttered. "I got the measure of you, all right." He grinned, and made the mock gestures of measuring a corpse. "But for one fact, you could be a great scholar."

"What fact?" I snapped, feeling a mite offended.

"Death!" He said flatly.

4.

Call me stupid. I probably was. You'd think I would have run out of the place, there and then. You'd imagine that I'd seen enough films or read enough books at least to be a bit wiser and less reckless. But – how can I make you understand – I had this overwhelming impression that I had just lost my virginity. When that happens, or at least the first time it happens, you just don't feel like mooching round the streets to find it again.

I listened to his story. Oh it was crazy and weird enough but, as I say, I was feeling a long way off my normal myself too. He made his living – or he resumed his own life – when and if he found someone who would take on the bet ... and lose. That was the come-on. If you won, you got his daughter – or his son – but if you lost, you got his job.

I was very quick, or so I thought. Whatever it was I had just had, I wanted it again and again and Amen! So suppose he said I would die in Cleckheaton. Where the hell is Cleckheaton, you might ask. That doesn't matter ... I'd go to work in Capri, or better still – Ceylon.

"Smart lad," he patted me on the back. "Then you'd double your chances of winning."

"Great," I thought, bouncing from years of pent up sexual eagerness. "What are my chances of winning?"

"Zero!" he replied.

I stopped bouncing. "Zero?"

"Zilch," he repeated.

I didn't need a pocket calculator. I could work it out in my head. "Two times zero is ... zero," I said.

"Correct," he conceded. "One of those mathematical quiddities that was invented by the Arabs. I'd blame them, if I were you."

I studied the problem a moment, wishing that I had paid more attention at school. What if I studied medicine, bought a private clinic in America, and took very great care of my own health?

"Oh in that case," he announced brightly, "you increase your chances by a factor of ten!"

I regarded him balefully. I saw him as he must have looked under a waning moon. "But ten times zero is still ..."

"Zero! Yes, but it is five times better than two times zero." He positively chuckled with glee. "Can I offer you some slight refreshment? A glass of wine? Or perhaps a biscuit?"

I shook my head. My stomach was upset.

"Would a chocolate finger tempt you?" I flicked my eyes at him. He made it sound so horribly suggestive. "Or some nice little 'snowballs' all covered in feathery bits of coconut?"

I left him with a long silence to play with. I hoped it might unnerve him, but I was wrong. He continued to regard me with that same professional smile, his elbows resting on the arms of his chair, and his fingers steepled in triumph.

"How do you choose them?" I asked bluntly. I'm like that, you know. Straight out with it, like James Bond. "How do you know which ones to trap by your advertisement?"

He said nothing. He didn't even have the courtesy to shrug.

"How do you predict my life expectancy? Like the insurance companies, is it? Do you take down my data – age, height, weight, health, occupation? Is that it?" I saw a glitter in his eye. "Is it sex?" I demanded.

He looked slightly lost, like someone who has found a dirty picture in his Gideon Bible. "Sex, Mr Foster? Again?"

He raised his eyebrow in surprise.

"I meant to say: is it a question of gender?"

"I beg your pardon?"

"Does it make any difference whether one is male or female?"

He paused. "Is that important?"

I was flummoxed and getting hot under the collar. "Not to me, no. But I thought it might count some way, in your calculation of ... things."

He peered at me very narrowly as if he were the one who had some wild suspicions. "What things do you suppose I calculate ... which require your sexual data? Hmm?"

## 5.

He played with me. I mean, in the way that a cat plays with a mouse. Nothing erotic in that, I hope. But no matter what I said to him, no matter what topic I raised, little by little he trapped me with his incessant and inescapable allusions to sex. Some of you might just find the idea erotic, I suppose – talking dirty in an undertaker's parlour! But that's not my idea of a great night out. Brass handles and shrouds do not turn me on.

What still galls me though is that he used my own sexuality to trap me. As cunning as a psychologist he was, the way he found out what I liked and what kind of person was my dream lover. That's part and parcel of the trade I suppose ... oops, sorry ... the "profession". An undertaker's clients are not the dead, but the relatives of the dead, and they are in such an emotional state: you have to guess what they can afford, and then sell it to them. It's like that with sailors, he said. A half bottle of rum, put a brassiere on the bolster, and you can charge them twenty quid.

"Sex!" he spat. "It's all in the mind!" I didn't find this anything to laugh at, but he chortled away like a maniac. "Has it never struck you? Has it never crossed your mind? You – that's right, You! You are the only person in the world who imagines that what he's got between his legs is so damn important!"

He grinned and leaned toward me slightly. "As our American cousins would say: what's the big deal?" He slapped his knees and threw himself back against the upholstery.

"Not everyone dies prettily, you know. Oh I'd say that less than half fall asleep, quietly, in their beds. We do the best we can. Titivate them up a bit. A discreet lace handkerchief laid across a cancer of the cheek. A foam mattress, impregnated with rose oil and cinnamon, for purulent sores."

He cast me a sharp glance and saw my face turning a strange colour. "After aeroplane crashes, we put all the bits in plastic bags and just share them out between the several coffins. So many kilograms apiece, and we make the rest up with bricks wrapped in cotton wool."

He paused while I vomited to one side of my chair.

"We don't even know whether we're mixing men and women together. When all is said and done, we have a job to do, we do it as best we can, and the family ... they are thankful that they didn't have to do it for themselves."

I wiped my face, and took some deep breaths. "What has all this to do with anything?"

"At least once in his life, every male should be obliged to lie naked on a table, lift his knees up, and hold a mirror to that part of his body he very rarely sees."

"Narcissism now?" I howled.

"No. The perineal suture."

I froze. I don't know why I froze. There was the tone of proof in his voice, like a barrister who has just told a judge the name of the one who did it.

"The perineal suture?" I echoed.

"A thin, red line, like a scar, that runs from the tip of your penis down to the anus." He looked at me a long time as I struggled to digest this puzzle. "We men ..." he spelled out with heavy emphasis, "are nothing other than women who have been sewn-up!"

He saw the horror on my face. He felt the self-disgust rising in my throat. "The Time is now," he shrieked. "The Place is here." The daughter grasped my throat. "Do I win or lose?"

## 6.

Yes. That's right. I am the Gamekeeper now. Clever of you to guess. I have been here for, oh, some forty-five years. I make it sound as if I were a prisoner, don't I? But the door of the shop is always open. I am free to go, any time I like. But I have chosen to stay. That is all. I needed the time to think.

I don't take very much exercise now. Well, facts have got to be faced. I'm on my way to seventy already. So I don't feel as spry as I used to. I tend to take a little walk from time to time. At dusk usually. You know ... the end of the day. What the Scots would no doubt call ... roamin' in the gloamin'. It used to be a song, that. 'Roamin' in the Gloamin', I mean. A man called Harry Lauder used to sing it. As a matter of fact, I seem to remember that they made him 'Sir' Harry Lauder, in the end.

I've got to go in now. One feels the chill much more as one gets older. But as I say, the door is always open. Come on round.

Pop in. Just for a chat, or ...

What do you say to a chocolate finger?

# The Tarot Man

*1.*

One of them was gay and the other was not. Or rather, what I should say, I suppose, is one of them was homosexual and very, very sad, while the other was not homosexual, but open minded, and even sadder. No. Gay doesn't come into it. As a matter of fact, the old word 'queer' would be more apt.

Why are we persecuted, they used to ask. Why don't they leave us alone? Why can't it be legal, for God's sake. Well, now it is legal, for God's sake. You can do almost anything you want. But they don't seem very much happier. They screech in public instead of slinking to their parties, and they put a lot more innuendo into their voices when they go shopping. Yes, there are more teeth and more twittering. But I couldn't really say that there was any more happiness.

The problem is, when you're gay – you are gay full-time. You never stop thinking about it. You keep your weather-eye open every hour of the day and night, always on the q.v. You're like a meteorologist looking for that one ray of golden sunshine amid a sky that is grey. It's not always pleasing either. You notice what you think could be an invitation in someone's eye and you follow him for miles. He stops to glance in a shop-window and "This is it" you think. He gets on a bus and so do you. You're out in the unknown suburbs when he strolls into his mother's house.

He never knew you were there. He never will. One more night wasted.

But we must not be morbid. God damn and blast anybody who is first to cry. Think of leather, think of lace! Think of flesh at all points of the compass, male flesh, swollen, hard. And the thunder that comes after the dreams. And that teensy, weensy drop of extra acid in your stomach that feels like a footballer kicked you.

A lot of queers, in an act of defiance, possibly against their father, change their name. They used to be Trevor, Jack, Herbert or Fred. But they want to be Julian, Sebastian, Roderigo or Giovanni. Never a Cecil, you notice. They don't go a lot on Basil, either. There are fashions in such things, or so I have been told.

You can tell what generation an old queen belongs to by reflecting on the kind of film-star she most likes to impersonate. Garbo, Dietrich and Mae West are out. Even Liza Minelli and Barbara Streisand are way, way past it. I couldn't begin to tell you who is in right now. But it will be a doll. It will be a person just right for hanging your costume on.

The queer one was called Jeff. The other was called Nick. Jeff had wanted for a long time to adopt some other name, but Nick had threatened to leave him if ever he did. And Nick was God. So Jeff stayed Jeff.

They'd been at school together, Nick and Jeff. They'd both been part of a much bigger gang, but in their mid-teens the others had started whispering and sniggering. Jeff began to get left out, and just because he felt sorry for him, Nick stuck by him.

"I don't think that mate of yours is much interested in girls," Nick's mother used to say. It was the nearest she ever came to asking him.

"Well I am," he used to grin and somehow this would stop her heartburn.

She found out it was true though. She saw him, one Saturday night, walking down the High Street with a beautiful lass. She didn't notice that Jeff was following them, hanging back, like a shadow in the dark.

But Nick knew. He never said anything – neither to the girl, nor to Jeff. He caught a glance in an angled window. If he turned in a dark stretch, giving the girl a hug, he could see him in the headlights of a bus. It was like going to school with the dog trailing behind you. It couldn't understand why you did not want its company, and you hadn't the heart to deliver a kick.

## 2.

It didn't exactly spoil things for Nick. After all, his friend never intruded or tried to cause a mess. But he felt an immense sadness for him and imagined what it must feel like – to be as bashful or as innocent as that. He needed a nudge of the elbow, a word of encouragement, or else a kick up the arse. So he would lead his girl to the sand dunes, knowing all the good spots where Jeff could do some watching. In the end, it became a sort of display. He would keep the girl's eyes averted while he put on a show for that hidden spectator. He argued, and he truly believed, that this might stoke Jeff's fires.

In fact, it must have driven Jeff mad. It dawned on Nick too late. One night, when he'd walked the girl back to her home, Jeff was waiting for him. Nick said nothing. He could not pretend that it was a surprise. They shared a cigarette and strolled back down to the dunes again. He lay back. His body was cupped in the sand.

"You're not fucking shy of girls at all, are you?" he accused.

Jeff shook his head. The dog who couldn't tell whether he was going to be kicked or offered a bone.

Nick realised that it was one of those things they could not possibly discuss. What could they have said? His mother had been right, after all. Trust a woman! He sniffed and put both hands behind his head. He was handsome, he knew, and although he was still slender, his physique was good. His posture was just the ticket – not blatant – but just a bit erotic. He presumed that this was what Jeff wanted.

"I won't do anything," he said simply.

"What?" Jeff blinked, the tension almost tearing him apart.

"I'm leaving it up to you," said Nick. "I won't do a thing."

There was a long silence, like that of someone in church who has been on his knees praying, and has suddenly heard

46

the stained-glass window speak. He was struck by the enormity of what his friend had said. He swallowed with a gulp. "That's all right," he whispered.

And Nick just tried to stare at the stars while Jeff tip-toed into paradise.

They were dimly aware of others spying on them – more and more openly too. But Nick wasn't bothered. They were not the sort to talk. And Jeff just hoped and prayed that they were jealous as hell.

That was how it began. Jeff thought of it as the beginning of their great romance. Nick just thought of it as letting a friend lend a hand. It was only masturbation, that's all. He did it anyway. So why not let Jeff do it, if that's what Jeff wanted. But Jeff wanted more, so much more. He was delirious that first time when he slowly bared Nick's body. He got braver and braver each time afterwards. Before very long he was licking with his tongue, sucking with his mouth, and inserting his fingers – and that supreme thrill when Nick crashed into orgasm.

But it was not enough. It was like a drug and the addiction gets stronger. Nick would never respond. You could do anything, everything, but he refused point blank to take any active role.

"Will you masturbate me?"

"No."

"Will you touch me?"

Shake of the head.

"Will you at least watch while I do it to myself?"

That's when Nick would stand up and turn away.

"You've no more feelings than beef in a butcher's shop!"

Nick would bite his upper lip and then go home. Jeff moaned in the hollow in the dunes. That is when the unknown shadows would edge in closer. They were warm shapes born out of the darkness, who clambered over his misery and devoured him. And after they had fed their fill – there was endless night.

3.

He didn't do it deliberately. Well, it might have been a bit planned but he wasn't really conscious of what he was about. He was weaving a web like a spider. He was trying to trap him. He'd buy him little gifts. Then it was big gifts. He'd make a suggestion, trying to develop their relationship a bit further, and after each suggestion he'd change the subject, let loose a lot of deep emotion. He cut down the chances that Nick would have time to refuse. He was training him.

He was hoping, he knew, that he and Nick would be forever. He was the one who rented the flat. He was the one who got Nick drunk and made him stay. He was the one who eventually got him to move in and stay.

"You can bring your dates," he offered generously, "if I can watch from the room upstairs."

He made sure he went out often, leaving Nick alone. It nearly killed him to do it, but he knew that the training must be gradual. He brought home bits and pieces of new furniture, nothing chi-chi, but all neat and homely and very masculine. He never wore make-up either, and fought back all temptation to buy a bit of cheap jewellery.

For Christmas he bought Nick some pure silk pyjamas – they were so nice for groping him. For his birthday he bought them a pair of tickets for a show in London.

"I can't keep on accepting all these presents," said Nick with a note of sour protest.

"Oh but they're nothing, nothing," insisted Jeff, his eyes falling. "You've been so generous to me. I could never repay you."

"You're not paying me!" snapped the other.

And something meant so very kindly would start a little quarrel. Nick would stomp out. Jeff would go into one of his agonies. Nick would come back past midnight, hardly able to walk, and Jeff would undress him like a mother, caress him like a lover, and weep into his pubic hair.

It was as if Nick wanted to be mates, like students sharing the same flat. But Jeff wanted never to be out of the other's company. When they did go out, Nick walked ahead. He would never walk side by side.

"One man and his dog, went to mow a meadow ..." Jeff would sing softly.

"Knock that off!"

The Sunday that Nick went home to have dinner with his mother, Jeff went down to the club to consult a friend.

48

"Just look what the wind's blown in," whooped the bar man. "The fifty-fifth feather!"

He sat at the angle just under the stairs, in what was called 'Mother's Corner'. It was a rule of the club that when you were sitting there, everyone ignored you. You had come for advice, a word of comfort, or something to stop you killing yourself. The rule was so sacred that they didn't even look to see who you were. They had all been there. They all remembered those who had never come back.

Mother listened to his story and shook her wig. "I'm sorry love, but if he's not gay, it'll be difficult to keep him. God knows, it would be hard enough, even if he were." She patted his hand gently. "You're very young, you know. You haven't realised it yet, but homosexual marriages don't work. One or other, or maybe both of you, gets tired. The best way, love, is to get out before the Christmas tinsel gets dull. That way, at least you'll have some lovely memories."

"What about Tom and Eva?" He meant two men in their late sixties. One was short and bald. The other was tall and lean. They looked like an advert for a certain building society. They were gay and were never seen with anyone else.

"Tom and Eva, my love, are very dear friends. The one likes young boys and the other likes policemen, which means they have to be very discreet." She cleared her throat like a female prime minister we all once knew. "As fortune would have it, Tom is a magistrate and Eva runs a coffee stall at one of the larger railway stations." She paused to let that sink in. "Each procures for the other."

This brought a lump to Jeff's throat. The news she had given him was causing several kinds of shock. It was like a transformation scene in a pantomime that had somehow gone wrong. All of a sudden, the world was so much plainer. He felt like a pilgrim whose luminous madonna will no longer shine.

4.

In an occult shop close to Covent Garden, he went to have his Tarot cards read.

"Do you just want a general reading?" asked the gangling young man in a sheepskin jacket and a lot of beads.

"What else is there?" asked Jeff;

The other visibly licked his lips in greed. "We can focus on one problem. We can have a look at your career. We can run through your karma and seek advice. We can look at your future in terms of money ..." He stopped as Jeff looked up sharply and stared into his eyes.

"How much does it cost?"

The young man knew that tone of voice. He had no job either. He saw the frayed collar, and the runs in the jumper. He saw that special hollow near the throat. He sighed as if letting air out of a balloon. All that was impressive, which wasn't much, left him. His shoulders seemed to drop and he just gave him the cards to shuffle. "Give what you can afford," he mumbled. His manner said it all. This wasn't going to take very long.

After the cuts and the laying out, he studied the cards lazily. "Your luck will change," he murmured, as if reading from a book.

"For the better?" asked Jeff.

There was such an unexpected urgency in his voice that the Tarot expert looked up. He saw his client's eyes. He began to feel like someone who has just driven over a baby. He turned the next card.

"Someone loves you," he recited in his calm, flat tone.

"Male or female?" demanded the other.

"Well, that's not easy – the cards don't reveal everything."

"Is he going to leave me?" said Jeff hoarsely.

The guy felt a cold wind, as the door opened and someone went out of the shop. You had to be quick at picking up cues like this. This poor sod was in a mess. The Tarot Man was not gay himself and you know, it is hard – it isn't easy for someone straight to understand the anguish of someone who is. But as Robbie Burns said – "a man's a man for a' that."

"Don't they always?" he said, with a bit of best Covent Garden philosophy, the sort that is made to order. "It don't matter who you love, mate. You'll end up losing them."

Jeff was silent a minute. His face was as white as the masks in a Japanese Noh theatre. The Tarot Man saw the sinews in his neck move as he tightened his jaw and swallowed back his pain. Now, he was very embarrassed. It's one thing to watch a victim of a car-crash die. It's different when he's awake and looking at you.

"What am I going to do?" he asked. His voice was like tearing paper.

The Tarot Man didn't know what to say. His cards were useless now.

"What am I going to do?" the boy repeated. "I paid you your money. Advise me. Counsel me. Tell me what to do."

"I'll give you your money back," offered the other readily.

"A contract is a contract, isn't it?" hissed the boy. "Even the Devil keeps his word."

And as he somehow knew it would be, the next card was "The Devil". The Tarot Man went green.

"And now 'The Twins'. That will join you and me together."

The man dared not touch the cards again. It was the boy who took the next one and placed it on the green baize. Exactly as he had said, it was 'The Twins'.

The boy's eyes burned in the deliberate dimness of the shop – the careful atmosphere that helped to put the clients in the right mood. He smiled a cold smile. It was the smile of a sailor who wrinkles his face against the storm. It was the smile of a ship's lantern that leers back at the lighthouse.

"Be seeing you," he said, going out.

"Not if I can fucking help it," said the Tarot Man, staring after him. And he didn't move for quite a long time. "Fuck me!" he gasped from time to time. In the end, he performed one of the popular 'banishing rituals'. It had worked once with the police, but now it did nothing for him at all.

To tell God's honest truth – he had not felt less like Superman in a hell of a long time.


5.


One evening there was a knock at the door. Jeff went down and a girl asked for Nick. He shouted up the stairs and Nick told him to bring her up. That night, she didn't leave. Nor the next night. Not even the night after that. Then Nick told Jeff she would be staying here.

For a few minutes Jeff wriggled and gasped like a fish on the quay side. "It's my flat," he reminded them.

"We'll move on, if you want," said Nick softly.

He gave in. It was no good putting on a show of bravado.

There was no point in arguing when you are more frightened of winning than he was of losing.

"I don't mind," she said, sounding so fucking generous and broad minded. "I don't mind at all." But Jeff minded. He minded like all hell.

Nick tried. He did his level best. The odd kiss, the rare cuddle. Once, when they were both drunk, they slept all three together. For a moment it was exciting to feel the real lust surging through Nick's body. But it was her he turned to, not him. Once the preliminaries were over, they both forgot about him. In the middle of that noisy, sweaty humping, her eyes opened and there was an expression of primeval triumph there.

He drew back. He crept away. The next morning he went back to the Occult Shop and saw the Tarot Man again.

"You knew I'd be back," Jeff told him.

"Aw shit, man. Listen." But the Tarot Man didn't know what to say. He'd read the book, that's all. He'd done a one week course with a guy who'd read a different book. All you had to do was adopt the right manner. "Nobody knows if you're for real or not," they told him. "Learn to smile as if you have a secret. Look sincere and tell them what they want to hear."

He paid half of his earnings to the shop owner. It was only fair, when you considered the rent and the local taxes. When he wasn't there, the shop owner took appointments for him. The Tarot Man was what everybody called him. He'd always wanted to be Ahab.

"Did you know," Jeff whispered without pity, "that the Tarot Cards have been entitled: 'The Devil's Book'?" Ahab shrank and his sheep-skin coat seemed to go limp on his back. "You've been meddling with things that are really none of your business at all. You've been dabbling with Black Magic and doing evil."

"God. Look. Aw, Jesus! Not me, man. Not me."

Jeff's face was bleak and drawn. He knew men. When you're gay, yes, you love them ... but as a matter of profound urgency you've got to understand them. There are ways, you see ... that you can seduce them without their suspecting a thing. It's as easy as doing the three-card trick. It's every bit as simple as selling fake 'French' perfume in Oxford Street. It's a question of using their fears, their greed and their needs. You have to find out what they are. You've got to 'feel' their soul as gently as a brain surgeon who excises splinters of broken glass.

Take this guy called Ahab as a case in question. He was dead scared of black magic. He would love to learn how to do the Tarot properly. He needed money. And to cap it all, he wasn't too bad-looking when you saw through the 'cool' disguise.

6.

"I feel a right fool," Ahab said, more to comfort himself than to offer yet another excuse. He was standing with bare feet, in the main bedroom of Jeff's flat. He was wearing just a t-shirt and jeans.

Jeff was facing him, and his expression was solemn. Just behind him, he could feel the edge against his buttocks, was a small table. There was a lighted, stubby candle that stood in bowl of shallow water. A tendril of incense curled in the cold air, making odd shapes in the draughts the were everywhere about them.

"You know what it means when we say cack-handed?" asked Jeff.

Ahab shook his head.

"Some folk pretend that it means dirty hands, shitty hands, or just left-handed."

"So what?"

"It comes from Greek, *kakos*, meaning bad or evil." He smiled and exuded all his best charm. "Now, I'm going to show you how to do it properly."

Ahab nodded. "Read the Tarot, you mean?"

Jeff took the cards in his 'wrong' hand, reached behind him, and did some manipulations to get things ready. Then he started to shuffle the cards, cut the cards, and deal them onto the table in an ancient way. Then, putting the remaining cards down, he picked up the ones that he was supposed to and turned his back on Ahab. He showed him the three cards in his hand.

"'The Twins'," he recited. "'The House of God'. And lastly 'The Devil'". He glared at Ahab. The young man was trembling violently as if he were cold. Suddenly Jeff threw the cards at him. And he changed.

He came toward Jeff and drew him down on to the bed. There was no hesitation, not the least bit of lingering. He flung himself into the timeless ritual of love as if he'd been doing it all his life. One by one each garment stretched and gave, almost as if in writhing together they had become two snakes who were magically shedding their skins. Limb wound around limb, as they slid and slithered in a glistening dance that had no end.

Light from the street flickered on their heaving muscles and the colours changed into the greens and blues of butterfly wings. They gasped and kissed and choked and licked as Ahab went mad with desire and Jeff lured him further and further on.

The door slammed below.

The two boys shuddered and throbbed in mutual climax.

There were feet on the stairs, a pause and a little laugh.

They went into the kitchen as he knew they would. There were small packages to put down. Things to go into the fridge. Then Nick backed into the bedroom, being groped and teased by the giggling girl. They were almost at the foot of the bed when Nick saw the Tarot cards. He spun round. He and the girl both gawped at the two naked boys lying on the bed.

Jeff got up very softly and walked slowly toward the door. "Sorry," he sighed, lowering his eyes. "Pure habit. It used to be my room." He turned round and spoke over his shoulder. "Come on, man."

Ahab hadn't moved. He just sprawled there, naked and proud, with his slackening penis lolling across his sweaty loins. The girl was gawping at him. Nick wanted to lean across and cover him up.

Ahab smiled warmly, deeply. "Hello, Miranda, my sweet."

Jeff turned. There was something in his throat, a big lump, which felt as if it was choking him. "Miranda?" The girl swallowed. She could not speak. "You said your name was Annie."

"No," said Ahab sadly. "That's the name of our baby, isn't it darling?" He stood up. He stood close. "She hasn't stopped crying since you left."

He glanced down at his naked body and then nodded at Nick. "I hope you're making him pay, doll. Six nights – must be worth a bit." He grinned and walked to the door. He touched his penis. "I'm on piece-work, myself. Bloody shame to waste it, eh, girl?"

## 7.

As soon as they were alone, she looked at Nick. She saw the grimace on his face. "Who is he?" he asked simply and closed his eyes.

"I don't know him from Adam."

"He knows your name."

"I've never seen him before."

"He knows your baby's name."

"I haven't got a baby." She blinked like a rabbit caught in the lights of a car. It was all going too fast. She ran towards him and slid her arms around his waist. Behind his back, she dug her hands into his buttocks. He always liked that.

"What's his name?"

"Who?"

"Your husband. Your boy-friend. Him."

"Listen, Nick, listen to me. I don't know who the hell this guy is. All right?"

He grabbed her hair, tugged her head back, and gazed at her viciously. "Which of you earns the most?" he spat.

That was when she struck the first blow.

In the other bedroom, Ahab seemed to be in a daze. He sat on the bed, leaning against the wall, peeping at the scene next door. Jeff's head was buried between his open legs, doing incredible things with his mouth, teeth and tongue. He moved his pelvis in little spasms, to encourage the other, to egg him on to still greater efforts.

Ahab stared at the violence unroll before his eyes. It was like being at a peep-show. He felt stimulated to a level he had never known before. But it was as if his face had become a mask. He could feel eyes behind his eyes. When he thought about where he was ... and when he remembered to what he was lending his body ... a part of him cowered in shame. But another part sent golden darts to different parts of his body.

He toyed with Jeff's head, pulling him down, further down.

"You stand by your promise?" he whispered, listening to the screams beyond the wall.

"Yes, yes, yes," gasped Jeff.

"Mine for all time?"

"Yours forever."

Ahab bunched up his muscles and watched through the hole as the man called Nick lifted the girl off the floor by her neck.

"Arrgh!" croaked the girl.

"Arrgh," croaked Ahab, slamming into a death-defying ejaculation deep inside the other guy's throat.

"Arrgh!" gasped Jeff, knowing that he was as close to death as he would ever be, and survive.

When Nick came out of his stupor, they had cleaned everything up. The flat was tidy. There were bright lights on the ceiling that came from the pub across the road. They could hear the sing-song and the tinkle of the old piano.

In the shop at Covent Garden, you can still have your cards read. It used to be a young man that did it. Wore a sheepskin coat, lots of beads, and looked a bit like a hippy. The word is that he went with some travellers. Others think that he went to try his luck on the French Riviera. The new Tarot Man looks a lot like the one that has disappeared. Except that he's very much older.

# The Underpass

*Think no more; 'tis only thinking*
*Lays lads underground.*

A.E.Houseman, 'Bredon Hill'

## 1.

Why do girls write letters to men they've never met? Is it because they have an urge to explain themselves? They're not too sure of their appearance, perhaps, and they don't want you to draw the wrong impression. You should read them. You should listen. Girls can be very grateful when you do not march rough-shod over their dreams.

Taking no risks, girls often say too much about themselves. Haven't you noticed how they go on for hours? If you want to be a success with the ladies, just ask them a few questions and pretend that the answer is as enthralling as 'Gone With the Wind'. They'll love you for it. They'll thank you for the very nice chat and invite you in. This is their weak spot, if you know what I mean. They are ever so interested in themselves. Buy them a drink and they'll say more than is wise. Also, like Wagner, they go on too long!

I'm sure you've heard all about those scandals where a famous political figure turns out to have a mistress? Well, you can take it from me, it wasn't the man who blew the cover. The scandal is almost always caused by the woman. Try it! In a public place, for example, the restaurant at Harrods, just cry out in a loud voice: "Madame, you have a lover!" The manager will have to send for a hundred new cups and saucers. And maybe some fresh waiters.

It's worse when they're in gaggles. They all talk at once,

yet they all hear what is said. They go at it hammer and tongs, nineteen to the dozen. Then all of a sudden they stop. Slowly their heads turn and their eyes fix on you! It leaves you in no doubt, does it? You know instantaneously what they've been talking about. I've seen nurses do it on a hospital ward, and the poor sod in the end bed has gone into rigor mortis. I've seen vultures do it in Arizona, and both horse and cowboy have laid down. It's the sort of thing that brings it home to you. Don't ask me what. Just put your hands up and wave that white flag.

"Now that you mention it..." says one, diving back into the rugby scrum.

"Well it doesn't show, does it...?" comments her mate.

"They wear things for it," says the full-back.

"Well Julie Nijinsky went and married a Pole," offers the wing-half, which is bloody obvious from her flaming name.

And so it continues. You go red, as does every other chap in earshot. Each is absolutely certain that they are discussing him – or his little weakness. The need for a dab of Brut gets more and more evident as the temperature rises to the level of an incubator for piglets. They shuffle their feet, and say "Aye", "Ah well", or "What did you think of the match?" Pipes get tapped on heels. Glasses get an extra clink. We all blow more froth from the top of our pints and smack our lips.

There's one old biddy who gave up rugby years ago, but she hasn't forgotten how it's played. She sits next to the dart board and, like the Boy on the Burning Deck, she'll only move for a gin and tonic. Her ears flap like Dumbo's mother. Her lips are pursed in a show of fuming outrage. Her eyebrows work like windscreen wipers and make you wish to God you were somewhere else.

It's at times like that you'd welcome an Arab terrorist, a Royal Visit, or a giant rat. Anything to break up the party or change the course of history but, as with policemen, they're never there when you need them! "But they are when you don't," my mother always adds, thinking of my Dad. Not that she suffers much from uncontrollable hungers, if you follow my line of thought. My Dad's best mate sees to that. I think she misses the candlesticks on which he was expert.

"Solid silver," he used to say with pride. And his voice

58

would tremble as if he'd made them himself at school. He would put them on the sideboard, the table, and even the television set. I swear to God, our front fucking window shone like the shrine at Lourdes! It was like sailing past the bleeding Wolf Rock lighthouse. When the coppers came to arrest him, they'd all been issued with dark glasses.

2.

The only reason they write to you, the girls, is that they think you're a celebrity. Most of your life, you've been nothing and your existence mattered to nobody. You know all about being 'a man in the street'. You should, you've slept in most of them. You were the first invisible man. Had you stood for election, you'd have been voted "the chap least likely to stand out in a crowd". Then you had to spoil it all by writing a couple of books. They learned about your dad, and fame came as the snows melted.

You never imagined that this would happen. You never planned it this way. I've had my fantasies, I must admit. But then again, who hasn't? I dare say mine were more particular than most. Do you remember those water beds? I'd have one filled with Guinness, and I'd prick it all over with the thinnest hypodermic needle that my doctor could provide. Then I'd fling a naked, buxom beauty on it, and make her writhe till she was covered in froth. The birth of bloody Venus! In I'd plunge, ready to open her oysters, and if he wanted, Botticelli could join us.

Three pints and I'm anybody's – seven and I'd fuck a hot drinks machine! My brother once told his girl-friend's mother that I was good at ousting moles from lawns! There's no point my going red in the face, or being ashamed. It's not as if I can help it. It just comes all over me ... and so do I.

I've been banned from Marks & Spencers: all because you have to pass 'Lingerie' to get to 'Men's Socks'. All that black silk made me think of Guinness. All that fragile lace put me in mind of froth. Not to mention the ample brassieres that were poking out of the very walls. But I got ensnared in some sort of folding metal contraption that had hooks, nets and wheels all over.

"What are you doing to my baby pusher?" an irate mother asked.

"The same thing it's doing to mine," I howled.

The Security Guard and a Plain Clothes Detective were not at all sure whether the thing that I seemed to be wielding was going into, or coming out of, my flies. They brought me down with the best flying tackle this side of Twickenham. Thinking the worst – or the best – it depends which way you look at it – I clamped my claws into their crotches and squeezed.

This was when the flash went off. And that was the photo that graced the front page of, first, the local newspaper and then, after, the nationals. "Local Man Traps Thieves Red Handed," said one headline. "Hercules Hot on the Trail of the Hydra", said another. The best came from a specimen of the gutter press: "Whose Bells is He Wringing?"

It was this incident which brought me to the attention of a literary agent. Or rather it struck a chord in her mind. I'd been writing for a year or two already, and she was one of the persons who had returned several of my manuscripts. Literary agents play very much the same role as exorcists: they send the ghastly back where it was spawned!

If you are lousy, you get what is called a rejection slip. It thuds like a dagger into your heart. If you show some vague signs of faint promise, you get a few scribbled words – "Next time you're passing through London, come and see me." The nearest you've ever been to London was a postcard from someone called Big Ben. But all of a sudden, you find an excuse for going. Your Cockney grandma dies, and you are 'passing through' inside three days. You get the "ten minute chat" and a coffee. But if you're promising, if you're the unexpected prodigy she's been waiting for throughout her career – then it's "the charming two hour chat" with a slap-up lunch.

When they let you see their legs, you realise you're in with a chance. If it's a male literary agent, then you know you're in schtuck. Speak to him only of cash or royalties and the fifteen children you've got to feed. I don't know why, but the fact that you have kids has the same effect on gays as botrytis on grapes. They wilt visibly before your eyes. It's not that I'm against gays ... but I don't particularly want to be, either.

Through the haze of smoke, a literary agent will often ask how long it is. Pause before you answer. Give one of those polite, little coughs and ask if he's referring to your manuscript or his own life expectancy. They usually take the hint.

## 3.

As it happens, I think my books are very good. So do millions of other people, if one judges by the sales figures alone. There are authors who have written only one book, called something like 'How to Do Joined-Up Writing for Money'. I'm not one to split hairs, but this is a bit like self-incest. But one must try to be fair. If someone is a lunatic, it might help more if his doctor were crazy too. That's what we mean by psychiatry: two ding-dongs ringing each other's bell.

Do you see what I'm getting at? You don't have to be a writer to be able to offer valid criticism. On the other hand, there are those people who call themselves 'book doctors'. You send them your manuscript and they do micro-surgery on it in return for a hefty fee. If they think your work is promising, they'll ask for a fee and a percentage. I used one once. It cost ten quid for a new title.

I can say without boasting that my books would have been good, whatever I'd written about. Or so my agent told me. "You have a flair!" she said, stroking me all over. "I can feel these things." She was certainly feeling mine. It was like being a cocker spaniel being hand checked for fleas. Of course, she said, she was tuning in to my vibrations. I thought she was trying to pull them out by the roots. Had I been a piece of rump steak, you could have said I was being tenderised.

So I'm not at all surprised when she says that she finds me very physical! Physical is all she has ever checked me for. I might also be intellectual, but we never get as far as my mind. It is only my body she likes. In itself, this is very weird. I know that you have no wish to have a look at it, but if you did see my body, you'd know that I haven't eaten much for several weeks. Not since I last sneaked into a funeral, in fact. They always assume that you're a distant cousin, and hardly ever get nosy. If anyone does ask what you're doing there, just slap your forehead and cry "Oh God! I followed the wrong hearse!" Then leg it. Can this be why she finds me physical? Not likely.

The last time I caught a glimpse of myself in the bathroom mirror, I screamed and hit it with a karate chop. I was in such fucking agony, I didn't even weep. I just writhed like a snake whose back has been bicycled. My Sensei would have been proud of me! If he's still alive, that is, because very few of us paid. It was while I was down there, on the bathroom floor, that I noticed a sanitary towel tucked behind the toilet.

Being a man, I hardly ever use the things, so I guessed it must have been left by a previous tenant or a visitor. More likely a visitor, I thought, because if the tenant had been female, she would have had one of those special little swing-bins that you operate by foot. You've seen them in hotels, haven't you? Every man who goes to the loo wonders what the hell it's for and presses the pedal. It's quite a shock to the system, I can tell you. You go back to your table staring away from the dessert trolley.

But while I was prostrate, on the bathroom floor, in front of the full-length mirror, I had time to reflect. I began to realise how useless I'd be if I were attacked by 'The Living Dead' or 'The Creature from the Black Lagoon.' Normally, when a man looks in a mirror, he cuts out all the unimportant bits and sees only his face and penis. The one hangs below the other like a circumcised wart or a dead thumb lacking a fingernail. He gives a quick glance like the sweep of a radar antenna. He takes in his looks and works out his chances.

Well, whichever angle I adopted, I could not quite see myself as having a starring role in anyone's erotic fantasy. I mean to say! We might as well be honest. I am not such stuff as dreams are made of. By the time I struggled upright, which means exactly what it says, I felt rather inferior.

Oh yes, there are men who like lads on the slender side. It brings back memories of youth and things that happened at school, they say. They like to pretend that you are younger than you really are. But this was a lady and so she was more difficult to analyse. Did she go in for barbecued spare ribs, or did she fancy my Spring Roll? After that, one has even stranger thoughts about the way these orientals use their chopsticks. I once saw a film where this guy trapped a fly!

## 4.

My golden opinion of my talents as an author is not shared by everyone. There are a few – sixty-three to be exact – who have taken the immense trouble of writing to me. To give me an example of their own literary skills, they usually begin: "You are pure shit"! This has even less charm than those notes from the tax inspector. At the outset, I used to think that sarcasm was a wonderful weapon, so I used to ask them what 'impure shit' might be. It turned out that I was that too, and lots of other things besides.

I'm a bit of a stickler, you know. I can't help it. When I was a lad, they taught me English. These days they train you in painting posters or marching like lemmings toward the line of police. Hence, to my ears, 'pure' is a curious adjective to use with 'shit'. On a normal day, I don't go to the trouble of saying anything other than just 'shit'. I am not a collector. I have not joined any clubs. I do not buy, sell or swap rare samples. Call me a barbarian, but I feel that shit is best left where it is.

But I'm only an amateur. I turn out only such and such a quantity per day and, unlike the Chinese communists, I don't want to up the production figures. So I have no wish to modernise my plant or enter into any kind of competition. Apart from which, my eyes are not what they used to be. I suffer from presbyopia. In common speech, it means I am long-sighted. There are some very awkward consequences. For instance, I have to cross to the opposite side of the road to read the name of a street. Now just think what this implies if ever I want a pee. You don't often see many men having to use a pair of binoculars! Even then ... I get very confused if there are other men at either side of me. It's not as if they wear a name-tag on it, and they do all rather look alike.

So I bow to the loftier wisdom of those who write these rotten letters. I salute the years they have put into their study of the subject. I am but a dabbler – whereas they have plumbed the lower depths. I also make a point of never contradicting them. Some write from prison, others from a mental home. So I just thank them for their letters and send a fast-breeding blow-fly by return. You know the sort I mean: the ones that brought down the Prophet, Job. They go by air-mail, of course.

It is tempting to glean a crumb of comfort by saying that one's critics are jealous. But for that to hold water, I would have to suggest what it might be that they are jealous of. Clearly, it is not my looks. To avoid such a dilemma, I have never once put my photo on the book-covers. This is to prevent them dropping the book in shock, and not to veil my charms. Of all the persons I might be, Salome I am not.

No doubt each of them nurses a private vision of what I am like in person. I can give them a hint and suggest that there is rather more of me than they might find useful. And it isn't all given over to herbaceous borders, either! Like the Leaning Tower of Pisa, time has taken its toll, and my foundations have slipped. To be more exact, my sub-soil has surrendered. I don't just tilt but, like Archimedes, I overflow.

I may yet outdo Marat. One day I'll get stuck in my bath and then they'll have to bury me in it. I imagine that this may pose quite a puzzle for some future archeologist! They may deduce that in this epoch we grew a shell, like turtles.

All this is beside the point. Although, to be quite exact, even that depends on your own angle of view. In my own eyes, I am special. I am still that drawn-out, gaunt, pale teenager, who looked like a photographic tripod, or a pile of unwashed plates. Oh I have tried all my life to 'think beautiful', and I suppose that, to some people, I do seem beautiful. One or two of them even say so – in letters. People who have met me, face to face, are strangely silent on the subject. They have nothing much to say.

### 5.

There is that certain class of girl who is ready to 'offer her all', for just an autograph. I tell them that I have sprained my wrist, which they do not understand. Or else I say that there's no more space in my freezer, which they understand even less. I have seen this 'all' which they are eager to fling. I have a strong suspicion that it has been flung several times before, and in some very far-off places. Obviously, it must be shaped like a boomerang because they always get it back – or else, what they are flinging is fraudulent.

Whatever else, I have never claimed to be a connoisseur of women – nor, for that matter, of men. If you can understand what I mean, when it comes to 'flesh pots', I prefer the type that have no handles. Apart from that, you could say I have always been cursory and a wee bit shallow. I just thank God and take what comes. And once in a blue moon, if I'm patient, it does. Come, I mean.

No, as regards sex, I've got to admit that I'm not at all your common or garden 'globe trotter', nor yet your intrepid 'opener-up of new territory.' I'm not in quite the same league as James Bond or Indiana Jones. The terms which spring most readily to mind are a sexual day-tripper, or your old-fashioned weekender. Not to put too fine a point on things, I am getting old.

Frankly, I have only just found out that a Hamburger is not quite the German equivalent of a Londoner. As for Frankfurters, they have always been my downfall. A rather bored waitress once asked me if I wanted one. "Frank's what?" I asked, aghast. She was rather naive and replied: "His Furter." I will never forget the speed with which that fast-food centre emptied. I've had the same sort of trouble with items that are 'finger-lickin' good. So I'm quite prepared to accept that a lot of sex passes right over my head.

This explains why some of my fan-mail catches me on the hop. If you'll permit a sporting analogy, I get wrong footed. Not that feet come into this in any way. I was a boy scout, I'd have you know. Well, a wolf cub, anyway. I remember the old motto, 'Be Prepared' which, when you give it some reflection, is rather vague. It was all left a bit loose-ended, if you take my drift. It's one thing to be given a training course but it's quite another to see what an older scout is pushing through the tent flaps. "Anyone doing owt they shouldn't?" he asked with glee. He then showed us what a woggle was for.

You remember Crocodile Dundee, the character who couldn't work out what a bidet was for? With me it was the lavatory brush. Ours was a wooden one shaped, if you will, like a freakish, elongated mushroom with a terribly long

65

stalk. The head, I remember, had tufts of black bristles sticking out in every direction. It was like a hedgehog impaled on an umbrella. Things like that stick in your mind, don't they? I had a faint fear that it might be alive. I wasn't too sure about the lavatory either. What was it eating, I used to asked?

For some strange and unwholesome reason, lost in the murky mists of childhood, I could never bring myself to say the word 'castrated'. At Wimbledon, I would shiver visibly, whenever the umpire called for "New balls." Baroque music stays a closed book for me, all because of the castrati. I have even been known to hit any girl called Eunice, which just shows how ignorant I am, really.

In the end, if you'll pardon the pun, I saved up and went to see a psychiatrist.

6.

No psychotherapist really knows what he is doing. He does it because that is how he was trained. He explains it away by means of unproved theories, but at the end of the day it seems that he lets you talk yourself into better health. Were they free to be honest – and not sworn to secrecy by their professional body – nobody who works in the field of mental health has any clearer idea. That people are sick is an undeniable fact. But why they are sick is a matter of fierce dispute. Indeed, there are a few academics who have gone quite ga-ga with rage.

To be fair to all concerned, nobody seems to have any greater success than anybody else. As always, the treatment of madmen is a hit and miss affair. In the nineteenth century they used to half boil them and then plunge them into ice-cold water, just as we still do with brussels sprouts and peas. Earlier this century, they strapped the patients down and either sent electric shocks through their brains or else made small holes in the head and twiddled about with knives like needles. Some thirty years ago we gave them massive doses of Lithium and ruined their kidneys. Today we just tell them they're Ecologists, and let them loose on the streets.

One professor has been rather outspoken on the point – "More madmen would get better more quickly if doctors concentrated on their crosswords and did nothing else." This is the kind of chap that makes tabloid newspapers rich. You may have noticed him on TV because he now hosts his own chat show. He says things with a gay carelessness which rocks the medical profession and makes the layman feel much more superior than he did before he heard it. It's always comforting to know that everyone else is much madder than you.

They all have a pet theory, of course. Just like the question of the possibility of life in outer space. Mental illness is so very gripping just because it is more prevalent than ever. We don't use the old, frightful names any more. In fact we're not at all sure what to call it. Some say it is all due to hormones or the biochemistry of the human body. Others say it can be put down to the social behaviour of other people. Yet others talk about neural transmitters, about trauma in childhood, or even about mystic Swiss herbs. You pays your money and you takes your choice. Except that it's impossible to choose because you know even less than they do.

This is why a total psychopath might try one last time by taking a splendid course of acupuncture. I've met manic-depressives who've been rubbing 'Tiger Balm' into their foreheads for many years. From what I can judge of Adult Education Centres, there are a large number of schizophrenics going to night classes on yoga. Do you begin to see what I'm driving at? The ones who are undiagnosed go to the ones who are unqualified and the result is undescribable.

I think that paperback books have a lot to answer for.

This is where Daniel was different. He was open to all suggestions, just as he was willing to take on any client. It didn't matter what the illness might be. A pain in the neck was just as welcome as a broken heart. He would tackle an alcoholic with the same zest as a bed-wetter. He gave no promise, of course. But then, what doctor does? He simply let it be known that no needy soul was ever refused his aid.

I can't say whether this was a commercial gambit or the plain truth but – he had more hopeless cases than any of his colleagues. There was a lady who walked five miles to work because the underground trains were too suggestive! There was a young man whose trouser flies opened of their own free will. There was an old woman of seventy-two whose husband had disappeared forty years ago, and who was sure he had disguised himself as a traffic warden. Last but not least, there was a young teenager who believed that his own droppings sought to re-enter his body whenever he fell asleep. He spent most of his nights watching the walls for signs of movement, and brandishing a red-hot soldering iron. No one had ever dared to ask what strategy he had in mind.

At this point in the story, it has to be confessed that the said Daniel's success-rate was very much lower than almost anyone else's. This may well be the reason why he adopted extreme measures.

## 7.

"I'm in a bit of a predicament," I said. I realised at once that I should have chosen my words more carefully.

"Predicament", he repeated slowly. "How very interesting." Of course, the fact that he had latched on to something did not necessarily mean that I had. I looked at him with total blankness as he asked "Are you quite sure that that is what you mean?"

Feeling strangely like someone who has just betrayed the Third Reich, I groped for a more colourful expression. "Yes", I said, beginning to doubt my vocabulary. "That or the other one, a cock-up!" Cock-up seemed to interest him even more. He had seized the syllable 'dic' in my first choice, and 'up' in my second choice. I felt like a comic's feed, giving him the right lines.

"You must think I'm spouting a load of rubbish," I offered with a smile.

"Spouting a load?" he echoed, frantically taking notes.

"I think I need my head examining."

"The head of what?"

I was by now pretty sure that one of us was not in his right mind, and it was a toss-up whether I cured him before he cured me.

Then I met Marcia. Or rather, when I look back, she went out of her way to make sure that we would meet. Now a man is not normally suspicious of women. That would defeat the whole point of there being two, different sexes.

No, if he feels his dip-stick rising, or if he gets this urge to rip off everything below the belt, then he is hooked. That's what happened to Mark Anthony. It was the same with Napoleon. And while I'm not claiming to be in the same class, I follow suit.

That went right over his head. But then, everything did when he was on form.

"What do you think a top psychiatrist would make of all that?"

I moved his query to centre stage and soaked it with limelight. "Fuck off?" I said.

### 8.

There was a pedestrian underpass. It ran beneath the big road. During the day it was quite essential, what with central streets resembling the Monaco Grand Prix. But at night it changed, and it was more like a hospital ward after a nuclear war. People lived there, you see. After dark, it began to fill up with the city's flotsam. These were the ones that nobody wanted to know about. These were the ones who dare not venture too far from the Social Welfare bureau. These were the ones with dead brains that had been killed by drugs, by shock therapy, or by a parent in a rage.

If you went down there – if you didn't know – it stank worse than the underground stations when they were used during Air Raids. You couldn't even make out the separate bodies because of the rags, the bags and the boxes of corrugated cardboard. There were empty bottles, a stench of urine, and always someone who would be doing the mumbling. In that tunnel shape, with walls covered by resonant tiles, the noise reminded one of a cathedral and of chanting far away. But the incense was wrong. If you half closed your eyes, it was worse than anything drawn by Gustav Doré. If you shut them entirely, it was worse than you could ever imagine.

When he took in the situation, he didn't like to turn back. He wanted to, of course, but that would have looked cowardly in the girl's eyes. She walked straight to the very middle of the tunnel, turned round and faced him.

"Let's do it here," she suggested.

"Here?" he repeated like a sick parrot. "But, but it's squalid – it's filthy."

"But so is what we're going to do." She lay down on God knows what and lifted her skirts up. He could see what she was doing but he couldn't make out the details. And although he felt nervous, there was always a touch of excitement in doing it somewhere that was strange or perhaps forbidden. He felt his penis stir.

"Drop your trousers," she whispered hoarsely. Not a soul moved. No one stirred. He grinned like a conspirator as he fumbled with his belt and then thrust out his manhood in blatant display.

"O-h-h," she groaned. "How fat and beautiful." She flung her legs around him and her hands mangled his buttocks. "What an arse!" she gasped, almost breathlessly. "What a fine pair of hams!"

He raised his loins and tried to aim his cock, ready to make that devastating first plunge ... when all of a sudden, she took hold of it herself. Her fingers curled round it, round his balls, and she started to pull. Aiiee...!


9.


His first thought was "perversion", but then he felt someone's teeth biting down extremely hard on the calves of his legs. He bent his head back to scream, just as a piece of broken glass started sawing at his buttocks. The people were coming to life. The whole tunnel was seething like wood lice under a tombstone. Young ones, lame ones, crazy ones and alcoholics – they all limped and lurched toward him like hump-backed rats.

"It was my turn to do the shopping," she said. At the same time she took his scrotum into her mouth and tore at the flimsy skin. He couldn't howl even though he wanted to. Someone was chewing his ears. Another was gnawing at his neck. It was impossible to defend himself. If he stuck out a hand, his fingers were cracked off like the claws of a crab. If he tried to roll away, he was held by too many mouths.

He was being eaten alive.

He watched in a state of paralytic shock as his body seemed to dwindle and shrink.

The girl was pulling back his foreskin and staring at his gland. "Help me," he managed to croak, and watched in revulsion as she bit off the tip. To his own astonishment, he had a weak orgasm and the sperm oozed over his phallus like a delicate, creamy sauce. She devoured it with intense gusto.

"You're so good," she crooned. Her face was smeared with blood and a gobbet of flesh dangled from her mouth corner. She giggled inanely as he fell flat onto the ground. "But you never doubted that, did you. You always boasted that you were the best!"

He stared at the shape that was drawn in felt-tip pen on the wall opposite. He kept his eyes fixed on it as they crawled over him, wave after wave. Finally they penetrated to the interior of his body. It was an indescribable sensation, all those hands clawing at his tripes. He saw his intestines being pulled away like the innards of a clock.

He felt the light going dim now. And all the time, the eyes of that drawing grew brighter and brighter, and a great splash of his own blood was being daubed across its hands. Who was it who said that dying was like ultimate orgasm? It wasn't true. It was a lie. And there he grinned, this insane image of the Father of All Lies.

When morning came, there was nothing left to see. It still stank of course, but the council cleaners would be round soon with their high-pressure hose-pipes. The early birds and the shift-workers clattered through the tunnel with distaste on their lips. They saw the graffiti and the jets of blood. It was easy to assume it was all due to delinquents and addicts who had hit an artery.

"It's supposed to be an underpass," snorted one woman in disgust.

"More like a public lavatory," sniped a man.

"You don't know where you're treading," wailed an elderly tea-lady who was just about due for retirement.

"They should put lights in," said someone in the dark.

"They did and they broke them," replied another shadow.

One simply didn't notice the odd finger nail, or the unusual tufts of hair. By nightfall, the rats had taken care of it all.

# Jingle Bells

*Yule : the Norse name for Odin's winter feast. During the ritual meal, a Yule Log was brought in, and lit by pieces of last year's log. This guaranteed the survival of right rule, and kept the order in the world.*

*1.*

The boy on the bed was stark naked and quite marvellous, if you like that sort of thing. But then again, most people are, when they're naked, wouldn't you agree? Quite marvellous, I mean. It depends, of course, on how many people you've seen ... lying on their beds, stark naked. It also depends on whether you are so afraid of nudity that even the sight of naked knee-caps makes you want to vomit. I'm told that many old ladies lose weight in the summer months, if you follow my drift. But then so do many old men, but for quite different reasons.

We have such a strange attitude toward our own kind, don't you think? It's good for mental health to remind ourselves that all religions have been engineered and devised by Man. In spite of this, the closest we ever get to spiritual rapture is during sexual orgasm. It is no good getting cross with me if you don't approve of the statement. I didn't invent it. But things being as they are, it's hardly surprising that different religions have different things to say about sex and orgasm. Most pious people are pretty sure it was God's single, biggest mistake. Myself, I think it was the blue rinse.

But there's no doubt that ever since we learned about art, we've been painting and sculpting the human body non-stop. Why, we even use it as a religious symbol. What is more, in the first few centuries, Jesus Christ on his crucifix was every bit a Man, and sported no tea towels! From an aesthetic point of view, there is nothing that inspires us more. From the moral aspect though, it has been labelled 'sinful'.

Yet we don't put ski-suits on Huskies, you notice. We don't fit Aberdeen Angus cattle with kilts. Come to that, we do not insist that snakes get kitted out in a long sock! This horror of nudity only applies to ourselves – and even then, only in Christian lands. Elsewhere in the world, they're far too busy dying from floods, famine and politics. We in the West, we've got it made, which may be why we brand certain bits of the body as 'improper'.

I have a theory that it isn't the nudity that worries us. I think it may be the clothes.

You see how difficult it would be if we all went around in the state of Adam. Police could not tell a director from a bum, a prince from a peasant, or a criminal from other policemen. Clothes are a way of saying who you are. They are a statement about your identity. If we all wore nothing, where would Traffic Wardens keep their sticky-tape? How would the Fire Brigade rescue cats? Would Members of Parliament still stand to raise their points of order?

The game of cricket would have to end!

Civil servants would have to be a bit more careful with those bloody rubber stamps. The dear, old A.A. would have to salute everybody. And local councils would have to fill in the slots on park benches or risk being sued for damages! Can you imagine? God's own handiwork on display everywhere. No brass buttons. No silk socks. No brand marks like 'Harrods' or 'Marks & Spencers'. We'd all look the same. Society would collapse.

It is in precisely these terms that I declare that the boy on the bed was beautiful. This was not a starving African. This was not a survivor from some Arab dictator's jail. Neither was it a Nazi remnant pretending to be a patriot in the middle of eastern Europe. If you have the eyes of an artist ... if you can still empathise with humanity ... then this naked boy was a summation of all that we believe in. He was our faith in the future of mankind – for which, they say, the Son of God died.

Had he been made of bronze, you would have dared to caress him. If he'd had nail-holes in his hands and feet, you could have put your arms round him and wept. Had he but been just dead even, you would have been allowed to display your loss and your love. But not so while he's still alive. Yet he himself was born because of someone else's nakedness. They had bathed him then and they would bathe him again when he died. Between the beginning and the end, between alpha and omega, he might just manage to create more life.

If that is not God, then is it not God within him? If ever it should cross your mind again, the crucifix, then you really ought to wonder. Would the Redeemer of the World have succeeded better if he had been dressed for Ascot, the New Year's Ball in Vienna, or the Red Cross gala in Monaco? I somehow think that the 'social impact' would not have bitten so deeply.

It is the mute appeal of his Humanity which makes the magic work. It is not the anatomy, nor the manly detail: it's what the nakedness says. It speaks in a universal tongue that we all understand, but none of us can explain. Priests and popes torture themselves with vows of 'purity'. Christian extremists would ban abortion, on the one hand, and castrate themselves with the other. Why not shout at God? Why not hold marches in front of his door and accuse him? "Oh Lord, why didst thou create sex, which so troubles us?"

They are quite unable to hear God's reply: "Verily, I made it simple. Who then has set fear in your hearts?"

If only they knew what harm they have done, and how much pain they have caused. There is such compassion in the charisma of Christ, yet so little in the souls of His followers. They interpret his words as they see fit. Yet He spoke in Aramaic, not that it worries them. Blind, bigoted and beyond all salvation themselves, they act as midwives to the birth of Evil.

They are not yet afraid, but they will be.

Just take a look at the books on the rough, home-made shelves in this sad bed-sit. There are the texts of Social Science, mixed with devotional works. Here is one on Economics and adjacent to it there is one on Sin. In the waste-bin he made there are pages from a magazine he's spent all night cutting up. There is a mound of fine, paper threads which even the landlady will not recognise – though she is certain to try to piece them together.

She likes puzzles. She is a born spy. When Peter left with his eyes moist and red, she just said "Good night, dearie", in her most sarcastic voice. The sun was up and the postman had already been.

She was Irish, the landlady, over fifty but under seventy, which meant she was sixty-two. It was hard to be precise with all the make-up she wore and all the Guinness she drank. Her hair was dull-red, like the tip of a joke cigarette. There were so many glints and hi-lights that it looked like a copper pan-scrub. She was a mess, but a very ethical mess. She'd thrown away her rosary when she was twelve, and bought herself a new one when she was forty-one and himself had left her. She was a case of 'faith renewed'. But if ever he came back, she knew full-well she'd flush the rosary down the lavatory again.

But, like a great many religious people, because she felt less than perfect herself, she had determined that her young lodger was going to be. She went to mass every day, or so she said. She prayed for him all the time and even lit candles. It made her feel virtuous. She told him, of course. She let him know. It's not a crime is it? They can't touch you for it. So far as she knew, there was no law against a bit of 'religious harassment'.

She seemed to know whenever Peter went in to his room. She'd knock on the door and offer to clean his room. She'd bring him some letters that she'd hidden for a week. She'd run the vacuum cleaner up and down the corridor. Oh, yes, she knew how to put people off. She had even thought about boring a hole through the wall so that she could catch them at it.

She backed up her frontal attack with more frequent assaults on heaven. She fell to her knees with a loud bang. She said her Amens like a High-Court Judge, and when she addressed the Lord direct, her prayers were more like nuclear missiles. She knew how to pierce each and every bloody breast-plate of righteousness all right.

It didn't worry her one whit when she heard them having words, and that Peter came out crying. "Oh dear," she

75

would murmur in mock sympathy. "Has he been nasty again? You go to church, dearie. Tell God all about it."

She just assumed that they were lovers. Well, it did look that way, didn't it? Not that this worried her, not in itself. She could easily guess what such people might do. She found it quite intriguing to guess. No, the simple truth was: she had found a soul that she was determined to save. She didn't realise that they were brothers. No one bothered to tell her. So she wasn't to blame for the things she assumed.

Truth was though that Peter, the younger one who came to visit and wept a lot ... Peter was afraid that his own God, Paul, might actually be going mad.

### 3.

There are people, eager to reel out the patter and make converts, who would do a damn sight better if they got their own last words ready. They should be working out what they are going to say with their last breath. "Into thy hands, Oh Lord, I commit my soul"? Something like that, I dare say. Something quavering but resolute, thinking that all the nastiness will be forgotten at the wave of a magician's wand.

And will it work, even though they themselves have been such stern, merciless judges all their lives, condemning others to a sense of perpetual guilt? Will the magic formula always work, no matter the hell you have done? One can at least assume that they place some high value on their own soul. As well they might! After all, they built a religion out of their own opinions. They gilded some trivial trash and bowed down before it, calling it Truth. And in the name of that truth, they felt free to destroy the happiness of those who did not agree.

God's word? They dare to call that God's word ... their own paranoia ... their proud delusions? Why do they think that what they believe is true? It's simply because they feel them so intensely. They destroy hope. They have attended on despair. They have been hypocritical wet-nurses to the whelps of the devil. There is no place in heaven for crack-pots or preachers who rant loudly – in order to drown their own doubts and convince themselves. Has no one ever asked why prudery drives us mad?

He lay face down on his rumpled sheets. The only light came from a lamp in the street. As it passed through the grimy, old window panes, it threw a chequered pattern across his flesh. The bed looked like a graph of the economy while the boy's back was a profit and loss account. One of the main points of male beauty lies in the curving necklace of his spine, and the smallness of his buttocks.

Women find a man's arse one of the sexiest things about him. Like a bull's neck or a stallion's flanks, it bunches sturdily and collects the power to thrust. The width of his shoulders lends it emphasis. His spinal column points to it like the arm of a railway signal. There are three great muscles in each buttock, and very little fat. That is how you might appraise your chosen sacrifice. That is how you take the measure of your man. Or your victim.

Perhaps it was the headlights of a passing lorry, or maybe a sudden gust of wind caused all the concrete lamp-posts to bend. At all events, the room seemed to heave, and the shadows in the corners seemed to readjust themselves. The finer detail of the chiaroscuro flowed as if Max Ernst were tampering with a David Hockney.

His back had the same sheen as the winner of the Derby. His lean muscles all had a touch of gloss. As for his arse, the twin globes gleamed like a pair of polished lemons as he stabbed again and again, downward.

It was only his pelvis which moved. That and his head which thrashed from side to side in frenzied jerks. He didn't stop. He went on and on. He was like an oiled frog on a bench, its brain pithed, attached to an electric current. He was a sexual martyr resolute and ready to die for his faith. He was like a kitchen gadget chopping up chips.

All of a sudden he stopped and gave a moan. It was not exactly a happy moan. It was hardly the moan of a man who is climbing upward toward an orgasm. Had he hurt his back? Had a ligament torn? Was it epilepsy? Did he have any kind of problem with his heart? He winced as he sucked in air via his flared nostrils. It was emptiness of spirit, that's all. The shadows by the sink seemed to slide closer to the wardrobe.

He was weeping. That is the top and bottom of it. A little boy sobbing salty tears. *Eine kleine nachtmusik*. He shivered though not from the chill of the small hours. The cheap alarm clock with Mickey Mouse fingers ticked out the rhythm of a slow march. His eyes had dark rings round them. But the dark shadows around the bed seemed to draw back a little, as if they were black sponges soaking up his sadness.

He was angry with himself and desperate. He couldn't quite reach orgasm. The absurdity of his plight enraged him and he felt furious at his sexual organs. He gave his cock a sharp slap and bent it downwards so that it poked backward along the mattress. He was punishing it, as if it were to blame. Other men smile, of course. It's only natural. When what you fear most – happens to someone else – then you feel such a great sense of relief. Banana skins, lavatories, God and death: the things that are ever fertile ground for jokes.

### 4.

It was no joke to him though. That is what filled him with wrath and rancour. He could feel himself filling up with an urgent need to spill his seed. It was like a boiler about to burst. But the valve wouldn't turn. He could not let off steam. The pressure and the hunger were starting to drive him mad. Hence the books, the magazines, and the dozen or so gadgets that he had tried and rejected. He was as desperate as someone with a cancer – except that this couldn't be cut out.

But what was the use of being frustrated and hungry and desperate? You couldn't just ... give up. That's not possible for a man, or he's got to be in a very bad way indeed. So he clamped his jaw shut and knew that he would try again. He must always keep on trying again ... and again ... because he could not live if it was never to happen again. That fear was like a knife in his belly. He held it back as best he could, parried it like a seaman in Shanghai, but even so he gave a yelp. The little, piping squeak of an enraged French poodle. His aching hips began to bang again.

The shadows seemed to draw in closer as if they too were aching.

He didn't know who he was fucking. It didn't matter. He was too handsome to care. They all loved him and wanted him. He didn't have to lift a finger or waste any time on chatting them up. A glance was all. A nod did it. A tilt of the head. A lift of the eye-brow. It was easy, easy, easy. He didn't need to do a thing. Some kind of strange force just drew people to him. The only question was: his place or theirs?

And what the hell did that matter? It met the need. That was the terrific side to it. A bit of snaking, a moment's shrimping, a few thrusts of the old pelvis and bingo! The bells rang, the wheels whirred, and angels sang as he hit the jackpot yet again. Wow-ee! Toes curled and dandruff jumped off your scalp. It was like being a vampire and banging the old stake well and truly home.

And after that, the thirty seconds of floating ... both the shortest and the highest flying lesson in the world.

The spirits were getting restive now. One or two of them gave little darts forward like hounds encircling a fox.

Yes, sad to say, he had forgotten who he was fucking. It had been like that for quite some time now. The very first time that he ever woke up to find a boy's head next to his, he recoiled so fiercely that he fell out of bed. When the kid had gone, he knelt in the toilet and heaved for an hour. After that he'd scrubbed himself. He'd even managed to give himself an enema.

Now, it didn't seem to matter. Nothing mattered. When he needed a fuck, anything would do ... a girl, a boy, or even a German Shepherd! He grimaced at the faint echo of his old sense of humour. He thought of the old Cliff Richard song, 'Living Doll', but replaced the two key words with 'Rubber Doll'. He wondered how many people would hear it with the same sort of tartness? Maybe someone should tell Cliff to compose a song about the rainy nights. Or else the cold nights and the lonely nights, and especially those nights when the moon was weepily blue. 'A Pillow Never Loves You Back'. That is what he'd call it. Maybe Cliff knew.

He was twenty-four, which is a very good age for virility. He was six feet tall, which is a height that has a terrific effect on most people. In addition, he was just about as handsome as they come. That was the problem though – he didn't come all that often. It gave a sad little down-turn in the corner of his eye. There were delectable shadows near to his nose. His teeth were still a blinding white but the springtime smile was tinged with autumn.

# 5.

They said it might be the drugs. That was the most likely explanation. They talked about the sympathetic nervous system and the weird things in the limbic region. If you tamper with things like that – well – you had only yourself to blame. Then again, when they didn't need to give him moralist sermons, they suggested it might be the drink. Yes, he thought, that just as likely as anything else. He imagined a bar with its jars of pickled pricks and spicy onions. Things to make you thirsty; things to make you drink more.

Oh perhaps he was just not getting enough sleep, a third had proposed. Well, he could go along with that all right, because he hardly slept at all nowadays. He was always tired. While he was still lying there, he felt too knackered even to get up. When he was up, he felt like a toppling tree – "Timber!" They used to ask him, wherever he worked, if he had just got over the 'flu. Someone said he must have been travelling all night. That was a bit closer to the truth. That's what it felt like. A long distance bus, London to Glasgow, or Marseilles to Paris, and your body twisting and turning to ease unknown bones and strange muscles.

"Do you eat enough?" the doctor had asked.

"What's enough?" he had asked wittily. He had failed in philosophy at college but was ever content to pretend that he hadn't.

But the doctor knew a bit of William Blake too. "Enough is a little bit less than you actually want," he replied. One would not have been surprised if he had known a bit about the esoteric mysteries, that one.

Well, in that case, he wasn't getting enough sex either, and that was more critical. But no, to be perfectly honest, that was not true. It all depends on what one means by sex, doesn't it? He was making bodily contacts still. His skin tried to set fire to other skin.

I'll explain it another way: he was putting his hands on more partners per week than most people had in a lifetime.

Like a matinee idol, he liked to have them waiting at the stage door. It boosted his courage to hear those sharp intakes of breath as he brushed by – and he was an expert at brushing by! That was a major part of the comfort, to know that you were still desired. And he was desired. Oh yes. No possible doubt about that. You could see it in their eyes. You could sense it in the way they touched you. You could even smell it. The same aroma as changing rooms, the Augean stables, the musk of animals in rut.

It was that which made it awesome: to think that they dreamed about him. The way they craved to finger him. The way they yearned to leap into his bed. It was like a carnival where everyone stood in line, waiting their turn to go five rounds with the champion. They could be penitents queuing on the banks of the Jordan, praying that the cousin with the charisma would come and take them riding bareback on wet dolphins.

Except that he had begun to fail.

The first time, he'd been delicately surprised and smoked a cigarette while she tried her magic arts. The next few times, faintly amused, he'd joked about Ben Hur flogging a dead horse. It took a little time for him to realise that something was going wrong. The moment the truth dawned, it was like someone plunging an icicle into his bowels. He screamed his head off. He tried to masturbate for hours on end, only stopping when his wrist got riveted or his cock was too inflamed.

These things happen, they all told him. He tried not to show his panic because, well, panic was starting. It was also the time that the shadows began to gather.

He tried everything that he could think of. At first, his partners thought he was teasing them, he took so long to reach orgasm. He tried to fool them into believing that it had all happened inside them. When that frown hit their forehead, he flung himself into the best bit of pretence they had ever seen.

They never doubted him. Why should they? Who would ever suspect it of a man? Besides, they all know that a man cannot pretend to ejaculate. Which is quite true, as far as it goes. But if they're not looking? If you distract their attention? You just make the right noises and jerk to the correct rhythm.

Under the mattress you've hidden a special tube of hair-gel that you have injected with cream and a teaspoon of bleach. It looks good, it smells good, and it has an ideal viscosity. They believe what they want to believe. They believe they have blown your mind.

## 6

Perhaps that was why the shadows grew bolder? He couldn't be sure about it. There was no way of telling. But he could see them more clearly as time went by.

He noticed too that on a few occasions, when he was playing with himself alone, he managed to achieve a kind of weak, residual orgasm.

His sperm was clear, more like paste for wall-paper. But, and this also frightened him, small gouts of goldish liquid oozed from his nipples and his navel. He found it on his forehead too, and his feet. It also spangled his pubic hair as if he had electric lice.

If he moved, it moved. If he stood up, it streamed down the length of his body. But it was slow – much, much slower than mercury. Not at all viscous, you understand, but slow like certain images in black and white films. It was why he thought it might not be real.

Except that the shadows seemed to react to it.

When it was really gold, as it had been at first, they recoiled. But as it grew duller, more tarnished, they grew less afraid. Sometimes, not too often, it was the colour of diesel oil, or meat-flies, and then they grew quite bold. They crawled closer, making sucking noises, and he ran stark naked through the midnight streets to keep them from licking his flesh.

People had seen him, of course, but very few. They were usually young, in which case they gave him a cheer. The others were tramps or drug addicts and they found it natural. One Security Guard had smiled and held out a can of beer. But he knew they would catch him, one day. That was more probable if they came to him during the hours of darkness.

So he tried with all his might not, at night, to let his mind roam toward sex. He burned sticks of incense in every corner of the room. He hung his walls with posters that sought money for famine in Africa, for flood victims in Asia, or for the homeless, the jobless or the helpless. He turned his room into a chapel of misery. He even stole a plaster statue of a Catholic Saint. He ate garlic. He hung crucifixes in any bare spot. He kept a plastic bottle of Holy Water in the toilet, and put seven drops down the pan before and after he

used it. He stopped up all the gaps round the edges of his windows with crumpled pages of the Bible.

He stuck mirror tiles on the ceiling just above his bed so that he could watch for anything crawling under it or sliding out.

He put Chinese rice bowls all around the bed to trap the black oils that were occasionally streaked with traces of gold when they condensed on his body.

He knew now that his mind reeked like a dustbin. If there was the least speck of eroticism in his mind – the shadows came, like pigeons in the park. He couldn't tell where they came from nor how they go into the room. Come to that, he caught sight of them in the streets, at a disco, or an empty car-park at twilight.

They didn't get out of taxis or step off of buses. They didn't crawl out of the drains. To be quite honest, they didn't really come at all. They thickened – like the clear glass of a bedroom window sweating over.

7.

It didn't take him long to realise that they were drawn by sexual compulsion. They seemed to be attracted by the merest whiff of orgasm, or the slightest shift in that direction.

He knew they were there. Was he supposed to see them? Did they know that he could see them? Did they give a damn? Or were they aware that it made not the slightest difference either way? By fair means or foul, it was obvious they intended to have him. It didn't really matter what he did – they were going to get him. He couldn't bear thinking about it, but yes, he thought of nothing else.

He got used to their being around. They were like the tell-tale spots that come before the fever hits. Whenever he saw them, it meant that the needs of his sexuality were grabbing the reins again. This caused a problem. It was getting very hard to answer those needs.

The circle around his bed grew more dense. The room was as dark as a railway station at night with a fog rolling in along the silent tracks. He moaned like a man in a hospital corridor who has just realised there is no way out. If you were standing at all close, and if you paid attention, you heard the terminal emptiness in his voice.

What am I going to do, he asked himself?

What will become of me?

And something, his own rancid emotions, or else the shadows, spoke to him from the tides and ripples in the darkness. "Play with it. Give yourself a treat. It will be good this time."

It crossed his mind that they might be mocking him, or making a fool of him. He couldn't even get hard. How absurd! He, who had been admired by hundreds. He had even been a model for one of those mail-order clothes catalogues. But look at him now. See the state to which he'd been reduced: a child going crazy as he tried like hell to toss himself off. How pathetic.

"Leave it to us," breathed the voices in the faintest of vague whispers. "We can show you things. We know your secret dreams and can flood your mind. We can take you to the further edge of excitement. Put your hand in ours and be divinely mad."

The shaft of his penis was as hard as rock and burned with heat. He'd never felt it so huge or so loaded with power. He stared up at the mirror on the ceiling as if it were a cinema screen. Yes, yes, he was as handsome as a warrior god, and stretched out on his naked bed like a living sacrifice. He took hold of himself as if it were a lever to move the mountains – and he began to rub.

Oh how the voices crooned, and what visions filled his mind! The strange liquid was pouring out of his body now, and he was surrounded by those iridescent, black beetle things. They formed a perfect ring about him like muddy piglets round a great sow. They made slurp, slurp, slurping noises as they sucked his skin over every inch of his body. He saw himself reflected in the mirror tiles – a pair of great, gawping eyes in a giant chrysalis cocoon.

And he felt himself coming. There was a sensation in the root of his penis like that of a great canon drawing back just before shooting a man to the moon. Then the explosion, the savage recoil, and the fountains of Versailles were turned on and sent out great fanning jets of semen.

There was a ruckus in the nest about him. His babies fought with each other to suck up the juicier gobbets.

## 8

The police telephoned Peter. They told him that Paul had collapsed and was being looked after in the Emergency Ward at the West City Hospital. When he went to Paul's room to collect his things, the landlady defied him. He had no legal right, she said. When he told her who he was, she went ashen and sat on the stairs. He guessed at once. He took great pleasure in giving her Paul's notice.

"He's not coming back," he said flatly. "He needs someone who'll keep an eye on him – not spy on him!"

She began to weep, and he saw her for what she was; a lonely, old woman who had dreamed up her own soap-opera.

"It's the name of our parish church," she bleated like a betrayed lamb. "Saints Peter and Paul."

"Go there again," said young Peter, shaking. "Go there! Stay there! Drop to your knees before your God who sees all and forgives all, you bigoted, mean, spiteful bitch! Tell Him exactly how you tried to help!"

She wailed like an air-raid siren.

He was only nineteen. So naturally, he didn't quite have the bearing to be furious or say what needed to be said. He was ashamed enough of the words he had just used. He touched her elbow in mute apology.

She hadn't pardoned him. She hadn't taken in the insult. She was thinking of other things and other mistakes. How big the house was! How small and frail she was. How empty she and it would be when the winter vacation began.

He left before he said anything worse. His old 2CV was packed like a picnic hamper. He smiled with fondness at the rubbish his brother had collected. And when he thought of his brother, he hurt inside. Things would never be the same again, would they? Childhood was gone. Now his teens were almost gone. One of these mornings he'd wake up as an old man, and wonder how and when his life had leaked away.

No one knew what was wrong with Paul, but they held out hopes of his getting well again. They murmured vaguely about anaemia and his standard of nutrition. It's like me with my car. When something goes wrong, I always say that it could be the fuel-pump. But I wouldn't recognise a fuel-pump if you put one in my hand.

The two of them said they'd get a place together – move in with each other. But they always said that. They went over the same ground during any holiday. They said it and they meant it but they never did it. There was an unspoken feeling that they'd cramp each other's style, or put strains on the way the other one lived. But the main restriction was that they were brothers, and they did love each other, and living together would be too much like never having left home. They would somehow recreate the nest which each needed to escape. They needed to love other people now.

Alone in her house, the landlady waited for the other three lodgers to come home. She wouldn't say anything to them about it. If and when they noticed, she'd think of a story to tell.

She listened to the scuttling sounds upstairs. "Bugs!" she said to herself. One could always hear them much more clearly in an empty house. And then it dawned on her cruelly. There is nothing at all 'Merry' about 'Christmas'. Get out the old folded tree. Deck it with the crumpled tinsel, the single star and the plastic face of Santa Claus. Above all, don't forget the two bottles, one of gin and the other of sherry.

Something upstairs went 'plop' as if it had fallen off a bed.

"Ah," she told herself, "it's only the music-box. The one that plays Jingle Bells very loudly."

# Chinese New Year

*Ganymede: a beautiful youth whom Zeus
abducted to be his wine-server in Olympus.
The gods gave him the elixir of life which
he may share with others. Under the
Romans, Ganymede was transformed into
Aquarius.*

*1.*

My real name is Fred, but everyone calls me Dancer. Fred
Astaire – get it? I'm the singer in a semi-pro rock band. We
think we're good. Or rather, we used to think we were good
but just lately we've been having second thoughts. Things
are not going as well as they once promised.

I'm not working just at the moment. Fact is, I haven't had
a job for nearly a year now. That's why me and a couple of
friends first got this band going. We get a lot of practice in,
seeing as how we're not short of time.

What we actually needed a while back was to make
what's known as a demo tape. We had to have something we
could circulate, especially to bods with the right kind of
influence in the trade. Normally they don't have time to do
much talent spotting so, by hook or by crook, we meant to
bring ourselves to their attention. After that, as they say, we
hoped to hit the Big Time and get rich.

It was Dave's idea actually. He managed to wangle an
invite to the Thompson party. He plays bass guitar and he'd
once been turned down by the biggest group of the day. That
made him cool. It also signified that Dave knew what was
what. So when he got us ready for the party, he told us we'd
have to go with the tide. There would be big names there –
people well on in the music industry. These were the ones

you had to know and be known by, if you were going to get anywhere.

"The reason they're holding this thrash is to celebrate the Chinese New Year," said Dave.

"I'm not Chinese," pointed out our drummer. They're a bit like that are drummers.

"The reason we're going," Dave went on, "is to attract attention." He let that sink in for a few moments. "So dress *attractively*, if you know what I mean."

"I don't know what you mean," said the drummer.

"Some of the most important people," emphasised Dave, "are a bit like *that*."

"Like what?"

"They might want to strum on your guitar strings."

The drummer thought this over. "But I haven't got a guitar."

Dave pinched his nostrils and inflated his nose. He also did this when he mixed Guinness with vodka. Normally, it was a storm warning to be followed, a moment later, by the sound of beer pumps being wrenched up by their roots. Any Yuppies in the area got heaved around by their FT Index. He had a short fuse, did Dave, in more senses than one!

He regarded the drummer as if he were either a police cadet or a freshly dropped turd. "Let them polish your cymbals," he snarled in a slowly mounting voice. "Let them rattle your tambourine ... let them tinkle with your triangle ... let them clack your fucking castanets!" His furious shout echoed and died away.

"What's a triangle?" asked the drummer.


2.


I got the message though. I have a 'D' in history, so I'm not thick. We went down the market and blew half my savings on some new clobber.

I got this white silk shirt. I swear to God you could see my nipples through it. But Dave said it was magic, just the job. I also bought some really tight jeans.

"Do they hug, you know, the figure?" Dave asked the Pakistani man who was in charge of the stall.

89

"They're fucking crippling," came the answer. He was a second generation Paki.

I went behind a curtain at the back of the stall. My God, they were tight! It took the three of us to get them on. They clung so close to my body, I felt indecent. They didn't just hug, they squeezed! Every part of my poor, pained person was portrayed as plain as day – warts and all.

When I looked at myself in the mirror, I had second thoughts, severe misgivings and cramp in a very awkward spot. "They could lock me up for this," I said.

"All's well that ends well," said Dave. He did the Daily Express crossword.

"You can see my sodding goolies," I barked.

"I haven't got any goolies," broke in the drummer.

We all looked blank.

"You can always tuck in a pair of rolled-up cotton ankle socks," said the Pakistani. The drummer looked at him, looked at us, and back at him again. "They wouldn't make any noise then," he said, walking off.

By the time I'd hobbled home, things were beginning to ease slightly. At least, I no longer had a fear of imminent gangrene. "What's the point?" I asked Dave.

He glanced down at my crotch.

"Are you trying to use me as bait?" He smiled at my crotch.

"What do you feed it?" he asked in a laid-back way.

I felt a cold sweat emerging down my back-bone. Dave was up to something. I gave him my 'Fistful of Dollars' look. "What's going on?" I said, loading it with menace.

"How much longer can we pretend to be a group if we don't make any demos and never get any gigs? It's essential we persuade someone to listen to us."

"Perhaps we're no good," I suggested.

"That didn't stop any of the others!"

I ignored his breezy wit and zoomed in on the bit that was worrying me. "Why the hell am I dressed like this?" I asked.

"Oh come on," he nudged me in the ribs. "Can't you guess?"

"Guess what?" I insisted, adding more pressure to my fingers round his neck.

"This is the best way to play it."

"Play *what*?" I asked in a voice of thunder.

He made a slight, Jewish gesture, as if about to lop off a few foreskins. "You're the bait," he said. "Big, blue eyes. Blonde curly locks. A nice, silk ribbon round your neck. You'll be the Rabbit that everyone will want to Roger."

It crossed my mind that maybe he'd dipped his fingers into our secret tin of Amsterdam floor sweepings, a.k.a. diamond dust. But of all the possible protests I could have made, what actually came out of my mouth was: "Who says I'm handsome?" And he knew then that he had me! I had to be the best bait because I swallowed it myself.


### 3.

He drove quite well for someone who built castles in the air. We took the full team, even the drummer.

It didn't seem fair, because the party wouldn't mean much to him. He'd just drum all night. That's all he ever did and maybe that was all he ever wanted to do. Some said it was caused by the noise. Others said it was the constant rhythm that did it. He'd been like it ever since we'd known him. During daylight hours, he was as thick as two short planks. But at night, with drumsticks in his hands, he was a genius. Perhaps we could pass him off as some sort of Hindu Mystic? Others had done it, with far less talent.

I'd stopped worrying about anything by then. I have phenomenal will-power. And Dave had supplied me with a couple of snorts of diamond dust.

By the time we got to the party, I was not only very pleasantly relaxed, I was also feeling a tad horny. It created havoc in the stone-washed blue yonder of my new jeans, and it had a fateful effect on anyone I spoke to. Some of them went rigid, like the King's enemies on catching a glimpse of the axe. Others tottered lightly, like opera singers who've swallowed the cork off the cough linctus.

One old dear, who looked a bit like Nefertiti's mummy, clawed at her pearl necklace as if it were choking her. For one short moment, I thought she was going to give it to me.

A Roman Catholic bishop went very red and mumbled "*mirabile dictu*". I won't bother to translate.

I was too relaxed to be too much bothered about the

effect I was having on other people. I caught sight of a prominent female singer in a far corner. I was hacking my way in her direction, when Dave grabbed my elbow and insisted on presenting me to a dreg called Robin.

"Robin," he said, "this is a very good friend. Just imagine, Dancer: his mother bought him his own recording studio."

### 4.

Have you ever wondered what a mongoose feels like when it's told to kill its first snake? That's what hit me just then. I wanted to bite the back of somebody's neck. I had to make do by grabbing the seat of Dave's knickers and screwing them up in a claw of steel. He must have felt he'd been hit by Terminator II. He knew why, all right. This thing called Robin was definitely one of *them*!

He seemed to have stepped out of an old cinema. He had no colour. There were dark shadows around his eyes, like a character from a silent film. You could even read the sub-titles as they moved across his forehead. His eyes gazed at my nipples and then at my dick. Clearly, his camera had no wide-angle lenses so he took lengthy close-ups of my crotch, my chest, and then my crotch again. It was like watching the crowd at Wimbledon with the TV turned on its side.

"Don't leave me," I said to Dave out of the corner of my mouth.

"I think he fancies you," murmured Dave.

"I don't care if he's stricken with starlight – you do not budge from my side."

Dave grinned and made a polite sociable noise for the benefit of the third party. He needn't have bothered. Robin seemed to have been struck deaf.

"Remember," hissed Dave needlessly, "he's got a recording studio all of his own to play with."

"He is not getting his hands on my acoustics," I said. I can be quite witty when I want to be. And when you don't know what else to do, I always say: be witty. I had the weirdest sensation that I might yet be auctioned off.

"I'll keep my fingers crossed," said Dave, sidling off. He's one of those who sidle off at the drop of a hat. He can melt into a crowd of just two people, if you know what I mean.

That very morning, in the Daily Mirror, I'd read my horoscope. "Your portfolio could do with some very careful handling," it said. Do the readers of the Daily Mirror have portfolios, I wondered? Apart from the proprietor, that is?

I'd been daft enough to scoff at it, would you believe. But my mother swears by their weather forecasts. "Wet and sodding windy again," is what she says at every breakfast, "And Arsenal have lost".

Only then are the rest of us allowed to look at the front-page headline. "Moral Dilemma Facing Government" it said this morning. I knew now that this had been meant as a subtle message for me. How do those reporters get to hear of such things? Or had this bloke Robin bought the paper as a new toy?

Robin was an idealist. He wasn't one to let grass grow under his feet. I was about to add he wouldn't let anything stand in his way – then I realised he might.

"That was my mate, Dave," I said by way of trying to make casual conversation. "He says you've got a recording studio." He neither confirmed nor denied it. It was clearly not the most pressing subject on his mind at that moment.

I felt as witless as the man who inquired of the Queen how she managed to keep the crown balanced. HM is said to have winked and replied that she'd had her head adjusted.

I couldn't be sure if my words had even penetrated his mind. He was still staring fixedly, first at my nipples, then at my crotch, then back at my nipples again. It's very hard knowing how to react in such a situation. More so when the public have noticed what he's doing and are leaning over to get a better view.

Even I had to take a quick look. You can't help wondering in a situation like that if your flies are open, or whether a sick pigeon has just splashed you with luminous raspberry jam. You feel so fucking exposed and your face goes red. And then, once your face has gone red, you get hot flushes everywhere as the blood in your body shunts pell-mell to every damn corner it shouldn't.

## 5

You sense the first twitches of an early spring so you try manfully to pray for frost or to occupy your mind with a hard maths problem. But the only thing that's hard is inside your pants, and it's doing geometric extensions like a maniac. What started out as the cube root of a worm is rapidly multiplying into an angry anaconda. Not to mince words, you've got a hard-on and there's nowhere handy to hide it.

Naturally, you try to brazen it out. You act as casually as if you'd brought this conger eel along to liven up the party.

Mentally, of course, you are mortified. You curse the thing, damn the thing to hell, and wish it would cancel its royal salute. It's quite unabashed though. Despite its girth, it marches to the centre of the stage just like Luciano Pavarotti, and gets ready to burst your zip.

As most blokes learn quite early in life, there are times when it's diplomatic to bend forward and lean on a piano or something. Or better still, sit on a sofa, slide into the Lotus posture, and cover your fluster with a few minutes of T.M.

The best thing of all is an ice-cold shower. But that's not the sort of thing they provide at the normal cocktail party. One could cling to an ice-bucket, I suppose, but you know how the skin sticks. You could also down as much beer as possible and pray for an attack of 'brewer's droop'. But they don't have beer at these kind of flings and those cocktails live up to their name. I tried a Tequila Sunrise, and it did.

What you really need is an excuse to get out of the house and drink in some fresh air, or thrash yourself with nettles. Try announcing loudly that the swine next door are shooting at the dogs again. Then stride out manfully, and go for a trot round the block. It's more convincing, and helps to keep up the illusion, if you do actually bring back a dead dog. The trouble is that most dogs still loose at midnight seem to have very much the same idea. If you catch sight of one eyeing you, just pray it isn't either hungry or rabid.

I speak as one who has had these problems since the age of nine. I was what my mum calls "pre-cock-ious". So I do know that these helpful hints tend to slip your mind when one of those strange blokes is actually taking aim. God alone knows what filthy project is going through his mind. It's bad enough in your own mind, where you can imagine him doing it! Your two separate visions are fed by two different fuels, of course. But you're both sweating as if suffering the same fever.

It hardly matters what the hell he might be dreaming about. It's what you *think* he's dreaming about that has the direst effects. An analyst would no doubt have many things to comment on. So inform him via your facial expression that if he breathes too deep, his days are numbered. This explains why most men in that line just take notes and turn them into thrillers.

Fuck Freud, that's their motto!

## 6.

As a matter of fact, it's really quite strange the sort of things that run through your head when you're mentally standing with your back against the wall. The emotional state I was in, I felt more afraid for Robin than myself. I would plead not guilty by reason of unnatural stress, I told myself. I stuffed the boot in where I did because I mistook him for a turkey, I'd claim.

I could read in his eyes that he was wondering if he might drop ash down my jeans and then offer to brush it off. I've done that myself with girls. (I'm not green, even if I look like a cabbage!) Besides which he was smoking a bloody giant cigar. Gives a whole new meaning to the word corona, corona ... or is that a song Boy George used to sing? Well, in any case, nobody's going to blame a boy for beating off a fate worse than death.

It's hard to say which disconcerts you more: a dick which jumps on stage to claim an Oscar, or the forbidden film that spews through the sprockets of your mind. They say that virtual reality is a new invention, but all men have known about it since their teens.

Back at the party, I realise with some panic that my nipples are now burning holes in my new shirt, so I spit on my fingers when no one's looking. The smoke makes my eyes run and I smell that special aroma of charred silk and grilled tit!

Frantic, I turn away from the spree to gaze at the romantic

scene just outside the window. The view opened onto the back-yard of a Chinese take-away. There was even a real Chinese chef taking a piss. The Yellow River. I gawped at him in vague curiosity. I don't know where I got the idea, but I somehow expected him to be using chopsticks!

As if hearing a call from ancestral voices, the chef raises his eyes toward the moon. Instead of that, he sees me, all of me, in crisp silhouette. This being the Year of the Ram, he must think he's beholding a celestial being. He rushes back into the restaurant and brings out the entire staff and clientele. They bow to me en masse. The old lady who spends her life making won-tun balls, salutes me with a bowl of Shark's Fin Soup, cackling like a tea-pot stuffed with crackers.

For my own part, I'm feeling very much like a tea-pot stuffed full of crackers! Robin has let his hand creep across the tight surface of my left buttock. I can feel the finger-prints! With a startled jolt, I jerk forward and stab a hole in a pane of the window. There's a joyful round of Oriental applause. Come to think of it, it *is* the Year of the Ram. I strive gently to extricate myself. The audience below reward me with a standing ovation and a rocket.

7.

I am now feeling a sensation that I last felt on the night of my eighteenth birthday party, some seven months before. As I suspect, my guts are playing up.

Until that day, I had only ever suffered two attacks of severe rectal panic. The first was when gastric enteritis struck on the top floor of Selfridges and the lifts weren't working. The second was when I dehydrated in the South of France and developed a severe case of concrete gut. Both episodes had been caused by the contents either insisting on coming out, or refusing to do so. The tide had now turned, so to speak, and I was grappling with the ghastly possibility that something might at any moment be forcing its way in. That, as the saying goes, was enough to make any man's knees tremble.

Robin is enjoying himself hugely. Having serviced one buttock, he does a long MOT on the other. I'm beginning to feel like the rubber bulb of a klaxon. I curl my fists into karate weapons. Problem is, Robin talks non-stop as he gropes non-stop, no doubt hoping that my ears will make me overlook the weird sensations coming from what my mum would call, down there!

He also grins a great deal too, as he reaches past me for ashtrays, matches, fresh drinks or framed photos. God knows where all these things were stacked but, without fail, his hands pass by, or go through, yet another erogenous zone. I felt I'd been well and truly trespassed.

He tells me what great after-shave I'm wearing, and absently taps his cigar into a black girl's Tina Turner wig. He doesn't even notice the bush-fire that breaks out, or hear the fantastic top C she screams as she plunges her head into the punch-bowl.

Which also bursts into flame.

With a girl guide's instinct for quick action, she flings the lot over the band. There's a mass stampede for any place there might be water.

"Why don't we all piss on her?" slurs a Mayfair accent.

"Steady on!" drawls another. "After what I've been drinking, I could be sixty degrees proof!"

The wisdom comes too late for a Scottish bloke with no trousers. He hoists his kilt, takes a sketchy aim, and then shoots backward through the broken window with a very loud WHOOSH! Luckily, he was red-haired anyway, and the Chinese thrash going on outside considers it a very lucky omen. I hear his Glaswegian accent roaring about Peking Duck ... or something that sounds very much like it.

"Don't worry," says one female voice to Scottie's erstwhile companion. "He'll handle it, he's into the New Age anyway."

"Well he's into the Guinness Book of Records now," says a second floozy boozily.

By now my pesky, would-be seducer has me tangled against some exotic greenery which, quite aptly, is a rubber plant. But Robin's the one with the tenacious tendrils! While one hypnotic hand flutters in front of my eyes, flashing a pea-sized diamond, five other hands are working away like Customs Officers. He doesn't fool me though. As Bananarama sang in the Clapping Song – my mommy told me! I knew damn well it was only cubic zirconium!

# 8.

Since both his hands are trying to claw my nipples off, I dare not for the life of me imagine what he might be brushing against my person! He goes rapping on and on about fame depending on a little talent and a lot of luck – or was it the other way round? Well, I'm not so thick that I don't get what he's suggesting. He's now grinding his out-thrust pelvis against me and I realise just how much luck I'm going to need.

The black girl comes bravely back. Her wig looks as if it's been chased round the block by a Chinese chef. The singed pianist gives a little tinkle on his instrument, as Robin does on mine. The lights dim for her rendition of a famous number by Frank Sinatra. I fix my thoughts on the words and ignore the rugby scrummage that breaks out between my legs.

Normally, if I were only joking about this sort of thing, I'd have no problem describing my sensations. If you'd asked me just one hour earlier, I'd have expected to be nauseated, enraged, driven berserk and generally pissed off. But I'd have been as wrong as the weather forecaster who said there would be no gales ... just as the studio blew away!

I can't actually tell you what it was like. There are no words, even in Australian, that would do it full justice. As the black girl warbled 'I Did It My Way', I underwent a new form of digital rape and battery!

He pushed things. He pulled things. Some things he moved about as if they were made of elastic. "I hope you've got clean hands," I spat with irony through gritted teeth. I was trying to display a stiff upper-lip but he took it for a suggestion. His head plunged inside my flies like a deep-sea diver clapping on an oxygen mask. "Bloody hell!," I yelled as I felt the touch of teeth on my rosary beads. The song, be it said, was also going down quite well.

Never before had my private parts been treated like rising dough. My testicles, which until now had always been quite chummy, felt as if they'd been trapped in the doors of different trains. My foreskin (I remember having one at the beginning) was pulled back like a nylon stocking on a bank robber. Another hand – how many did he have? – was working at my arse-hole as if changing a tyre.

98

I would have liked to scream. I would very much have liked to scream. The fact that I did not was due quite simply to my being paralysed. I had the distinct feeling that if I moved a muscle, or even blinked, there was a serious risk that I'd turn inside out. I could only lean there weakly, with the leaves of the fucking rubber plant up my nostrils. As this deviant villain did those naughty things, I made a low, slow groaning noise like an Arab bee-hive that's been flung into a synagogue.

## 9.

He kneaded my cock like a French baker determined to make bread. Out popped his dripping, sweaty face. "It's a fucking beauty," he whispered hoarsely.

"If it's all the same to you," I choked, "I'd like to have it back."

"I'm just finishing you off," he explained needlessly.

"Give it two undercoats and a metallic finish," I somehow managed to quip.

"Geronimo" he yelled like a happy cowboy and flung himself back to his work. He went at it hammer and tongs. I never dreamt that a poor sod's parts could go through so much indignity and live. He was like an antique dealer searching for fraud. He was like a cattle breeder de-horning a dangerous bull. He was like a part-time plumber close to tea-time.

That he was an expert, there can be not the slightest doubt. He had the touch of a master, as they say, and he also had one knack if not two. Fuck the 'shrink' and the Daily Mirror. I remembered what my mother had said. "It's enough to make grown men crack!" She was describing her personal reaction to 'Gone With the Wind', which had moved her tremendously. Outside the window, down in the yard, my eye caught a glimpse of shapes moving about, just outside the Chinese restaurant. It might have been turtles, I suppose. Or some other delicacy that they like to keep as fresh as possible. I had other things on my mind right then. "Frankly," I croaked on a rising note as I clawed at Robin's head, "Frankly, my dear, I don't give a damn!"

I made a noise like two tubas mating, and donated

enough cream to last Wimbledon a fortnight. Well, I thought, so much for tennis! As I tottered down the steps to the yard, I remember wondering if the latest mega-star – the one who'd had everything lifted – had ever met Robin? I also wondered if Robin had pulled out any surgical stitches? I felt like I could use a few myself.

### 10.

I passed the window of the Chinese kitchen. The chef was oiling his wok while behind him, a steaming Scotsman was trying to re-pleat his kilt.

"You like crispy meat-balls?" he invited.

"Where did you get them?" I croaked.

That's the trouble with the Chinese. They speak like characters from a Kung-fu film and are very foreign. That means you can't scrutinise them. I mention it in case you try.

Do they know more than they're saying? Where did their slant-eyes come from anyway? "It pays," as Gladstone said to Queen Victoria, "never to forget the Yellow Peril." Queen Victoria, who seems not to have been too fond of old Glad, is said to have replied: "I think of very little else!"

The grinning chef was intent on welcoming in the Chinese Year of the Snake. Have you noticed how suggestive the names for their years are: the Cock, the Ram, the Goat? This explains why so many Chinese babies are born every day. Hence 'the yellow peril'.

"Chow mein?"

"Oh yes, officer. He certainly did."

He gave me the strangest look. It was a bit like the Dowager Empress about to signal the start of the Boxer Uprising. "Not turn round," he said.

"What?" I asked.

Then I heard what I thought was Robin's voice – "Look, Sweetheart ..." It was cut off by an even stranger noise – like someone crunching the crackling off roast pork.

"Not turn round," said the chef, gripping me by the wrists. "Very fine English boy accept to enter kitchen and eat my guest?"

It sounded ominous, but he was being nice enough. I sat side by side with the inebriated Scot and we ate until we resembled those fat, beaming, Chinese Gods Aleister Crowley once tried to imitate. I've since celebrated quite a few New Years at that Chinese Restaurant. The chef never mentions what it was he saw over my shoulder that night, and no one has seen hide nor hair of Robin ever since.

---

> Who saw him die?
> I, said the fly,
> with my little eye,
> I saw him die.

'Who killed Cock Robin?' A children's nursery song about the death of King William II, The Rufus, in 1100 A.D. His brother, Robert, was the elder, but Rufus used black magic. He was buried without rites in the centre of the choir at Winchester Cathedral. Here he lies for eternity amid a circle of mocking, Saxon kings.

Tyrell, the man who killed the King, was smuggled out of the country. Wherever he spent the night, the famous phrase 'Kilroy was here' was marked on the door. Kilroy was a mongrel term of mixed Norman/Saxon descent which meant: the King-Killer. In pagan times, King-Killer was someone heavily disguised who made the royal sacrifice. In folk-memory he also became the Whiffler.

# Pearl

*Persephone: the daughter of Zeus and Demeter who was taken to be the Queen of the Underworld. She was able to spend part of each year in the world of men. This story represents the ripening of a sleeping seed and, in occultism, the awakening of forgotten truths ...*

### 1.

Her new pool was fabulous. She all but lived there. On a hot summer day the air around it shimmered with humidity, and a thermostat cooled the water by just the right amount.

She always bathed naked. If anyone called, she refused to see them unless they were naked too. Why should they get an eyeful for nothing? That was her philosophy. One took a big risk. There were the odd sights that could make the eyes sore. Like her fat, Jewish agent. Oh, didn't he just love to waddle onto the patio wearing nothing but his briefcase! He couldn't quite believe that his briefcase was all that interested her.

"Is it pig-skin?" she asked just to make him cross. He was Jewish, one must remember.

But he could always turn a quip to his own advantage. "No, pure alligator, with a very long tail!"

"They shouldn't have left the hair on." He was very hairy. "It looks more like yak or camel."

The trumpeter with the band though, he was something else. And she liked to invite any lead singer round, anyone in a new group looking for a bit of patronage – and a leg up. She was quite partial too to any nice lad met at a party. Anything, in fact, between seventeen and forty. She was only twenty herself, which explains why she never strayed beyond these rather narrow limits.

From where she sunbathed on the patio, she could see visitors arrive. She moved her lounger so that it faced the sliding glass panels right on. It amused her to see their faces when the Philippino maid told them that either they stripped or left.

"Madame has not clothes, so cannot receive you."

It was a lovely way of putting it. She cannot receive you. Oh, but I can, she would giggle. I can receive all of them in a big bunch.

It tickled her fancy to see grown men shamed. It tickled her fancy to see men. She'd heard it said on a television programme that women did not find anything erotic in a naked man. Yes, well, that might be the official Feminist line, but most of them were lesbian. As far as she herself was concerned, naked men were much better than ice cream cornets. You could lick them all year round.

She chuckled to herself gently. She had a filthy mind, thank God. But when people looked at her, it was not her mind that drew their attention. It was her quoit. That, at least, is what she herself called it. It sounded much more classy and up-market. It had started at a village fete a few years before. While waiting for twilight to fall and for the dancing to begin, someone had shown her the game of quoits. He was coming on pretty strong. The vicar was going the colour of a turkey cock.

"It all began thousands of years ago," said this leery-eyed chap. "When the spring was too wet or the summer too dry, they made an appeal to the gods and goddesses of fertility. They brought out a set of hoop-la rings, whittled out of oak, and selected a lad to fill the central role."

She asked him what the central role was.

"Why," he grinned easing his collar, "to be the peg, of course!"

He went all soppy after that. After describing a scene so close to his own heart, his ambitions got the better of him, and he had pulled her behind the Tea Tent. The vicar had seen them go. He just hoped that no-one would see them come. He went inside the tent himself to cause as much fluster as he could among the Mothers' Union.

"You'd be a natural," the man said as he showed her his rampant peg. Without so much as batting an eye-lid, she scored at least one hundred – using only the one quoit!

## 2

Now here she was, with many millions, and the unsung champion of quoits! This is why it didn't exactly worry her that there was a building, just the one, which overlooked her swimming pool. She could shield herself from the other neighbours by trees, real or plastic, or by a dainty trellis wound about with man-made roses. But one hundred metres to the north-east was the high-rise hostel block for students at the City Medical School. No doubt they, the students that is, would be grateful for a few extra lessons in Anatomy, Physiology or Quoits.

The flash of sunlight playing on the lenses of field glasses and telescopes could be quite erotic at times. It lent an air of dappled jungle to the coloured tiles of the patio. She pretended not to notice of course – which wasn't easy. When there were so many spots of light twinkling on her, she felt like Mae West in 'Diamond Lil'. She played the part well. She played to her own special gallery, doing the most outrageous things under the guise of innocence all alone. Mind you, she also did some of them with the tall young trumpeter while he practised fingering his instrument.

If ever those medical students passed their exams, it would mainly be due to her. She always wore dark glasses of course. That way, they never knew that she was also watching them. There were the shy ones who peeped from behind curtains. There were the brazen ones who stood in full view, also naked, hoping to attract her attention. Finally there were the ones who didn't give a damn. They went at it hammer and tongs, and seeded the flower-beds below.

"I sometimes think that never blows so red, The rose as where some Caesar's seed was shed!" She often misquoted things. It showed that you dare take risks. An admirer, back in the days when she could support admirers, had made her a present of 'The Rubaiyat of Omar Khayam'. He'd meant to flatter her intelligence but he was struck dumb when they made love while she was reading poetry! She had now learned over a hundred verses by heart. It came in very handy, and it impressed the Americans. It was also quite a wow during interviews. She was deeply moved by the words although she didn't understand them all.

She liked to appear brainy. But when she couldn't take the

risk, then she played at being deep and mysterious. Most of the time she got it wrong. It didn't much matter though. She was terribly rich. She had lost count once there were more than seven figures. When you were as rich as that, you have to rely on other people to handle it for you. You pay them. But you don't trust them.

It had amazed her at first. I mean, she didn't really believe that she had a thrilling voice. Even now, after her fifth golden disk, she still didn't believe it. The songs were good. The mad crew at the recording studio, they were good too. Hence she was a woman of some substance and not yet twenty. The figures had lost all meaning for her. All she knew was that more came in than went out and that she was rich.

She had chosen the name 'Pearl Virgin' herself. It quickly became a gimmick. It caught the creative fancy, and of course ... she helped it along. They had asked her during a live television interview why she had chosen the name 'Pearl'. "Oh, it reminds me of sperm", she answered quick as a flash.

It had happened too quickly to pull the plug. Her words had already gone out into thirty million homes. Next morning she had even bigger headlines than the future Queen.

That one outrageous comment, made up on the spur of the moment, was enough to turn her into a legend. Far from banning her from the cameras, she was more sought after than ever. She might not be brainy but she realised why she had hit the jackpot. She also knew what they were expecting from her.

In the course of another interview, where a well-known DJ was trying to tease her towards putting her foot in it, he asked: "Tell me, Pearly: do you love all the men in your audience?" She fanned him with her eye-lashes and smiled so innocently. "I'd like to but, of course, there just isn't enough time."

That made him laugh. Up to that moment he was happy with her naivete. "Listen, Pearl, if you hadn't become a singer – what would you like to have been?"

"If I hadn't become a singer, darling, you wouldn't be poking that thing in my face." Here followed a naughty giggle and she added, "There're no cameras, folks, so you'll just have to believe me. It's only his microphone – worse luck!"

3.

The public went totally mad about her, and not only the men, although they showed the biggest reactions. The girls began to model themselves on her too. Her words started appearing on T-shirts and hats. Her quips and asides became a kind of cool philosophy – the latest substitute for Kahlil Gibran. The sauciest fashion for men was to stitch tiny pearls or sequins down one trouser leg.

"What does it represent?" asked a new girl from one of the commercial channels. As often happens, she knew she'd made a mistake the moment the words left her mouth. She tried with great aplomb to change subjects. "Thank you for coming," she blurted out. This too became a catch phrase for a few weeks.

Then, one evening, at a massive concert in a stadium, there was almost a riot. When she walked on stage, several men exposed themselves and roared their proposals at her.

"Darlings, please," she pouted. "I'm not a nympho-maniac!" They laughed. "But I'm taking lessons at Night School." They went crackers.

Her backers were terrified but the crucial thing was – she got away with it. It sounded so very 'off the cuff' and not at all like a pre-set script that had been rehearsed. Each of her 'pearls', as they inevitably became known, was as fresh as spring mint, as hot as cayenne pepper, and spoken in a tone of utter innocence. She was playing with fire and everyone waited to see if she would get burnt. But no, not at all. The guys went crazy and their girls did not criticise.

"Do you use condoms?" someone yelled from the seething mass of ribald faces.

"Why on earth should I?" she replied sweetly. "I've got a heated swimming pool."

Statements like these could mean all things to all men, and each made his own interpretation. Normally, from the stage, you can only ever see them – the fans – en masse. At big concerts it's like standing on the cliffs and singing at the ocean. They are all of a oneness. Each head is but as a grain of sand along the sea-shore. But they are individuals, every single one of them. And many of them were lonely ... young and lonely ... or to be more precise: timid, young and lonely. She was now well on the way to becoming their new fantasy figure. First she was idolised, then she was sanctified, and finally she became deified.

Most stars are perfectly aware of the role they play in the private dreams of their fans. From the great Clark Gable to Tom Cruise or from Mary Pickford to Madonna. If you can but wheedle your way into their hearts, you're a winner. If you can but be the main component of their 'do it yourself' kit – then you're a success. You have to become the main character in their private erotic fantasies. That is when the true magic begins.

If your name appears in graffiti, or if you figure in those stories on lavatory walls, you will be a phenomenon. "I saw John Travolta in the showers," says one. "I worked in Joan Collin's hotel when she sent down for some sandwiches," says another. A smart agent sends the cameras in. The smartest sends in lads with black pencils! Pearl's agent went one better. He had the hottest ones blown up and coloured and used them as a back-drop for a portrait. It was dirty, it was daring, and it did the trick. Rumour has it that was the night Saatchi and Saatchi tore their own hair out.

They all know, it's their job to find out, that the most popular religion in the world is nameless. Among its many members you'll find pimply boys, gauche girls, gloomy couples, and some senior sex maniacs. Each of them makes unto himself a bedside altar and there he doth set up his holiest icons. These may be pop stars, film stars, or stars from television.

The devotees gaze at photos, fondle sacred relics, kiss 'genuine' autographs and rub themselves with letters they got via a Fan Club. Their fervour may take them further still, even to a visitation during the long, hot night. The faith is endorsed by a little trip to glory. It is a sex religion, pure and simple, and not a hundred miles from Voodoo.

For there are Gods, old ones, dusty ones ... ones that are all-but forgotten ... who feed on grief, and need, and solitude. And there are other Beings, loftier than us, to whom human anguish is as exciting and refreshing as nectar to the Gods.

108

They come from nowhere, like spiders in the top-floor of a high-rise apartment block. They come mainly at midnight, when you are not looking. They come as silently as moths drawn by the dying down of some strange, invisible light. They come like damp that seeps through the angles of your heart.

## 4.

Pearl Virgin was made into a miracle.

Nobody knows whether or not it was true. She was on a feminist chat-show and they weren't being all that friendly. They pretended to ask fair questions but they weren't. She cottoned on at once. She was quick at picking up the 'vibes'. They were aiming to make her look ridiculous. In this way they planned to boost the morale of their housewife audience, most of whom led drab, unlovely lives.

"Do you possess the secret of making men happy?" It was a wicked question and they were ready to pounce on whatever her response might be.

"Well – all I can say is – men seem to think so."

"But how could you possibly know that?" they probed. "You're so well protected and none of them actually get near you, do they?"

"Not face to face perhaps, but lots of them send me their condoms." She sighed a sad sigh and gave a Marilyn moan. "The poor darlings feel so sad, and I suppose it makes them feel closer."

The interviewer was stunned. She was turned to stone. One almost heard the hat-pins drop from her hand. Silence reigned throughout the studio, and in their little cabin the production team had all gone hoarse. It was like the stillness before a tidal wave hits the shore. It was like the shrug in the land one feels before an earthquake. The air was tense as the earth held its breath and the sky throbbed with suspense.

"Used?" asked a bodiless female voice from the control box, with something like a sob.

Pearl looked round to identify the source. "Beg pardon?" she gasped, for all the world sounding like a dying butterfly.

"Are you saying that men send you condoms that are used?"

Pearl was dazed. The woman seemed so naive. "Well," she explained with great pains, "they tie a knot in them, naturally."

The lady producer was lost for words, and that's putting it mildly. There was a slow, swelling mutter among the male members of the technical crew which grew into a gale of open, helpless laughter. The whole situation threatened to get out of hand, to break down into a complete fiasco. The lady in charge felt her anger spilling over into her stabbing voice.

"What the hell do you do with them, may I ask?"

"I just cut off the tips with my manicure scissors."

"And then ... ?"

"I empty them all in my pool."

Now, even the men were stunned. The entire personnel, including fully paid-up union members, all stared at her with awe, as their breath came hotly and their reveries ran riot.

Pearl felt called upon to say more. Although she could see by their faces that nobody was going to voice a question.

"It's their way of offering their love to me. Each one of them is sending me his personal tribute and sacrifice." She smiled and shrugged her shoulders. "So I empty them all in the pool. It's the least I can do, don't you think? Besides," she added with triumph, "Elizabeth Taylor bathed in asses' milk when she played the Queen of Egypt."

"Do you – swim in it?" asked a strangled voice from the control box at the back of the studio.

"Well it's not for effing goldfish!" she said in some surprise.

"You mean – you dive in and frolic?"

"It's the closest I can get to them," she said with an angelic smile. It's my way of having intimate contact. I feel as though I'm making love to each and every one of them. It does wonders for my skin. And it makes me a more desirable person."

It was all she could think of so her voice trailed off. It was all that the staff could think of. They were as silent as the grave. This is not good at a peak listening time, so in a moment of panic, someone switched on the National Anthem.

The evening papers were the first to hit the streets. 'Pearl Virgin Makes Love to a Thousand Men' howled one headline.

'Dive In, the Water's Divine' cried another.

The most vulgar and tasteless one – the one that sells best – just announced 'This Girl's Got Spunk!' It's shares doubled on the Stock Exchange.

There were new bids from alert commercial firms who were beginning to glimpse the answer to most of their problems. A company that made beauty products offered her a colossal sum just to endorse a new line that was going to be called 'Pearl's Cream'.

Even the evening news programmes gave her a mention now, though one could see that the sedate announcers were having trouble with their mouth corners. Witty remarks were printed on badges. Hat bands flowered in the night. By the next morning, Pearl Virgin was a triple, world-wide celebrity. The telephone line to her agent's office was hot with bids and offers. One wanted her for a week at a cabaret club. A second wanted her as a guest on a famous chat-show. A third wanted her to model his clothes in Paris.

A couple of sheiks sent diamonds. A South American dictator sent emeralds. A member of the British House of Commons sent her tickets for 'Phantom of the Opera'.

All that, plus two thousand condoms which came the first day. The Post Office had to find extra transport. Very considerately, Pearl thought, they hired chilled meat wagons for the job. Evidently, the trade union was feeling a little outburst of solidarity for all men everywhere.

Pearl herself took on two more Philippino maids: one to slit the envelopes, the other to clip the tips off the perishing bags. She also employed an ex-snake handler who wrung them out into the pool. Until quite recently, he said, he had been squeezing out poison from cobras and Fugu fish to make an exotic Japanese sauce. There's not much call for it outside of Osaka, though.

There was a wee bit of trouble from the local council. They could not keep the buses running because of the crowds of men who formed queues outside her home. On the spur of the moment, they had formed a secret society dedicated to keeping the swimming pool topped up! They were sponsored by a certain petrol company who gave out t-shirts with the slogan 'She'll Give You Power', or 'She'll Do Your Piston Good'.

The watch-dog committee which keeps an eye on publicity received no complaints and took no action on their own behalf. Someone had a bit of common sense. He decided that any legal attempt to stop the slogans would be so farcical that their impact would be tripled and push the profits still higher. Which was not what the committee was there for. It was very difficult for them, mind you, especially when a new slogan appeared: 'She'll Absorb the Shock'!

Pearl Virgin's pool was well on the way to being one of the seven wonders of the modern world. Helicopters took aerial snaps and, just to oblige, she lay beside it dressed only in ecstasy. Postcards of it were sold at every concert. The music of her most famous songs was published with each note printed like a falling drop. Many words now took on a double meaning – a shared secret between Pearl and her fans. 'I'll Kiss Your Tears' soared to Number One, as did 'Cry First, Smile Later', 'My Weeping Candle', and 'Pearls on Your Petals'.

Several city councils had to close down the municipal swimming pools because of – and I quote – "a sudden spurt of insanitary practices"!

6.

If it wasn't the beginning of the end, it was at least a warning that the end was drawing nigh.

One of the more burly medical students loosed his bolt too quickly and with too much force. Like the Scot who forgot to let go of the caber, he tossed himself with it. He went clean through the window and fell into the bed of lovely Dorothy Perkins. He was, as the newspaper put it, "almost pricked to death", but worse still, he was smitten with Black Spot. Hence the expression: "he was a marked man"!

No transplant was necessary. Which is just as well since it is odiously difficult to find donors for that sort of thing. When you ask relatives if you may remove certain organs, they are already quite reluctant. But if you should mention that one in particular then the male kin collapse and the women have mass hysteria.

In this case though, it wasn't necessary. The other medics rallied to the call, and by means of some quite stunning surgery, their young colleague ended up a slightly twisted, but much wiser man.

The hospital itself, the team of junior surgeons, and the theatre staff, became famous all over the world. For reasons not yet fully understood, all of them resigned en masse, and went to Sicily to organise a luxurious private clinic. It was not that far away from the site of Aleister Crowley's famous Abbey at Cephalu, though I don't see any connection. Unless it was the drawings on the door?

They made a most lucrative career for themselves, adding to, or taking off, the charms of famous Hollywood film stars, especially those with family links to Italy. It was noticed by chance that policemen and many other enemies of the Mafia were wont to vanish in broad daylight. It was also remarked that when they reappeared they had a heavy limp. They never said where they had been. They never gave a hint if anything had been done to them. One could only observe that they had lost most of their old cockiness.

As for the film stars, pop stars, and men of industry who are filthy rich: it was all very well for their grins to become as wide as a banana overnight. But those in the know hinted that their reputations hung by a very slender thread ... which is a different tale entirely.

As for our own dear Pearl, she stayed in the Number One position, right at the top of the charts, longer than that book about the origins of the universe. I don't know if she and the author ever met. If they had, I calculate we'd be sliding into the middle of a 'black hole'.

I understand that an offer was made, on behalf of an ex-rock star whose guitar was becoming as heavy as lead. He wanted to buy the pool – lock, stock and filter – along with all future offerings. There was no let-up on these. Nobody on the local council could find a paragraph anywhere in the by-laws that forbade anyone to ejaculate into private pools. They'd even been to see the Minister of the Environment and put these problem before him.

"It's a question of legal niceties," he reminded them

sagely. "If we were to publish a private bill – can you imagine it being read in the House? Can you imagine the newspaper headlines?" He sat back and quoted ...

"This house hereby declares that no person of the male gender may ejaculate into a public or private pool. Nor may he conspire to cause others of the male gender to ejaculate. Nor shall he or they ejaculate from a distance – or send samples by post, rail or road. Not even if the package is stamped with the words 'Danger to Health'!"

He studied them with amusement. "What name would we give to this new felony? Have you thought? Let me throw out a few random ideas. What do you say to 'Reckless Tossing', or 'Wanking with Intent', or then again, 'Getting Your Rocks Off Without Due Care and Attention'? We could always list it as a new sort of firearm, of course. Or we might just get away with it if we charge them with 'Causing a Hazard to Low-Flying Aircraft'!"

"There will be thousands who would claim they couldn't help it. They will plead diminished will-power, or extra stress from ill-made underwear." He shook his head with reproach. "No, no, no, gentlemen – this whole thing could blow-up in our faces."

He ushered them toward the door before he was obliged to offer them tea. "Try your best to think of it as a fortunate form of birth control!"

7.

It was one day later that Pearl announced she was pregnant! When they asked her who the father was, she just gestured toward the frothing swimming pool.

"D...?" began a reporter from the News of the World. He had fiery, ginger hair which somehow seemed quite right. "D..." he repeated. "Do you? Do you? D-d-d-do you mean ...?" One had the impression that his freckles were moving.

Pearl nodded demurely. "All of them," she murmured.

There were three immediate impacts. First, married ladies with fertility problems began sneaking in for midnight dips. Second, everybody else stopped swimming all of a sudden – in the sea or anywhere else. Three, the value of shares in the making of pools went through the roof of the Stock Exchange!

114

There were lesser insanities, of course: like the enterprise at Croydon who invented a product that changed the water of your pool into "the next best thing!" It was a combination of wall-paper paste, dried milk, a certain brand of hair-gel, and ground-up shrimps. An Irish girl filled her bath with the stuff and told her family that a miracle had happened. Her father flew over from Cork, shot the bath and made the Jamaican inventor marry her. The chap had been a Rastifarian but he became a Catholic before evening fell.

The only real hitch in the whole affair was the fact that the damned stuff proved alluring to tortoises. No one realised it at first. Even when the first tortoises began to march, nobody made the connection. It wasn't until a week had passed that the penny dropped. The favourite food of the turtle family is krill, shrimp and prawn! Millions of the beasts began to trek toward the nearest pool with the dedication of the fools of the First Crusade. What is more, their retractile heads send women into swoons! There was a knock-on effect which caused a boom in mole-traps, slug pellets and 'Primal Scream' therapy.

When the baby was born, a little girl, Pearl called her Pearl as well. Her musical career took on a new lease of life as her promoters made great play on the phrase 'Mother of Pearl'. Not to be outdone, thousands of men began to wear discreet, nacreous lapel badges on which were engraved the immortal words, 'Father of Pearl'.

Nobody ever noticed that the group's trumpeter could now play 'The Flight of the Bumble Bee' faster and higher than anybody else. The strains would sometimes float across the surface of the waters in the still of the night.

"That's a good omen," said one of the bathing women.

"No, it's not," said her friend, "It's Rimsky-Korsakov!"

# Quo Vadis?

*Because God was the origin of all, mankind had nothing of his own that he could offer in sacrifice except, possibly, the miracle of life itself. Thus, men and women could act as 'sacred prostitutes' for a period in their life. This practice was known throughout the whole of ancient world, and the practicians were known as 'the slaves of God'.*

## 1.

He was trying very hard not to show his anxiety. He spoke softly. He moved calmly. But his upper lip had a sweat sheen on it. His knuckles were white, and he gave out a typical, not unpleasant smell. It was the sort of smell that excites rats and sends them into a killing frenzy.

"You're frightened," said the man behind the desk in a flat, matter of fact tone.

"No," shrugged the young man airily.

The man studied him for a moment, smiling at the end of his cigar. "You're frightened," he said again.

"I promise you, I'm not," repeated the young man, with a tiny touch of annoyance in his voice.

The man was silent a moment. He let his eyes wander all over the other's body. "Then you should be," he said. "If you're not, that makes me worried. Why aren't you frightened?"

The young man was cornered. There was no point in wriggling. "I'm nervous," he conceded.

"How nervous?"

"Very nervous."

"Almost frightened?" smiled the man.

The young man nodded and licked his lips.

"Which bit frightens you the most?" The man was

117

enjoying the situation immensely. He liked to torment them and to watch them squirm. "Which bit makes you want to run?"

The young man rubbed his hands along his thighs. "I suppose it's about knowing what to do." He sniffed and shifted in his chair. "I don't know the first thing about it, you see? I don't want to look a fool."

"Ah, then you're not reluctant about actually doing it? You are just worried about the method concerned?"

The young man blinked and glanced around the room. "And the way that we go about doing it, as well."

The man grinned and finally gave up on the cigar. "You're shit scared, aren't you? Come on, come on, you might as well admit it. It's no skin off my nose, either way. It might even count in your favour." He leaned forward and lowered his voice. "Some of our clients are very, very keen on – er – new recruits. They call them 'virgins', which just goes to show what original thinkers they are." He grinned like an ally. "Myself, I like to think of you as beginners."

The young man sucked on his cheek and looked down at the carpet. He was abashed too.

A sudden flash of insight shot across the man's brain. "Are you married?" he asked. He beamed with delight as the other blushed bright red and then nodded his head.

"And she doesn't know, does she?" He almost laughed with triumph. "She doesn't fucking know and you never want her to find out! That, matey, just about puts you in the palm of our hands – which makes us very happy."

The eyes looked up. There were broken diamonds in them. He bit his lips as he shook his head.

The man lounged back and almost purred. "Well let me tell you something," he murmured with a gurgle, "it just about doubles your value." He stopped suddenly and leaned further forward. "Don't tell me that you've got children?"

The young man shook his head, eyes downcast.

"But she's expecting, isn't she?"

The blue, splintered eyes stared straight into his. "First one due in seven months." There was a long pause. "That's why ..." he spread his hands.

"Say no more!" said the other warmly. "You'll do all right with us. I'll see to that. You work hard and we'll pay you in gold."

He pressed a buzzer on his desk. A nasal voice answered. "Will you take Antony to the studio, Annabelle? And while he's having his piccies taken, get some forms ready: a contract, the usual insurance, and the waivers. Do the full set."

He walked round the desk and shook the young man's hand. "My secretary will see to all the papers. With any luck, this time tomorrow, we'll be making you dates with your first clients." He grinned and slapped his back like a chum. "So, welcome to the Best Escort Agency in town ... and keep your pencil sharp!"

## 2.

A few weeks later, he was inspecting a rather grubby kid of seventeen or so. He looked like an urchin who had stepped straight from the pages of a novel by Charles Dickens. He was not too tall but skinny. His long black hair hung in greasy curls on his shoulders. He wore a red-check shirt, "Chosen by men who work in Canada's forests" the label said. It was a few sizes too big, but then he'd stolen it from an open stall.

The man showed him the button that would start recording their meeting on video. He took no risks. None of them would ever get away with claiming he had lied to them. Sometimes, as in this case, it was safer to record them in the process of lying to him. "Listen kid," he said, his finger poised on the button. "I won't be able to help you unless you do some convincing acting." He pointed to the camera in the corner of the room.

He paused a moment to let the significance of the camera sink in. Then when the boy looked at him again he winked, and the kid gave a grin and a nod.

"How old are you?" he asked.

"Nineteen," the lad answered. "Twenty just after Christmas."

"You don't look nineteen."

"That's what the doctor said."

"Why did you go to the doctor? Are you ill or something?"

"One of the hostels I stayed at, they asked a doctor to check me for lung disease."

"And what was it?" asked the man.

The boy laughed. "Lack of food. He said I wasn't eating enough. I could have told him that! He said that youngsters like me, we get physically retarded or something. Always young looking. You know, skin like a fucking girl." He laughed and winked rudely. "Then, round about thirty, we suddenly get old. From then on, nobody believes how young we are still. That's all." He shrugged. "Swings and roundabouts, when you come to think of it."

"Have you got any means of identity? A passport, a students' union card, a bank account or ... even a letter from the Social Security?"

"I've got my driving licence. Will that do?"

As the man took it, the boy smiled at him like a secret agent.

"So this is your name then, and your current address?"

"It was my address when I passed my driving test. I'm dossing at a mate's place right now. You can get me at short notice though. He's got a telephone."

The man was torn two ways. Yes, there were plenty of clients who liked them this young. And the lad was quite right, the lightness of his build did make him seem younger still. Almost a school-boy. Have a pair of short trousers made, and a school blazer – he would go like a bomb. But the police might ask questions. That's why it was necessary to take every possible precaution.

"On your application form, you write that you have not had a single job since leaving school?"

"That's right. One of the two million unemployed."

"When did you leave school?"

"Three years ago. When I was sixteen."

A sharp one this! He could think on his feet. "Did you win any diplomas?"

"Just one for swimming."

"That's not much good for anything, is it?"

"It keeps me fit and I look good in trunks. What few muscles I've got are nicely firm and in good nick."

For a fleeting second the man wondered who was playing with whom. This kid was really on the ball. He'd make a great cock-teaser if he had the wit to play his cards properly.

"It says here that you need money..."

"Yes!"

"... and you're willing to do anything to get it?"

"Yes."

The man raised his eyebrows. "When you say – anything ... ?"

"I mean anything," the boy grinned, for all the world like a tart in Paris playing with the stem of a champagne flute. "So long as it's legal, of course. I wouldn't want to get into trouble."

Bravo, thought the man! Exactly right! And so natural too. Another cold shiver ran down his spine. "You do know what sort of place this is, don't you?"

"Course I do. It's an agency."

"But what sort of agency? A Typing agency? A Private Detective agency? A Musical agency ...?"

"An Escort agency."

"A *Male* Escort agency!" insisted the man heavily.

"Not much point my filling in the fucking form if you was looking for bleeding girls!"

The man swallowed his smile and continued, a bit heavily. "Our clients are looking for male company. Often they are overseas visitors. Often they are women. You take them wherever they want to go. You pay all the bills with a special card that we'll supply. All expenses are added to the final fee."

"And what cut do I get?"

"You get fifty per cent of all that you earn. That includes commission we get from taxis, theatres, night clubs and eating places."

"And the hotels?"

The man's eyes flicked toward the camera. "What hotels? All we do is arrange for people to meet, and do our best to fill the client's requirements. We do not allow our personnel to work for other agencies at the same time, or to make private deals with clients. We can and we do check up on you. We have over two hundred names on our lists. You stick to the house rules or else we kick you out. All the clothes that we provide will stay ours too. You give them back when you go."

"When I'm wealthy, I'll buy my own."

"That is allowed, as long as we approve your choice."

The boy shrugged. "It seems like I'm going to be your slave."

"Not at all. You are free to go whenever your wish and there is no penalty clause in your contract. We pay you in arrears, you see, and we just deduct the clerical expenses."

The kid was passed on to Annabelle and she took him to the studio.

## 3.

New recruits turn up pretty regularly. Old ones leave, many to make it alone on the French Riviera, others to go with clients who have made an offer they can't refuse. In any one year, we see the whole spectrum of mankind, which is to say, every type of man. There are students from all corners of the world. There are tycoons who like taking risks. There is even the rare Biker who wants a night to remember. Quite often, there are those pasty, pale, artless virgins who come like stray lambs looking for something to eat. You can even have psychopaths on the books – they do it to revenge themselves on women. Not to mention army officers who do it to revenge themselves on their mummies. And even one or two real sex maniacs who have to carry special insurance cover.

You even have the occasional policeman. The manager always recognises them. They think they're good at disguises but it's obvious. A copper stands out like a sort thumb!

Of course, the manager can never be sure whether they've not been sent – part of their official duty, that is. It's unlikely in fact, and in any case all the firms have good lawyers who could make legal mincemeat out of coppers who incite crime. No, it's pretty certain that any copper turning up is there on a purely private basis. To be sure, he might have convinced himself that he's out to show some real initiative, and intending to disclose the truth. He probably thought that he would rip the place apart once he had unearthed all the sordid little secrets. One does not bat an eye. One does not even say a word. They learn soon enough how and why they were mistaken.

It's all an excuse anyway. They do really want to live the life, but they need to justify it somehow or else they would be crushed. One feels a slight pang of sorrow for such guys. The firm had a deluxe catalogue, not for sale, from which clients could choose the escort they preferred. Along with a top-class photograph or two, there would be a few that showed an interest in fine detail. Coppers often say that their main work is as "a security guard".

One kept an eye on them, that's all. They would be given a first date at a special address where hidden cameras ran some super quality film. If the man was genuine and happy in his work, then they might propose to market these films on commission. But if he was a wrong 'un, they would give him a private showing and then wish him well in his police career. The films were kept as a guarantee of his good faith.

The ones who are wrong in the head are difficult to handle, and there were several of them about. In many cases they're quite easy to spot, if only because they make themselves so obvious. A small handful were in a very bad way. They ought not to be free to roam the streets. One or two were downright evil. Their minds were more than squalid, they were wicked, and they yearned to do odious things. In a shadier world they could be kept in a cage, and allowed to mount depraved spectacles for a wealthy and bored clientele.

Outside of Europe, they would have been popular as 'gifts of vengeance' whom one sent to someone one didn't like. How great they would have been as a more lethal version of the strip-a-gram. One could have sent them on a date with a nosy policeman, for example, or put one in the arms of a fractious wife. Not in very good taste, I agree, but – it has the makings of the perfect crime – and similar things have happened.

### 4.

If you're running an escort business, you have to be ready for anything. Problems can and do crop up from time to time. Take suicide for example – that's not as rare as you might think. They choose such bizarre ways too. One young fellow, (they're usually young), whipped out a scout knife all of a sudden and then hacked his genitals off. He lay there for an hour, sobbing like a baby, and slowly bled to death. The client was either paralysed by fear or else in a hypnotic trance.

They weren't often as messy as that though. Whether out of respect for the company or simple courtesy as regards the client, I can't say, but most of them just swallowed pills.

They didn't leave any notes. It must have come over them quickly. One client too many perhaps? Or someone who touched a raw nerve? Nobody had any real idea but of course they all gave opinions. Somewhere behind it all, there had to be a reason. They just couldn't take it any more.

It was very significant, all told, that they very rarely did it in front of the client. They waited until he'd fallen asleep. Actually, it was a much greater shock to the system to wake at some ungodly hour and start touching up someone already stiff with rigor mortis. They went mad! They climbed up the wall! More than one corpse had been attacked in fear that it was a vampire.

What the Agency did then depended largely on what the client might have done already. Had he called the police before ringing them? Had word got out? How private was the situation or how public? Was the client spiralling up toward a crisis of panic? Was it a hotel which called, the client having done a bunk and one body left behind? What was the scenario? Did it bode a calamity or could it be handled at the level of a small tragedy?

Something could usually be done. There was a special fund, with a large sum in it. It was called the 'EMV Account' – short for "eyes, mouths and vacuum cleaners"! At all events, you can understand why clients had it drummed into them that discretion was the motto of the house. And it worked both ways! "You say nothing, and we do the same," said the manager. It was actually the kind of mutual tact on which good business is built. In other words: if any shit gets slung, we're better slingers than you. This worked wonders for one's peace of mind.

Then there were supposed to be 'the special ones'. One had heard about them, but hardly anybody had met one, face to face. They might just be a legend. Oh yes, every walk of life has its legends. Some of them were just extensions of a lonely man's dreams. Like the client who dragged every seventh escort to his lawyers and made a new will. Or the handsomest, most gorgeous, perfect guy you had ever seen who would tell you he understood why you did it. He understood those reasons that were too deep ever for you to glimpse. And he would sweep you up in his protective arms and be your best friend, your brother, your father, or your playmate for ever more.

124

For such were their secret dreams. No matter how hard they seemed, all these virtuoso veterans who rented out their bodies had been searching ever since childhood for the one person who would stake his claim. They pretended to sell themselves but they wanted to be owned. They offered to provide you with any erotic pleasure but they were yearning to be found, to be recognised and to be taken home. That is why these myths are born. They act as a sovereign antidote to the slow poison one has ingested all one's life.

The Special Ones were something like that. Just as godly folk cherish the myth about angels knocking on your door, or Jesus himself waiting for shelter – so these escorts had a personal vision of God. He would know it all. He would forgive it all. He would put it all to rights. He would be a good farmer who would nurse even the twisted seed to full flower. He would be a good shepherd who would not cull the tainted wethers of the flock. There would be no more shunning, no more ostracism or mockery. No more pointed sticks and no more cruel stones. There would be arms – and arms. All the way would be arms. Open arms. Haven arms. Arms that held you and made you throb with Alleluias. Arms that made you feel as eternal as a live statue sculpted by a cocky Michaelangelo.

That was the best point for boosting our sales. Our agency was said to have the biggest percentage of specials in the whole of Europe. We never discussed it. If any client asked us straight out, we told him politely that we didn't know. "How would we tell?" is what we asked him. "That is something only our clients can ever learn."

I have to tell you that a special is someone who is looking for a permanent relationship. He is a lost boy, like in Peter Pan, and he is constantly on the look-out, even when he's on the job. One of them told me about it once. "It's not planned," he said. "You go out with whichever client has booked you. But you can't help wondering why he picked you and not someone else among the two or three hundred others."

"Does it matter what he looks like?" I remember asking.

"Oh no," he shook his head. "Not at all. This is a love that's grown in the darkness. It's not the eyes that are hungry but the arms. It can be the way he sinks his nose into the corner of your neck. Or the way he sheds a tear or two of shame. You know then that he likes you. That he's driven by something which may very well be the same something that drives you."

"Is it love?" I asked naively.

"More than that," he hissed. "It's worship."

I've heard some strange things in my life, but this just about took the biscuit. I think I got the flavour though. I remembered enough from my Sunday School days to make a weak attempt at wit. "And the Word was made flesh," I whispered.

He turned his eyes on me. I don't know whether he was just disgusted with me or whether he felt a deep, religious loathing. "And vice versa," he spat, his lip curling.

## 5.

It was round about then that our first 'boy' vanished. It wasn't the police who informed us. It was the client. He came in to the office the day after his date and asked to book the same escort again.

Normally, you understand, it's the boy who comes back and tells us. "I've made a hit," he will say. What he means is a client has been smitten by him. Now and then they will even claim that they have fallen in love, but in our opinion they're just having a little fantasy. They liked what they got, and they hadn't had it for a long time – and so on. When a second booking was made on the spot, the boy concerned got a little extra commission. If he could get himself engaged for a week, his commission was doubled.

That's why it seemed bizarre that this man came back to the office to reserve the same guy again.

He'd forgotten the boy's name. This doesn't surprise us because they are almost all 'made up' names, only every used for the job. Brad, Hank, Big Tim and so on. This one asked to go through the catalogue and soon picked out the one who had rung his bell.

It was Cameron, a boy from Miami, who described himself in the glossy brochure as both a keen surfer and a lifeguard. It wasn't our place to verify these facts. Even when we knew that he was a failed acting student from a nearby drama school.

"Didn't you tell him yourself that you'd like to reserve him again?" we asked.

The client dropped his eyes a bit sheepishly. "He never gave me time," he replied. "We went back to my hotel – for a drink, you know?" We nodded. We understood. Most of the boys would go back for drinks – and make it last a couple of hours.

"Well," he said. "Later – "

"After the drink?"

He looked at us oddly and nodded. "He went into the bathroom to, er, tidy himself up."

This too was part of the routine we taught them. As soon as possible after any date, they should take proper hygienic steps.

"He never came out," said the man blankly.

"Do you mean he did a bunk?" This was not unknown. "He robbed you? He stole your wallet or something?"

"No. Nothing like that. He just never came out again."

My colleague and I looked at each other with a worried eye. "Is he still in there?" I asked, fearing the worst.

"No," said the man. "I went in to see. It was empty. Just empty."

"Then he buggered off through the window."

"There isn't any window. It's just a small, neat bathroom, between the doorway to the corridor and the bed."

"If you were shagged out – if he'd pleased you – maybe you wouldn't notice if he went into the bathroom or the corridor."

"He was stark naked," said the man. "With a huge erection."

Yes, well, he had a point there. This was not the kind of thing one often came across in hotel corridors. And certainly not this one, which was very chic, very high-class, with security cameras on every floor.

We tried his home telephone number, of course. We made enquiries with any friends that we knew of. We learned nothing new. This was a real puzzler and we were quite flummoxed. There was nothing we could do. He was a free-lance escort. We paid him commission. Apart from that we had no obligation whatsoever. We didn't even have any next of kin listed so there was no-one we could get in touch with. To all intents and purposes, Cameron had faded into thin air.

127

"Maybe he's gone back to America?" suggested my colleague.

"Via a deluxe bathroom?" I asked with biting sarcasm.

"Was he wearing a snorkel?" asked my colleague.

## 6.

He was only the first.

There was no advance warning so we were not the least bit alert. Had we suspected that it was going to spread then we'd have tried to take some appropriate action. I can't think what that might have been. But at least we'd have been on guard. We could also have told the lads to be more vigilant.

The next one, called 'Davy', just melted away in the back row of a cinema. The client had some weird nostalgic streak. In the middle of the big picture he fell to his knees among the empty soft-drink cartons and lollipop sticks. He began to nuzzle like a gun-dog amidst our Davy's legs.

The next thing he knew – he was wildly unzipping a pair of empty jeans. He put it in a much more direct and graphic manner. "I opened his flies," he gasped, "and all I could find was more denim ... plus the lower edge of an equally empty T-shirt." He blinked at us in pathos. "I was staggered," he added. I said that I bet he fucking was too. We wondered if it had anything at all to do with the film they'd been watching. It was called 'Terminator 3' which sounded very ominous.

Hal soon followed, and then, in quick succession, Greg, Jason, Meat and Pete.

That was still only seven of our best numbers. When the figure got to seventeen, we started to panic. We hadn't actually said anything to the rest of the stable, but the weird thing was that they all sensed that something was wrong. We closed shop for the day and called them all in. Not that we had a room big enough to hold them all, so they spilled out into the corridor and the other offices.

There was stunned silence for a few moments and then Randy raised his hand. With a name like that, you just knew he was American. "You can put Foster on your list as well."

"And Steve," said someone else.

We soon realised that many more guys had vanished while doing a few private jobs on the side. There was no rule against it, of course, as long as they were available from late afternoon to midnight. All told, about one third of our stock was gone. We would have to mount a campaign to recruit new stock before there was only me and the accounts clerk left.

"Do you think it's one of those religious maniacs?" asked Tony. "Are those freaks knocking us off one by one?"

"What about a blubberer?" asked Nathan. "You know: one of those guys who gets crippled with guilt the moment it's over?"

"What about a bloody maniac," said Stewart. "It could just be a nut-case who goes too far and then gets rid of the evidence."

"The problem is," I reminded them, "the clients do not run away. They are the ones who tell us about it."

"Could it be the devil?" asked Sean, an Irish boy. Everybody looked at him as if he had just dropped from an aeroplane. "Well it's a thought, isn't it?"

Indeed it was. You could tell by all their faces; it was a thought they wished that no-one had mentioned.

"It's probably the hotel staff," suggested Jorgen. We reminded him about Davy who had simply dissolved in the back row of the cinema. There was Gerard too: he'd been at the opera. During the last act of Madame Butterfly he'd leaned over the edge of the box and hurtled toward the stalls. He had never even landed. Our client had been hustled out because his wild howling had ruined the aria 'One Fine Day'.

"I don't see that there's a lot that we can do!" This was Troy. His real name was Toby and he worked in the office. He sounded terrific on the telephone – a voice like rum truffles – but he was nothing at all to look at. He didn't agree with us, naturally. When we told him the bad news and offered him work in the office, he assumed it was because our other lads would be jealous. Even so, we changed his name. Toby isn't exactly the kind of name on which we could build our image. Toby, you remember, is the chap in the Bible who met with an angel. Wherever possible, we avoided the names of apostles, angels, saints or the seven virtues. Who wants to go out with a stud called 'Thrifty'. It's much more commercial to change it to 'Thrust'.

"Well," continued Troy, "have you ever thought of letting one client meet another? Neither of them need know. We could always explain that our escorts are men of the world who are only available when they pass through London."

"They're not much of an eyeful," I told him. "Guys who are willing to pay our prices are not exactly built like film stars."

"Double chins," moaned someone.

"Bald and fat," said a second.

"But very, very rich," reminded a third.

That was when Troy surpassed himself. "Then from now on, we send our studs out in two's. You pay for one, you get the other free."

This idea had a kind of piquant appeal to it. "Triolism?" I mused.

"Not at all," said Troy. "It's called the Sandwich!"

It passed through my mind to wonder how on earth Troy would know about such things, but the idea itself had a lot to recommend it. One guy could keep an eye on the other. We could make sure there was no hanky-panky by giving each team a Polaroid camera complete with flash. If all went well, we could sell the souvenir postcards. If something went wrong we'd have some sort of visual evidence.

Not that I'd missed the commercial potential. "You could even allow the client to take shots of the two of you," I said blithely.

7.

Boys did still disappear. But now they went two by two. We couldn't fathom it out at all. Now and then we got some shots of themselves in full, rampant romp, if you take my meaning. But nothing that showed them fading away or turning into a blue mist. There was just one thing that was odd. In general, the camera vanished too but when it did stay behind, the counter told of more photos than we could unearth.

In short, at least one shot was always missing.

It was Prong who gave us a clue. Prong was the name he

had concocted for himself, of course. He was ultra macho. He was so macho he walked with a permanent strut, a bit like a matador. They had thrown him out of the Marines just because he carried things far to far. When they gave him a gun, for example, his finger froze on the trigger. He could not relax it until he had let off two hundred rounds. He had simply seen it as a handy way of showing off his virility. He hadn't even had time to take aim but – he'd managed to wing the Commanding Officer. He had also drilled a straight line the full length of an omnibus, and knocked off a whole parliament of rowdy crows.

He had much the same attitude as regards sexual matters. Let me put it this way: if any clients went out with him, it didn't matter what exotic tastes they had or how insatiable their appetites were – they stopped smoking!

I have served them myself at our Reception Desk. "Do you know our personnel?" I would ask. "Is there any particular man that you prefer?"

"P...!" They would stammer. "Prrrr...!" they would gasp. "Ah, you mean Prong?" I'd smile, and they would go white and give at the knees. Prong, it seemed, had this kind of effect on people. He was just about our most popular line, and he made quite a small fortune. We held him in great respect because, of course, he made even more money for us.

"It could be a thingummy," he offered.

One has to be patient with Prong. He'd make a good navvy but he'd wreak havoc in a book shop. "What thingummy?" we asked calmly.

"I've had them all my life, kept on feeding 'em," he explained smugly.

"Where?" we pursued, hoping to God he wasn't going to say anything about lice or viruses.

"Beetles," he said.

There was dead silence and a few slow glances one to another. "Did you say – beetles?" I asked in a high voice.

"Yeah," he said. "Them things in the pictures." He pointed at the pile of Polaroid glossies lying on our desk. I suppose our faces told it all because he suddenly got nasty. "If you don't believe me, see for yourself." He snatched one of the snaps at random and held it in front of my nose. "What's them?" he asked, stabbing the image with bad grammar and his index finger.

"Shadows on the floor," I proposed.

"On every sodding picture? In every bleeding hotel? With every fucking client?"

## 8.

We glanced at one or two of them. Then we began scrabbling through them like someone looking for a lost lottery ticket. At the end, we just stared at each other in amazement.

"I didn't even notice," said one.

"I thought they were stains on the carpet," said someone else.

"Oh no," smirked Prong. "Them are thingummies!"

We got it out of him in the end, and it was true that he'd had them all his life. He'd first become aware of them just before he learned how to toss-off. In Prong's case, this had begun at the age of nine. Whenever he played with himself, they just seemed to come. No, they didn't crawl out of cracks or holes, they just congealed, in the shadows. They would just appear, and gather round him in a circle.

Was he afraid of them, we asked – but no, apparently not. He was so used to them, he took them for granted. How did he feed them, we asked? Was it with his sperm? He looked at us as if we were daft. This made us feel very queasy because we were all pretty certain that the daft one was him.

"They eat the silver," he said, in the kind of patient voice you'd use with very young children.

"What silver?" we all said together.

"The silver that drips off your body once you get close."

"Close?" we echoed.

"You know," he grinned. "Close to letting it rip."

He meant orgasm, of course. His face glowed with some sort of sweaty virility and we could all feel his body-heat. For one short second, we saw through the open doors of the mad-house. I felt a cold sweat just in the small of my back.

"I know what they want," he went on. "I know how to feed them. They hang on, you know. They're like little pigs or puppies, except there's hundreds of them. They try to drain you dry, so you've got to learn how to give them just enough."

132

Our eyes were huge and round as we gawped at him. I don't know whether we were horrified by what he was saying, or by the fact that he was saying it out loud. We just couldn't take it in. Those words of his, and what he was trying to make us understand – we dare not let it penetrate.

"I'm not really as randy as you think," he said quietly. It sounded almost like an apology. "I'm not such a glutton for it. They make me do it, you see, and it's just got worse. There's more of them every day. I try – I try to squeeze out enough of the silver. But soon it's going to be too much."

"What will happen?" I tried to say but it came out more like a croak.

"Some go mad," he said flatly. We all swallowed noisily. "And some just disappear."

I'm sure each of us felt as if the world had suddenly tilted. We were not so sure any more.

We decided to close down the agency. Nobody wanted to keep it going. Not now. We never saw Prong again after that last meeting, and we never spoke to each other about him. I suppose we were scared to face the idea that he had raised. We never stopped thinking about it though.

I kept the photos – not out of prurient interest, you understand. My God, I'm well past that! But there are times, especially nights, when I look at Victor, or Demetrios, or any one of the hundred others. All gasping in some sort of frozen climax. And I look at those strange shadowy shapes and I wonder. Have I ever seen anything similar in the dark doorways where rent-boys lurk, in the centre of town?

I can't be sure, you see. None of us could be sure. But so many of us have changed our lives. I have heard on the grapevine that a few of us have either gone away, or been taken away. What I mean to say is: I doubt if we'll ever get to Bali.

I think we just get eaten.

I know. It sounds crazy when I say it, just like that. Believe me, I have learned not to tell it to very many people. As a matter of fact, I don't even mention it any more. You can see my problem, can't you?

Besides which, I can never be really sure about it. Nobody can ever be sure, can they? That's what life and death is all about, I suppose: not knowing for sure. Perhaps that's the reason why we think about it so often? It was mentioned on a television programme once: this morbid fear of death and the dark. They said it was just a neurosis. And they should know because they had real doctors talking.

That was the title of the programme too: 'A Morbid Fear of Dying'. But what's so morbid about it, huh? Do they think it's healthy to smile, wave at the camera, and then dive off a cliff? Aren't you afraid? Aren't the doctors who treat lunatics nervous? I bet you they're all screwed up inside. From the day we are born until the day we die, we spend our life just shitting our pants! That's not bad for a philosophy, is it? Can you tell me who first said it? Did anyone say it? You, yes you! Have you ever even thought of it? Maybe we should. You know what I mean? I don't want to spoil the party or anything – but – it's getting closer all the time.

This was quite a few years ago now. Much water has flowed under the bridge, as they say. For instance, in the meantime, someone has opened a new escort agency in the premises we used to occupy. Naturally, they've chosen a new name though. It's now called 'I'll Come With You', which is rather clever, when you think about it. But it does still rather beg the question, doesn't it? "Where are we going?" or, as Saint Jerome put it when he wrote the Vulgate, the first Latin version of the Holy Bible: "Quo Vadis?"

It would be nice to have an answer.

---

### Why Cry When I Could Be Laughing?

*I believe, and therefore it must be*
*That my great God looks very much like me.*
*What others dub sin, I rub into my skin,*
*And the two of us together knit our own reality.*

*Am I in His Good book or am I in the Bad?*
*The preachers who speak for Him say it's very sad.*
*I shall die if I worry much, And die if I never such,*
*So why worry needlessly when God and we are glad?*

*They say, of course, that I am very odd*
*Others, more bluntly, call me: That Old Sod!*
*It must do them some good, Like touching holy wood,*
*But I listen to my love beside me whisper "Oh My God"!*

Aleister Crowley, on a birthday card, January, 1937.

# Fives

*In ancient Greek tragedy there are only five characters. These are the Agoniser, the Organiser, the Chorus Girl, a Doctor and a God who drops off a crane to end it all.*
(Answer given in a test on drama.)

THE GIRL: I caught his eye on Oxford Street. I wasn't sure, straight off. You have to be careful anyway. Some of them wink, or smile, then they come right up and they ask: how much? Some don't ask. If they're not worried, it's best not to tell them. They'll stuff some notes into your hand afterwards and ... brush their teeth, I suppose.

At any rate, if somebody sees you, and wants you, you've only got to ask for a light – or ask them where the Number Eleven bus stops. If it's a nark, he grins. "What you playin' at then?" Then it's a fine. Or if you're lucky, he'll ask for a freebie any time he sees you. If they reply and then turn away, that's the tricky one. They could be shy, see? It might be they're not used to this game. Or they could be annoyed, offended – in which case, you daren't really try again. Which is a pity. I mean: we get cold too.

THE MAN: I was picked up, in London, while I stood gawping at the lights. It was close to Christmas and all the shops were open late. Their windows shone like jewels, and people's faces were mottled as if they were clowns. The Season of Good Cheer was being churned out everywhere – and I felt so desperately lonely. Angels, bells, carols and candles .... oh, the shallow tinsel and sparkling dust.

I should tell you, of course, that I always get depressed – at Christmas, New Year and my birthday. I'm not too sociable either. What some call a good neighbour who minds his own business. What others call that weirdo who never even passes the time of the day. I'm just rather shy, that's all. I've been this way all my life.

THE YOUTH: That song: 'If They Could See Me Now', what show's it from? I think it must be 'Hello Dolly!' or was it 'Funny Girl'? I'm not sure. I hardly ever go to the theatre. If they take me anywhere, it's usually their hotel bedrooms. If they've got relatives with them, a partner even, we go to the cinema. You'd be surprised what goes on in some cinemas.

It's one way to keep busy if it's raining. Slip into one of those seedy sex cinemas. It's all men there. Pathetic old men. Yes, I know: who am I to call the kettle black? But I hope to God I don't finish up like that. You wait by the door to let your eyes get used to the dim light. Then you find a row that's almost full, just one empty seat further along. And as you push past, in the dark, it's like running the gauntlet. Who'd have thought that old men had so many hands among them?

THE LADY: I caught sight of this young man. Nothing special about him. An ordinary, straight-forward sort of chap that you wouldn't notice normally. Except that I saw he was looking in my direction once or twice. It didn't even dawn on me that he could possibly be looking at me. But then he smiled. Briefly, fleetingly, in a way that you could be mistaken, and he looked into the shop window sharply.

It's what strangers do, I suppose. You know how it is when you've been day-dreaming and you realise, with quite a start, that you've been staring at someone. You shake yourself, give a half smile, and hope that they don't think you meant anything by it. Once, on the train, that happened to me, and I went quite red. I stood up to go to the restaur-ant car and I said to him I was so sorry. He hadn't even noticed. He got quite uneasy though because he felt then that I was trying to chat him up. I was terribly humiliated. I don't like people getting the wrong ideas about me.

THE GIRL: I knew. He knew too. As soon as he told me the time, not noticing the huge clocks everywhere, I could tell he was embarrassed. It wasn't so much that he was rejecting me. He just couldn't handle me. It was a situation he'd never come across before. It does happen. There are men who're doing it for the first time. Every time you turn out, there's always one or two.

THE YOUTH: On the whole, I don't think I like it. Of course, you mustn't let them know. They've got to believe you're in a seventh heaven or some strange erotic paradise. I found that out very early on. They're all capable of believing that they actually turn you on – that they possess some charm, some allure that they didn't know about until you started to writhe in their arms.

I was stunned, the first time I did it – put on the act, I mean. They measure all things sexual by their own gauge, I suppose. They find it so tricky getting excited, that the moment you have an erection, all their doubts disappear. All you do is make your mind blank. Concentrate first on your own nerve endings and let the client feel how you grow hard. If they groan, you're home and dry. They open you up like a sliced loaf bought at a supermarket and they explore your body crumb by crumb.

They remind me of myself as a child. Me and a few others, pressed against the window sprayed with artificial snow. We could actually see the things we dreamed about, but of course, we couldn't touch. It's as if they were touching for the first time too. Their fingers trembled. Had they never played with a prick before? Didn't they know how sensitive balls were? And so many of them – the majority of them – loved to stroke your buttocks with the flat of their hand.

Almost as if you were a child, and they were remembering.

THE MAN: God, I wish I didn't talk to them so much. There's no need. You pay them the going-rate and they're glad to earn it. Ready cash. No taxes. I bet they even register as unemployed. But why the fuck do I talk? Before I've taken them wherever we're going to do it ... I've told them more than anyone's ever known about me. They never show it if they're bored.

All part of the job to them, I suppose. Part of the tricks of the trade. I asked one once. The head was buried in my loins and trying desperately to lick me, suck me, swallow me ...

and it didn't work. I don't know why but I was just so fascinated with the head of hair.

There are times when you wish they'd stop, or at least go easy. But once the fee is agreed, the quicker they can get you there, the sooner they can look for someone else. If you're wise, you ask how long you get for your money. They usually say: as long as it takes. They don't want conversation. Just cash. And even if you pay them for the whole night ... they play with you incessantly and expect you to do extraordinary things to them.

I don't think they know how to listen.

THE GIRL: They can't get you undressed quick enough. They're like drug addicts. They're like somebody bursting for a piss. I sometimes wonder why we even bother to turn ourselves out nice, and make the best of what we've got. The clothes, the image, the packaging – they can't rip it off quick enough.

You can't help asking: can they possibly be as hungry as that? They're like animals – like rats. It's hard not to turn white as they stare at you. Some of them are expecting you to be wicked, in which case you've got to do some pretty wicked things with your body. It's not as easy as you might imagine. You've been treated like dirt so often, you feel like shit. And you look at the wonder in their eyes as you twist this way and that – stretching, opening, moaning – and you almost begin to believe it.

THE YOUTH: But you mustn't be silly. You learn the truth soon enough. The way they get rid of you when they've had enough. You used to be amazed how much you could ask for. I mean, you look at yourself in the mirror and you wonder: I can't be as good as all that. And yet there's someone, somewhere, who feels ready – almost to die to possess you.

The money's a kind of revenge. If truth were told, I'm not always sure that I didn't start doing this because – I was looking for love too.

THE LADY: I love the young ones. The ones that have stopped being boys, but they've not yet started being real men either. The muscles are there already, but they're silky

138

rather than rough. Also, they're less likely to think of causing you trouble. They're still innocent enough to hope that they can do it well enough to please. And they're still inexperienced enough to ask for too much money. I give them what I think and I tell them: "You were worth every penny!"

THE GIRL: Do I have a regular boy-friend? That's what they often ask. That's if they actually accept that I do it only for the money. They're curious, I reckon. Some of them want to make it feel less like having their car serviced. They want to build a kind of relationship. In half an hour? Can you believe it? So I've got a standard story that I tell – how I was corrupted and the horrible things my elder brother did to me. If they've paid for thirty minutes, there's no way I'm going to let them cheat me. I don't care how near he is. When the last second is gone, I down tools, so to speak, and I get dressed.

Oh yeah. One or two have hit me. Most of them fumble for a few notes extra. I mean: if you don't have pride and standards, God knows what you'll start thinking about yourself.

THE LADY: You must never pretend you have a lover in your arms. However good he is, and however well endowed ... he's not driven by lust but a deep desire for money. You buy him. You hire him. You pay about as much as for a good meal or having your hair done. He may look like a Greek statue – or even a Greek beach-boy – with everything ripe and luscious. But you pay only to cross from the dull mainland to the jewelled isle for a spell.

So I think of them the same way I think of a telephone or a common hot-water tap. They are available. One uses them. That's all. One snaps one's fingers for a waiter. One waves for a taxi. With these accessible young men ... one simply smiles.

THE YOUTH: We all know each other, of course – the ones on the game. We meet up in certain coffee bars or sandwich places. We even talk shop. The strange things that have happened, the close shaves we've had, or the ones who fall in love with you and give you a pile of notes to meet you

139

again tomorrow. We stick by each other you see. It's like a club we're all in. And we never touch one another. That's one of the unspoken rules.

We do have our regulars but – there are no emotions involved. Well nothing deep anyway. Fun, fun, fun. And not for sweet charity either. Don't judge us by what we do. Ask rather, do we give value for money?

THE MAN: I was born in the house of my grandparents. My mother and father were too poor yet to pay a rent of their own. Then, when I was two, we moved into a small slum house. The bedroom was behind a curtain. After that things got bad. My father just went out one night and he never came back. We sold his clothes and his Indian clubs and went to live with grandma and grandpa. Six months later, the council moved us five miles away. Two years after that, I moved to a better school. Then I went into the army. After the army I went to university. And by then, it was too late. I'd never had a friend for more than two months.

THE LADY: I married too early. The family was so anxious, they all but pushed me into it. They looked up the name in 'Who's Who' and that was it. You'll learn to love him, my mother said. Afterwards, I was so sickened when she asked me intimate details with a smile like someone from a Noel Coward play.

She chatted him up. Can you imagine that? My own mother had it off with my prick of a husband. I said I'd sue for divorce on the grounds of adultery and name her as the co-respondent. We all got paid off – papa, my hubbie, and me. "You're not a woman," she said. "With me, he actually liked it for once." I felt furious but I didn't kill her. I didn't kill him. I didn't love either of them enough for that.

That's why I pick my 'purchases' carefully. What I want for my money is a gladiatorial display. I so enjoy playing the role of Messalina, and I always give them the thumbs down. When I've done my worst ... they go to bed for a week. I destroy their pride ... their cocky, swaggering pride. Oh, you can take my word for it; I've made a fine study of the subject. I know how to ruin men.

THE MAN: While I was still alone, before I met the young girl, I saw this woman with a young man. She must have been in her mid-thirties, while he was much closer to twenty. I felt a sharp spurt of disgust. It was like acid in your stomach.

Which of them was the one who paid? Him, street smart, looking cold, with hunched shoulders? Or her, in a Dior coat, and costly jewellery decking her person? Why not me, I thought. I would have been much more suitable.

It depends what she was looking for, of course.

THE LADY: I saw this shadow of a man, a non-entity – a man like my husband, cut out of dark grey tissue paper. He was with a kind of girl. One instinctively knows the type. She was dressed in things that would come off easily and she almost, but not quite, wore a price-tag on the end of her nose. I find that sort of thing disgusting.

Oh I'm not a fool. I realise of course the comparisons that might be made. But that girl, she contaminates herself with each client she goes with. At the end of a day she must be like a dust-bin or a slop-bucket.

My boy is the only one I take and he must like me or else, you know what I mean – he wouldn't be able to do it. I mean to say, sweetheart, there's no man in the world can make himself hard just at the sight of money! I have known gigolos – my God, show me a gigolo I haven't had – who use a sort of gadget. They stick it in a glass vessel and pump out all the air. It's supposed to make it bigger. What none of them will face up to is: it also makes it softer. It's like a cake that has risen in the oven. Fine to look at, but nauseating to touch – like a bath sponge.

That's why I do rather go for the inexperienced ones. Fruit that hasn't been fingered in the market is far less bruised.

THE YOUTH: There are times, doing what I do, when I could just let go and scream and hurt. You think you don't mind. You tell yourself that it's an easy way of earning a living. "Money for old rope," as my mate puts it. We laugh a lot, the members of the club. We horse around and giggle. But it's all pretence. We're as sick as parrots inside. I mean, fair's fair. They pay and so you deliver. But somewhere along the line, you can't help feeling that you've been cheated.

What I mean is – is it right that someone like me – has to do what I do – for people like them? I can't rightly say if ever I've loved or liked anyone myself. When they play with me – when I pretend to be going delirious with delight – there's no special dream that I think of. Do you cotton on to what I'm saying? If you asked me what turns me on – I couldn't honestly say.

There's a kind of fog comes into my mind. It's like seeing a statue looming in the rain. Who would I love? Who would love me? And I don't know if I'm crying or not. Others can't tell me. My face is wet. With my fucking desirable, lithely muscled physique and handsome manly face – that's what I put in an advert – was love still a possibility? Or had they all killed it?

THE GIRL: I like Phil. If I had an older brother, I'd want him to be like Phil. In looks, you know. In the way he carries himself. If I wanted a boy-friend – not that I have many hopes in that direction – but if I had a boy-friend, I think it would be nice if he were like Phil. Phil has that look – as if he'd be lovely to cuddle up to ... as if he'd make you feel deeply, deeply happy, like a woman should.

He's on the game, like me. When we see each other on the street, or with someone, we say nothing. Not a flicker of recognition. We're blind. And when we have a coffee in Dan's place – it's the one thing we never mention: what we do, who we do it with, and how much we earn.

I've seen him with wealthy women. I think, lucky women. I've seen him with older men, the type with well-fed double-chins and nicely pressed suits. I think, poor Phil. No one's ever told me what they do, men, when they go to bed together. I can never quite imagine it either. It strikes me as comic. I always want to laugh or turn my face away. Don't things get in the way?

But I've been with women, you know? It's sad really.

I have an idle dream. Honestly, it's nothing more than that. On a bad day, a nasty day, when there are no clients about – I wonder: what if I had enough money to pay for Phil? Oh it wouldn't work. I know it wouldn't work. If a couple on the game try to set up together, jealousy begins.

One or other has to stop. Or both stop. You try to get ordinary jobs. And then you bump into an old client. No. You can't escape.

But isn't it strange? Of all the men I've met and slept with, the only one I even dream of loving – is the one I can never have. I asked Old Hicky, one night. I bought him a coffee. "Is that what dreams are all about?" I asked him. "Things that are impossible?"

And do you know what he replied? This old geezer that sleeps among the dustbins. He said: "We would never let ourselves believe in the impossible." If you ask me, he's been to school, has that one.

THE MAN: I sometimes think – well, it often crosses my mind – that people like me have no right to judge others. Whatever the rules might be, we're outside them ourselves. To pretend to be offended by what others do – what's it called? – "conspicuous outrage"! As Hamlet said: "the Lady doth protest too much". A sure sign of a guilty conscience.

They're hungry. So I buy. But what I buy – it ought never to be offered for sale. And that is our fault. There's no emotion. They smile like assistants in a travel agency, anxious to fulfil your dream and earn a commission.

It's not even happiness. And it stopped being a relief a very long time ago.

THE OLD TRAMP: My name is Old Hicky. That's what the kids call me. I don't know how it began. I can't tell you how old I am. I don't remember who my mother was, or even if had one. I have faint wisps of memories, like puffs of steam that hover above drains. I think there were once better times. I can't say for sure. But I don't think that I've always been like this.

Old Hicky. It seems to be friendly. They do seem to be fond of me. There are scores of us, hundreds of us – I dare say the world is full of us ... but my kids like me. They buy me coffee. They give me a meal when they can. One lass gave me a fur coat last winter. "It's no longer the fashion," she said. "It's coloured plastic raincoats now". Well, I wouldn't know about that. "It's only fake fox-fur," she said.

"I love fake foxes," I said, and she laughed for a long time about it.

I knew what she meant by giving me that. Help to keep me warm. And it did. But I unpicked it. You know. I have a little pen-knife and I took out all the stitches. There were thirteen whole foxes in that one coat. I used the silk lining as a blanket to keep them warm. They used to cuddle up with me. One big bundle, with little black noses everywhere. Such loving eyes. Such happy smiles. And those sweet, lolling pink tongues.

Luckily, they knew how to fend for themselves. They'd set off, in the small hours and come back with bellies all round and fat. If it was cold, like now, they hunted in turns. Half stayed to look after me, and half went off like things that you only ever see in your eye corner. I wasn't frightened for them. Even if they were seen, there are no hunters in the centre of London. No one to come galloping through the trees. And very few trees, come to think of it.

I miss trees so much I ache inside. I talk to the ones that're in the squares because they're lonely too. They bow their branches, slowly, so that nobody else notices.

THE YOUTH: I was with this posh woman and she suddenly screamed. A policeman came running toward us. There are plenty of them at Christmas.

"I saw a fox!" she said aghast.

The policeman smiled. He'd hoped I was robbing her. "There're no foxes here, Madam. Just cats and the occasional dog. You don't have to worry about that."

THE GIRL: "Did you see that?" hissed my client, nodding down the side street behind the Soho restaurant. "It was a bloody fox, I swear."

You never contradict a client. Always humour them. "Wild animals are coming in from the country," I said. "It said so in the Sunday paper."

If it had been a fox, I'd have run a mile.

THE OLD TRAMP: Where men build their cities, there they bring their new Gods and they build their Churches, their Temples, their Meeting Houses, their Mosques and ... whatever other place they need in which to house them. I could understand that. That is human nature. But do

144

they think that before they came, there had been no Gods at all? We were there first – the Gods of the Wilderness.

It used to be forest all round here, with a few boggy patches because the river was low-lying. There were men. There was a tribe up there, where they now have their government. There was another tribe down there, where the first king built his first castle. Come winter, when the river went hard, they used to come out of their little towns and they would bow down to me.

"God of the Wilderness", they used to chant. "The food we have grown with our own hand will soon be done. There is only the seed-corn left." And this was true. They had been good husbandmen and they had taken good care of their fields and their kine. But it was all done now. All that remained was my land – the land they had not tilled – the land they had not paid for.

"Oh Wild One, Oh Horned One, Oh King of the Beasts, we bring you gifts to honour thee," and they'd leave me a fine maiden or a splendid youth. "Please may we stray onto your land, in order to live until Spring?"

I rarely touched their offering. It was enough that they had remembered me. When they came by next day – and if the girl or the boy was alive and warm – they knew I was pleased. They were free to hunt – but for food and never for pleasure. If they took any pleasure then they too would be hunted. I had my wolves. I had my hounds from hell.

THE LADY: "Why on earth are you bringing me here?" I asked with distaste.

It was one of those terribly narrow alleys that are allowed to exist because of some ancient, mediaeval laws or something. There were no doors at all. It was a long time since it had been used to take a short-cut. There were stinking piles of derelict rubbish and at the next turn I could see one of those filthy old men.

"Don't you find it exciting?" whispered my Lancelot, starting to press against me, and work his hands up and down my back.

"But if anyone should come?" I objected feebly ...

"It's the risk we must take."

And I swear to God he stripped off in the moonlight. His penis stood out like the handle of a sword and I was the

Lady of the Lake. He moaned when I took hold of him. It made me shiver. It sent a shock wave through my body. It is a most amazing thing. In what is it rooted? How does it stand so hard?

He undressed me too. All my lovely things, they cost the earth at Simpson's, he almost tore them off me. Then he held me as if I were a wild boar or something – he took aim and he drove it into me, *slowly*, like the thrust of death.

THE MAN: "We can't stay here," I muttered, trying not to be heard, and I nodded toward another couple who were having it off further along.

"They're not going to complain if we don't," she giggled, and began to undress me.

I can't explain why I let it happen. I can't begin to tell you what I felt. She knelt on the floor, her legs open, and I was paralysed. I knew that she was young enough to be my own daughter. I just closed me eyes, and felt more than physically naked.

THE YOUTH: It was horrible. I withdrew from her. She looked afraid – no – she looked panic-stricken. She tried desperately to fondle me and awake more interest, but although I stayed hard I knew that my soul felt revolted.

I turned her toward Old Hicky. He was standing there, at the next corner, and a light that came from somewhere else surrounded him with a silver halo. It was like one of those wonders they talk about in the theatre. One of those visions that you never forget.

I heard a footstep and, instead of feeling shy at being stark naked, I just drew to one side, and the man walked by. He was naked too. He took hold of the woman's hand and they just ... stood.

THE GIRL: I watched him come toward me. I realised that we were both as naked as babies, but it wasn't his nakedness that made my spine curl and twist and quiver. It was his beauty. Oh my God – was there ever a man so perfect?

He held me in his arms, and everything from the past was pardoned. He pressed against me, and his hard penis tapped against me like the nose of an animal begging to be stroked. We just – how can I explain it without it sounding silly – we

146

just slid our hands all over each other in amazed wonder and worship.

We kissed each other. And then we kissed each other. After that, we just went on, and kissed each other. The two people watched us. Old Hicky had pointed, and they had turned. They both wept. It felt as if we were rolling in leaves and moss underneath a great tree. He was in me, like a plough, and I was clawing his small man's buttocks, drawing him in further.

We were oblivious of everything else but each other, and even there, we two were melting and becoming one.

THE OLD TRAMP: I called my foxes home to me. They came, and brought their friends with them. You'd be amazed if you knew how much of my old kingdom existed still between Bond Street and Covent Garden – between Marylebone Road and the river. You do not see it. You are looking in shop windows. You do not hear it. You hear the dance music from the cafés and the clubs.

They came in their hundreds, and pattered over and around the boy and the girl. The wilderness respects what is sacred. The man looked at the woman. "I think we are going to die," he said. Her jaw was chattering and she just drew him against her.

They made me a signal – a kind of salute. I raised my own hand ... and the walls and floor became alive. The couple dissolved in the moonlight, nibbled away by hundreds of sharp teeth. Then the foxes crunched the bones into a hundred pieces, and they were carried away, strewn like leaves or bleached twigs, all over the West End. Any blood just trickled between the ancient paving-stones and was sucked up by the soil and sleeping acorns.

Thy day will come.

THE GIRL: He came very close and regarded us. Phil – he was now my Phil – pulled out and let him see it in its full, burning splendour. The old man nodded with an approving smile, and Phil impaled me again. I cried, as I died, and sighed as I was reborn again. He was shuddering in his own death throes and his life juices were pumping into me. He was like a volcano as he sang a wordless lullaby. I felt like an ancient field being split apart and planted with liquid monuments.

"Oh God," he whimpered like a baby. "I love you."

"And I love you," I managed to gasp, and held on to him, never wanting to let him go again.

"Here", said Old Hicky, delving into one of his many pockets. And into the palm of Phil's hand he put five simple rings of gold.

THE OLD TRAMP: And at that moment I told them the secret of the rings. That two of them were theirs, to wear always and so form a union. That two were for their own, individual spirit twins, as a gift of invitation. And that one was for me – if they would be so kind – and that I would wrap them round with roses wild and let them drink of my own cup.

---

Extract from a Sunday Colour Supplement:

"As we all know, it is becoming less and less fashionable to live in the centre of a city. As more and more land is given over to commerce, ministries, and shops – so people are moving out and becoming commuters. At the same time, wild-life is moving back in. Scientists from Warwick University have been studying a family of foxes that live off Cambridge Circus. At the same time, more and more stories are coming in of pumas being sighted in Surrey, Sussex and in the region of Gatwick airport. Unofficial sources say that these may be animals which have escaped from quarantine while being shipped to zoos around the world.

A couple of night revellers swear that they saw a huge male figure wearing antlers near the site of Berwick Street Market. The police point out that the couple had just spent five hours at an office party."

# The Old Lady

*Urd: one of the three Norns who resembled the Three Fates. She is an old crone, very much concerned with extending the past into the present, and seeking thereby to help shape the future.*

*1.*

She was not just old, she was obsolete. Her clothes dated back to a time that most people had forgotten. She wore her hair in a style that echoed an old newsreel of royalty. Even her speech and manners spoke of a different age.

She walked through the street market on a Saturday morning, poking at this, prodding at that. She would hold out a cabbage snootily. "Take the yellow leaves off before you weigh it," she would order.

"I don't weigh them," said the man. "I sell them at forty pence per head."

"Then you take ten pence off for all the yellow."

Or she would buy some apples and the black woman would tilt the pan of the weighing scales. "Where do you want me to put them, Grandma?"

"In a bag," said the lady in outrage, "and don't be pert with me! You are to address me as My Lady." She said it as though she meant it, so that's what everyone did. She was 'My Lady' to all and sundry. There was a small darn in one of her stockings.

It was the same at the Food Store. As she passed through the check-out she told the girl to come round and load her trolley. When the girl explained that she was not allowed, the old lady sent for the manager. Rather than suffer a scene, he helped her himself. "I am pleased to see that someone knows his job," she told him, handing him a coin for his trouble.

Little by little, in fact, she had trained the entire district. She passed along the streets like a Queen. When she went into shops, the staff pandered to her every whim. "Morning, ma'am," they would call in the market. "Morning, milady," said the young police officer as he helped her to cross the street, stopping all the traffic. The lady at the florist's always gave her a little posy. The stems would be wired and then wound around with silver paper. It was really very sweet of her.

## 2.

The man at the paper-shop had a dark skin and hailed from the colonies. He knew his place though and was very correct. Each and every morning he offered her a good quality journal that had been used to bind up the others.

"How kind," she would murmur, and try to hand it to a servant. "Oh dear. Why doesn't he stay at my side."

"He needs some stick," explained the owner of the shop.

"Yes, yes," she smiled. "Perhaps a little beating – but not too heavy with the blows, eh?"

"I'll see to it myself," he smiled, looking as though he might cherish that.

The nuance did not escape her. "Ah, you like putting them across your knees and smacking their brown bottoms? Partial to that sort of thing, are we, Ranjee?"

The man gave a grin and oozed a scented oil. "It will be done with great prudence," he whispered, "and the Countess may observe from the other side of the screen."

He would chuckle and she would join in. Their little conspiracy gave him a thrill, and she did seem to understand him so well. Indeed, that is what everyone would tell you – that she really understood them.

She was not really a Countess. Just the wife of a former civil servant who had been given a knighthood when his career had ended. She had a perfect right to be called 'Lady' but felt it demeaning to give the explanation. "It marks no honour of my own," she could imagine herself saying at tea.

"They gave it to my late husband for working his bollocks off turning a black savage into a Head of State."

Despite her airs and graces, she had a vulgar streak in her.

She would not add that he'd been struck impotent within three months of arriving there. Bitten on the buttocks by a mosquito that didn't know best Eton rump from common Aldershot arse. Her mind was even more vulgar than her words sometimes were. The men had liked that. The stewards found it made her less distant and much more human. She was in charge of all the domestic staff, of course. They looked to her for their orders. She ordered them, all right. She put them through their paces. As a matter of fact, the other wives had told her: "The men quite like your particular kind of discipline," they said. And they did, too. No complaints in that department!

She smiled with a courtly nod of her head at someone who doffed his hat with a flourish. Could he but read my thoughts, she mused. Her lace collar had a dash of cologne but her mind had the stench of a dustbin. So long as it is hidden, she assured herself. There is no disgrace so long as things are kept tidily hidden.

3.

He was already in by the time that she got home. The student, that is. The student with long legs to whom she had rented a room. Well, that was how it started, renting the room plus free use of the toilet. Then she had invited him to use the kitchen to get his little meals ready. Then they had come to an understanding, just as she had done with the soldiers. Now he had the free run of the house.

She liked long legs on a man. She had liked them even more in the old, tight uniforms, when diplomats wore a frock-coat. They looked as virile as tulips. But her student fitted the bill quite perfectly. Terribly polite, cultured, and with jeans that looked as if they'd been painted on.

She asked him once. "Aren't they a little, er, *restrictive?*"

He'd been at a loss for words until she gave one of her wicked winks, and like Captain Frobisher, all those years ago, he'd grinned in amused complicity.

After that, she offered to have his washing done by one of

the house boys. He hadn't seen a lot of her house so as far as he was concerned there might well be hordes of servants. She did them herself though. By hand. Lovingly. And she shook one drop of a rare African perfume right on the spot that counted.

It was not very long before he was taking breakfast with her. Yes, she still took meals. She did not eat them. She also partook of the occasional bon-bon which she obtained in Brixton. She had friends in Brixton, who remembered her from the old days. She would offer the student one.

"Would you care to taste a special bon-bon?" she asked, proffering the cut-glass bowl. "You must not chew it, but being a man, you are allowed to suck it. As we used to say in Africa: a Lady does not allow herself to suck anything in public."

It had amused him enormously. And he no longer blushed. That was good. That meant the perfume was working.

She informed him he could bathe on Friday nights because he would have the house to himself. She and a few friends met to play bridge. Of course she didn't bother to mention that they were only next door. Someone before her had made a desultory attempt to split the house into three, to make separate flats that could be rented out. There were still some stairs though. They led up to the apartment that was next door to his, and she had adapted it slightly. She had bored a hole through the wall.

The bridge party consisted of herself and one black lady who, instead of saying ma'am in the proper fashion, insisted in calling her Mama.

3.

The bathroom was huge. The bath was huge. The lavatory, the wash-bowl – everything – was a matching set, made out of flowered porcelain. It would be worth a mint on the antique market. Even the pull to make the toilet flush was an object of beauty in itself.

He liked using this room. First, there was the pleasure of just taking a bath. But then there was something special in the air – a feeling, a scent, or a hint of music. It was sensual

152

and exciting. He would undress slowly, watching himself in the mirror. Knowing that no one could see him, he did a knock-out strip. By the time he'd whirled and twirled and let the towel drop, he had a raging erection.

Even in the bath, with soapy water all around him, his prick refused to slacken. It inclined this way and that as he scrubbed himself. It bobbed like a buoy on the surface of a sea.

In the end he gave himself a hand-job. He had to. He let some water out, of course, or else his threshing about would have sodden the floor. As he got closer he arched up and then – for some unknown reason – he seized a tissue from a box at the side, and ejaculated into that.

He had meant to come in the bath. Easy to wash it off his belly. He also meant to flush the tissue down the lavatory. But he left it on the walnut shelf beneath the mirror.

As he went out, the water was still gurgling away, so he didn't hear the door to the hot-water cylinder open. He didn't see the black hand take the tissue away.

He could feel himself changing but he didn't quite know how. It was nothing to alarm him. He assumed it was to do with his age. But he became less and less attentive at his lectures and his marks started going down. One of the tutors had a word with him. Instead of being meek, he'd insulted the chap, and one more note was added to the list in his academic dossier.

He started turning up late, as well. He missed four lectures in one week. The tutor sent a written warning but he just threw the note away. His name came up at one of the staff meetings. They didn't want to lose a very promising student so they asked a lady from Welfare to call at his lodgings. They would send Mrs Whitaker.

"Lady Cecilia?" she enquired graciously.

The old lady nodded with a charming smile. "If you are collecting for some charitable cause, my dear, I'm afraid I cannot help you. In spite of my title, I am just as poor as any other old-age pensioner. With a house like this ..." she waved behind her, "... I even have to take in lodgers."

The visitor picked up the cue nicely. Within five minutes they were seated at a cane table, sipping cups of Darjeeling tea, though not from Fortnum & Masons.

She was obviously an extremely tactful old soul but, when

153

persuaded, she told Mrs Whitaker all that she needed to know. There was a strange smell in his room that reminded one of incense. He had been very dreamy lately. He was three weeks behind in his rent. He ate less and less. And so she chatted on and on.

Mrs Whitaker wrote the word 'Drugs' in capital letters in the dossier.

"Are you content to let him continue living here?" she asked with concern.

"Well ..." Lady Cecilia hesitated and bit her lip.

"What is it, my dear? Please, tell me everything. We're very anxious to help him."

The fragile old lady dabbed her eyes with a piece of lace far too delicate for sneezing into. "He hardly ever comes home. He stays out two, three nights without letting me know." She blinked with an old lady's concern. "And he has sold so many of his things."

"His clothes, you mean?"

"His electric gramophone, his books – and things like that. I wondered if I shouldn't contact his family? I feel responsible, you see. I've tried to be a grandmother to him."

And then she wept.

Mrs Whitaker held her in her arms and mentally cursed the ungrateful brat who had so cruelly deceived this sweet old lady, the university, and the state! If she had her way, students would go to prison. They'd be forced to repay all monies. Then they would be flogged.

### 5.

As a matter of fact, he *was* being flogged – but very lightly, and not with leather whips, but little bundles of herbs.

He was hanging by his wrists from an overhead beam in the old wine cellar. He was as naked as the day he was born and didn't give a damn. It was true that he was under the influence of drugs – but he had not taken them. He had been given them forcefully. He'd tried to refuse. He'd done his best to spit them out and clamped his teeth shut. The negro priest had just grinned. Then in front of his face, he had mixed powdered herbs with pork dripping and formed it

154

into a bullet. "Five minutes in the freezer, man, and then is you going to get a thrill!"

They pushed it into his anus and rammed it in very high. He had felt humiliated. The shock was both physical and emotional. He trembled like a rape victim and, when the fever hit him, they took him to the old Lady.

Her face seemed much more beautiful now – more like the pictures she had shown him of her on a verandah in Africa. He was too woozy to think rationally. He just submitted to her charm. He made love to her – so slim – so slender – and even while he was still shuddering with a thunderous orgasm they pulled him away.

He was tied to a table. They stood a coffin by his side and she pulled on the hinged lid. "My husband," she announced. Inside was the remains of a corpse that had been gutted, and whose head had been thrust into the abdominal cavity. "My dear, impotent husband. Got lost in the bush you know. Too much whisky. They said that wild animals had killed him."

She gazed in homage at the decomposed horror and laughed. "Sir Alfred, in person!"

The African woman came closer, shuffling, half bent, as though terrified of the white Lady. "Mama, mama, mama," went her endless whisper while the other people said "Mama-lao," like the rustle of leaves.

She fondled the helpless student. "Look at you, what you can do, and you are only twenty." She giggled lewdly and tied a short string around his genitals.

"He was seventy when he died but he was still in good voice. You should have heard him scream. A whole day and night they tormented him. Now his soul is as safe as a Jinee in a bottle." She laughed softly. "The Arabs got the idea from Africa, you know. Allah let it happen to hundreds of them. Slaves," she howled. "Phantom slaves. Doomed for ever to do as I wish."

"And when you die?" spat the boy, in a rash display of bravado.

"When I die?" she screeched with laughter. "I was a debutante at the court of Queen Victoria. The new Princess Alexandra was god-mother to our first child. I lost my husband in 1923, when I was sixty-five years old." She slapped his belly with the flat of her hand. "I will never die, as long as there are young, sexual fools like you about."

156

Her fingers played with him even more urgently, teasing his testicles and kneading his cock. "If I can corrupt them then I may keep them. If I keep them, I am allowed to squeeze out as much of their life-force as I can manage, for my personal use. I will show you before you die. There are rooms down here that are full of them."

His throat felt tight with fear. "Why must you kill us?" he croaked.

"They want a sacrifice," she murmured. "And if I am the last woman you make love to before you die ... they feed me."

His mind thought furiously. "Then why not just emasculate me?" She was rubbing him now, making fun of him, mocking his manly nature and offending the creative powers of good. "Wouldn't that be a suitable sacrifice?"

"Oh but we do cut them off, during the ceremony. It's essential that we make you suffer as much and as long as possible. The greater your agony, the stronger the force I can gather." She giggled now, almost drunk with the bubbly power rushing through her veins. How favoured she was! How much more blessed than any other woman! To still be feminine at over a hundred years, and to bear babies with which to recompense the gods!

6.

The drums were thudding out like the heart of a great factory. People were chanting, mostly in a high, nasal tone that sounded like a whistle. Most of them were naked and they danced. Except that this wasn't dancing in any sense that a European might know. It was more like a rhythmic, concerted shiver, with hardly any moving from the spot.

She sat on a throne of pain. Each ivory tusk had been used to impale a victim. Each cord had strangled. Each peg or nail had been hammered into a living skull. She sat there, like the Dowager Empress of China, and waited.

She mulls about her kin and how the grandson of her grandson had babies. There was no-one alive who knew her any more. If there were records, then it was assumed that errors and omissions had been made. She was thought to be long dead. No, not thought to be – no-one thought about her any more. She was the past. She belonged to the past. She was dead, even though she was alive.

She knew the terrifying power that had its abode inside her. She acted out her role of the eccentric old lady with lavender scent. But she positively purred with the secret knowledge that she could kill, maim, send mad all who displeased her. She was very selective, of course. And extremely discreet. It wouldn't do to be certified and sent to spend her days in a mental hospital. It might be difficult to get the young men! She would have to break out and then, people would start looking for her.

The table had been placed before her so that she could feast her eyes on him. She was amazed herself that desire could still tremble through her limbs. That was how they had first recruited her, of course, all those years ago. Juju, they'd called it. How close to the French, Dieu Dieu. But this was the religion of the Dark Continent. They can be Christian, Muslim or Jew, but if they're African then they also believe in Juju. So do many Europeans – people who worked there for gold, diamonds, tobacco or cocoa. When they went back home, if ever they went back home, there was Juju in their blood. Sometimes they attempted to use it.

When she was there, all those years ago, with nothing to do except drink, dream and go slightly gaga, she'd gone out into the bush alone. There was a filthy, small shelter among the trees. It looked for all the world like an abandoned chicken roost that had never been cleaned. They showed her to an ancient black man. God knows what he saw since his eyes were white with cataracts. She made him a promise and the very next day he sent her the son of an Italian exporter. She had no intention of resisting him, but the way he made love, she could not have resisted anyway. It had been violent, painful, and ecstatic. She gave them the baby as she had promised and in return they gave her back her husband as an eternal slave. In the records at the Foreign and Colonial Office, should you care to look, he is presumed to have been killed by wild animals.

She had over one hundred such slaves now. You gave them extreme joy and then extreme pain. Somehow, magically, you trapped their souls.

Exactly as the current young man had reminded her, there

were moments when she wondered how it would end, assuming that it ever did. But her people knew the truth, and the gods sometimes spoke to her. "Never," they told her, giving her the sweet stroke of half an orgasm. "It can never end."

7.

She had managed to make him climax again. It was often difficult, so soon after having made love. And at the moment of supreme climax, they had tied and knotted the cord extremely tightly. The pain stopped everything, like a stone falling into the clockwork, and sperm were inside his organ, to be kept there forever. He was still erect, of course. He could not now go flaccid. The tumescence would last forever, like that purple God from Egypt. They need only cut it off and slowly dry it. It would shrink in size as all the tissue fluid evaporated. They would disguise it. In the end they would sell it as a monkey's paw, or a rabbit's foot. So much the better if some punter bought it for good luck at Chepstow.

She had supplied a famous racing driver and he'd been killed in a crash. His widow wasn't told, but they'd taken his genitals too. Mutilated – that was the word the police used. Somehow or other, they always assumed that dogs had done it. That made her laugh. Dogs, lions ... what difference did it make?

"Now, my sweet buckling, we're going to slit your skin into strips, a quarter of an inch wide, and we'll rip each one off very, very slowly." She shivered with a sexual frisson.

"Stop!" shouted the boy.

"That's lovely," she encouraged. "Scream, screech and howl as much as you wish. The greater the pain, the greater the ecstasy before you die."

"I am not a worthy victim," he yelled. There was something in his voice that made everyone stop. It would be a disaster if they made the least mistake. "I never made love to you," he sobbed.

"Ho!" she snorted. "Ho!" she scoffed. "Everybody saw you."

"I was drugged. You made me see what my heart wanted

to see. But that wasn't me, old woman. I didn't love you. You used magic. You used force. I was not a willing victim. I didn't do anything of my own free will."

There was silence now. People looked at her sideways, wondering what she would do. "I drew out your sperm!" she said in triumph.

"You can do the same to a billy-goat! That doesn't mean he loves you."

There was a murmur among the people. There was sense in what he said.

"It's no use trying to talk your way out of it. The Gods have chosen you!"

That was true. That convinced the people. They relaxed again. They grinned again.

"What?" he roared. "They chose a man who loves other men?"

This time every one's eyes opened wide.

"I think you were too hasty," he hurried on. "Your birthday was getting too close and you forgot to ask me about my private life." He grinned at her defiantly. "Dear Mama-lao, I regret to tell you that I am homosexual. Therefore the Gods will spit on your imperfect gift and they will be very displeased!"

There were howls of terror, and someone cut the cord tied around his genitals. It had been six minutes or less. The tissues were not dead, and the blood was able to start flowing again.

The Old Lady glared at him bleakly. Then, with a sudden grin, she took hold of a handsome black youth and shoved him at her student. The black youth understood and began kissing the white boy carnally, his own body sliding all over the other's.

To her horror, the white youth's cock was growing hard again, and she just gawped at it, feeling sick.

The head, inside the belly of her husband, popped out and rolled across the floor.

"No!" she screamed. "These things are not true!"

But the people pointed at the two young men, locked in a tight embrace. They all knew the law. They opened the doors to the farther rooms and started hauling out the coffins.

A male priest, a baba-lao, opened each one. Some of the

160

cadavers were like ancient mummies. Others were more recent. One of them still stank to high heaven and there were still grubs and larvae wriggling in the crevices. The Old Lady was shrieking now, but two of the women held her in her chair.

The Baba-lao began chanting and everyone moved or tramped in a circle, carrying the student along. The smoke from the candles moved in spirals as if drawn to follow them. The student felt that he was riding a horse on a roundabout again, and waving to his grandmother in the crowd.

The first time round, her teeth fell out. The second time round she had no hair. After that, her clothes all rotted. Then her skin was as thin as finest silk and tore as the threads retracted. Her eye-balls shrivelled and her nose went thin and bony. And all the time there was a rising, sighing sound as if a hundred souls were being set free from bottles. Each head popped out of each abdomen, and each time it was like there was a clap of thunder. There was a whoosh of something diving through the room like a flock of unseen birds, twittering and fluttering like things released from a cage. You could hear them, no, not hear them, but feel them, whooshing past your skin like arrows.

## 8.

She sat there still, what was left of her, like a long-dead Miss Haversham. The finery was stained by nameless fluids. Her skeleton was fractured so that she tilted, like a clown seen in a broken mirror. There was no more elegance and no more terror. One looked at this thing which had once been wicked and one only felt a slight, very slight, touch of sympathy.

There was utter silence. They all stood still and far away, like a distant playground, they thought they heard a faint cry. They turned to him. "You have powerful magic," said the priest.

"No," grinned the student, easing the black boy away. "I have a liberal mind, that's all."

"But the spirits believed what you said."

"I don't see how they could, since it was a lie. She did though. She wasn't sure, and so she believed." He gave a little shrug and an apologetic smile. "I don't know anything about your religion but – no man's truth can be built out of lies."

The priest drew him out of the cellar. Once upstairs, there was a faint rumbling sound, like a passing underground train. The cellars collapsed.

After that, the people faded away. There were doors he didn't even know about. They went back to their suburban houses and flats, to their electric freezers, to their gas-ovens and to their ancient, black Gods. They watch football on the television. Once a month they drink fresh blood.

He was not one to be afraid of imaginary noises or bumps in the night, but he didn't much fancy the idea of staying on in the house. There were smells, and memories of smells, and it was all a bit too big anyway. There was also the little problem of whether he should tell, and if so, whom?

In a locked drawer of the bureau, he found many bundles of Student Union Membership cards. There were also lots of letters from uneasy parents, along with warnings from tutors, and even the Tax Office. How many had not escaped from this house, he wondered? How much joy had been used to bait how many traps?

He decided to crash at a mate's place for a few days. He decided to say nothing to anybody. He would keep his mouth shut and leave it all in the lap of the Gods.

There was a knock at the door. An eighteen year old student was holding a note from Mrs Whitaker. The Welfare Officer would collect the rent herself and send Lady Cecilia a cheque each month. The new student was a girl – and very beautiful.

But that, as they say, is a different kettle of fish.

------

When an African dictator was toppled in the recent past, it was widely reported that heads and other parts of human corpses were found stuffed into ice-boxes, in several parts of his palace. Among them were former political opponents, army generals and persons who had held positions of power.

Many European countries once had colonies or territories in the dark continent. British, Belgian, Dutch and German colonial officers have written books. In one way or another, almost all of

162

them mention the weird, barbaric practices that they came across. One of the more gruesome habits among Kings, Chiefs, Sheiks and other leaders, was to keep bodies of former enemies as if they were trophies. But the corpses of close family members were always disposed of in a respectful fashion – and the graves guarded.

One author, Isaiah Oke, (in 'Blood Secrets', 1989) states that kidnapped white men have been used for this magic. Isaiah Oke was a babalorisha, or Juju high priest. Many of the 'religions' in the area of the Caribbean and Brazil, contain African beliefs that have been mixed with local indian beliefs: Voodoo, Condomble, Umbanda, etc.

# Bethlehem

*Bedlam: a mad-house or a place of great uproar. The word was derived from 'The Hospital of Our Lady of Bethlehem', which was in London. Whence 'Bedlamite': an insane person or an inmate of a mad-house – often thought to be 'marked' or 'specially blessed' by God. In Hebrew, Bethel means 'The House of God'.*

*1.*

It was dark in the streets outside. There was a light drizzle on the tarmac and against the walls of the buildings. It filled the air with the murmuring sounds of a far off waterfall.

A hundred years ago, when they first built it, the hospital had been a long way outside the town. They had not meant it to be obvious. As a matter of fact, they had wanted it hidden – like an attic, or a cellar, or a garden shed. After all, they explained with great refinement, the poor inmates had to be sheltered from the idle gaze of the morbidly curious.

That sounds rather strange when you consider that, only a few years before, genteel families could bring guests to have a look at Bedlam. One gave a coin to the porter and he would walk you through the corridors, between the chained victims. But lunacy had lost its power to amuse. The world had become shrewd because madness had acquired an aura of shame. For this reason, the hospital was built where visitors, if any, could come and go unseen. The basic sentiment was: insanity may befall the very best of families – but one needn't flaunt it.

The town had grown though, and the hospital had aged. What had once been a tiny deformity, discreetly tucked away among some trees, had now become a blatant wen on the face of civic progress. The trees had gone. The fields had been swallowed whole. The asylum and its own staff housing had been grafted into the body of the town. No-one liked this new ordering.

There was an alarming number of staff who left. The faces changed almost as often as the bed sheets. It was a very rare bird who wanted to work here all his life. There were fewer and fewer white personnel, but more and more coloureds, some of whom took great delight in scaring the patients. It was not the sort of place where careers are made. You went there in order to be forgotten.

No-one ever came to see it. Quite simply therefore, no one ever got it ready to be seen. The main entrance hall had once looked like St Pancras' station, with tiles everywhere: lettuce green, sulphurous yellow and a luxurious red like a plum. The noises were similar too – what with murmurs, metallic clanks, and the far-off shriek of brakes. Perhaps it had looked better by gas-light?

Today it had been adapted to better use. There were no civic visits any more. The area had been divided up by plywood panels and grey metal straps. A huge net had been stretched across the whole in case any glass fell from the glass roof that imitated a dome. All in all, it still looked like a Victorian public lavatory, or an annex to the Royal Albert Hall.

Efforts had been made to tart up the general appearance of the whole hospital. Little bits had been added on, here and there. Like the pleasant little memorial garden with clumps of uncut grass, cinder pathways and one tragic hydrangea. There was also a saintly statue with four holes that had held a plaque. Apart from that, there was nothing to indicate in whose memory the garden had been planted.

Someone else, the Pope perhaps, had kindly donated two television sets – one for the 'male side' and one for the 'female side'. The two sexes did not mingle. Mingling was frowned upon. So really, under the surface, very little had changed in the last ninety years. Everything was much as it always had been. Even the faces were the same.

2.

There was a church next door. It had been built to serve the hospital. By one of those strange quirks of history, the

Chairman of the hospital still held the right to appoint the priest. Not that there was ever much competition, you realise. It was not a rewarding post in any sense of the word. In theory, there were over four hundred souls to care for. But many of them thought they were priests too. One or two even thought they were God.

Hence the church was most unusual in never seeing a couple married, nor any baby baptised. The pews had been used once upon a time. They did indeed show some signs of wear. But that went back to olden days, when patients were herded in by force. That had long since stopped. There was too much titter. There were too many bodies sliding under the pews. Not that the staff minded. They were paid extra. Now though, not much ever took place, apart from the dreary, standard funerals. Over the years, the cemetery had been enlarged as often as four times. Very few of the inmates ever went 'home'. The family was so shocked when someone was admitted but, if they got well, there were a thousand reasons why they couldn't go home again.

There were several visits to start with – as many as one a month. But they seemed to drop off steeply. What's the point, relatives would ask, when she doesn't even know me? But she knew them well enough. It was just that she had nothing to say, and she saw them so seldom she was terrified to say it. All people are born with the gift. They can turn into strangers so easily.

They would come on her birthday, until they forgot the date. They would call her by name, until it began to embarrass them. Then it was just one or two greetings cards, which she mistook for some sort of official document and tried hastily to fill them in. After that, it was nothing. That and only that – just nothing.

She wondered what they expected of her, but they gave no clues. She noticed that other ladies grew older and older, until someone came for them, usually at night. The next morning, their beds would be empty and stiff with clean sheets. Her favourite doctor went away, just like that. They said he'd gone to work somewhere else. The nurses she liked, they too were taken away "to work on other wards", or so they said. But she knew better. They were still trying to punish her. They would never forgive. That's why they put any friendly people into the stews, the soups and casseroles.

They were given food that did not require a knife or fork. It was always plastic spoons and she knew the reason why. So that bits of gristle could never be named.

This was why she decided to be fat. It was the quickest way to make herself succulent. The faster she grew, the sooner the cooks would take her to the kitchen. So she sat still. She did not move. She saved her energy. "Oh dear," said the daftest of the nurses, "she's turning into a vegetable," and inwardly she sang an Alleluia. They gave her medicines to hold her back. She made sure her mouth was dry and kept it all under her tongue. She spat it down the lavatory! It was a nice lavatory, with a bolted metal grill. That was to stop people putting their heads in ... or else to stop the nasties from getting out.

Once they had found a dead baby in there.

3.

They took her to the cemetery once. Another girl had shown them how to cut her gizzard slowly but cleverly with the pages of a book. She had watched her do it. She cried because the paper was too soggy for her to copy the idea. They thought she was a special friend, that it might help her if she went to the funeral. She was the only one there. Plus a nurse who knew she did not need watching.

She listened to the vicar talk about tears. But there were no tears. The nurse winked at the man who brought the trolley from the morgue. The vicar was talking to his black book. That book was no use. It's pages were too thin. She did not actually know what was going on. Unless, of course, they were giving her a trial-run. Is that what it was – a rehearsal? Maybe she was supposed to watch and remember so that when her turn came she'd lie still too. It was only a cardboard coffin, all of a piece, folded, and held in shape by staples. It put her in mind of boxes for keeping shoes in. "Could I have mine now?" she wanted to ask, "with somebody nice in it." She didn't though. She hadn't spoken for years. Not one word. They weren't going to catch her out as simply as that!

A lot of thought had been put into the design of the graves. They were simple slabs, engraved with a simple name

167

and a date. At first they had been pieces of dark granite. But the War had brought many changes and now they were simple slabs of grey concrete. The surrounds were simple gravel which made sure that no unsightly grass would grow. Vases were not allowed, so there were no dead flowers to clear away either. If anyone had bothered to look, they would have noticed that many graves were marked with several names. They looked a bit like library bins, in fact, or those great tanks where they collect empty bottles.

One stuck to essentials, which is to say: one vicar, one hole, and one body. Only once in ten years was there ever a mourner. That was usually for a young biker who'd had a badly damaged brain. The family was always officially informed, to be sure, either by registered letter or via the police. But life had moved on, and the family with it. They no longer lived at the last known address. By law, they had done their duty, and were not obliged to search further. There was a budget limit which governed these niceties.

There was a gate between the cemetery and the main road. It was painted black and never used. It did rattle though. Most of the local people thought it rattled rather more than gates of that sort should. They noticed these things. They took great care always to walk on the opposite side of the street. They didn't actually talk about these things, you understand. As a matter of fact, no one ever does. You don't, do you? In some way or other, it is generally agreed that there is nothing very helpful to be said. One knows there might be things. That is to say, one has evidence that certain things exist but – let's leave it at that.

The gates were as solid as those of any prison. But then, they had to be since they served the same purpose. They existed to keep what was inside in, and what was outside out. The world was a clear-cut as that.

4.

If ever you visit a mental hospital, or a psychiatric unit as they now prefer to call them, you find it hard to remember that these people are sick. They look so normal, so ordinary, and their behaviour most of the time is exactly what you'd expect. The staff have much the same problem. Nurses, orderlies, aides and cleaners, all find it hard to remember that these people are normal, apart from their sickness.

That is what Anna found. Anna came from a rural Irish family which was staunchly Catholic. The mother wished her husband looked more like the Pope. The husband wished his wife looked more like Jezebel. The children wished there were fewer of them, so they'd have more to eat and new shoes. No-one could say that Anna had been spoiled as a child. As a young woman, she had done her training by hard slog. She always sent half her wages home. She was a model daughter. Her mother said so.

But her mother didn't know that Anna had trouble with boys. At three, she'd been allowed to play with them. At ten, they'd dragged her away from them. Throughout her teens they had kept her aloof and told her never to have anything to do with them. Then in her twenties they told her it was time she began thinking of them again. "Surely to God," her mother would ask, "there's one that catches your fancy?" That was the hitch. She fancied them all. God damn the priest! God damn her mother! She had thought of nothing but boys for the last fifteen years.

There were lots of nurses who had the same feelings. The male nurses too. Women weren't allowed to work on the male wards. It wasn't safe. They'd be raped. As would any male personnel who went on the female side. Most doctors had their flies ripped open at one time or another. The danger was the filth on their finger nails and the ghastly infection that a simple scratch could cause.

Their male colleagues were very curious, as you might expect. When they ran into each other, in the canteen or the gymnasium, they would always probe for obscene details. Were there any nice girls on any of the wards? Were any of them obsessed by sex? If so, what did they do? The female nurses laughed up their sleeves and wove the most erotic stories which kept the men enthralled. The male nurses in their turn also set out to astonish. They spoke of the athletic, immodest young gods who exposed – nay, displayed – their charms to all who would look.

"There's a youngish chap on Ward Twelve," said Albert, "who's got the most colossal cock I've ever seen. I think he knows it too. At least, he never stops showing it off. Night and morning, it's like the raising and the lowering of the flag. We can't stop him, you see. We can't watch him all time."

"Is he handsome?" the female nurses asked, wondering how they would react if they were confronted with such a spectacle.

"Judge for yourselves," grinned Albert and opened his white ward-coat.

The girls screamed, but not too loudly. They were not as cross as they pretended. Later, as they walked back to the wards in a group, they had a giggle about it. "Not bad," said Dolly wistfully. "Oh I've seen bigger," said Sarah, more wistfully still.

Sometimes Anna used to wonder if they were not being depraved by the quality of the work itself. Or did one just get used to it? Did the skin get thicker with age? She also had doubts about religion.

5.

There was one ward that everyone was curious about. It was always referred to as 'The Special'. Most of the time it was staffed by some of the older personnel – male and female together. It made one think it must be a soft option. It was one of those duties given to those who were getting close to retirement. One never met them. They didn't live in the Nurses' Homes. They all had cottages or flats. Most of them were married with grown-up children. That was why very few of the younger staff were ever asked to do a turn there. When it did happen, they came back ... changed. And they would not talk. They had been sworn to secrecy.

There were rumours, of course, as there were bound to be. Some said that the ward housed an obscure member of the Royal Family. Others said it was for mental patients who also had AIDS. That's one more of those things that most people forget: that mad minds are not in the least bit proof against the normal physical illness. It doesn't seem fair somehow, to know that demented maniacs do die of 'flu, cancer and the other ills. The mad do get sick. The worst thing is: they will not cooperate with any treatment you try to give.

One man, who needed his appendix out, had almost throttled the surgeon because he had not swallowed the pills

170

they had given him. As far as he was concerned, the man in the mask was hurting him. You had to be ultra careful with all surgical instruments too – and just about anything else that might be found in the kitchen, the bathroom or the laundry room. They had found one woman, only nineteen years old, who had stuffed a soup-ladle into her vagina. "It's mine, it's mine," she screamed with outraged logic when the doctors tried to release it. Similarly, on the male side, one poor soul had been in agony for days before they discovered a bottle of vinegar up his rectum.

If one laughed, it was not out of cruelty. Nobody truly mocked these people. One laughed, one made jokes, in order to fight off the fear. Working with the ones who were physically ill was a whole new ball-game ... or a different kettle of fish, depending on your age.

But there were 'Medical Wards' for them. There was even an obstetrics unit for women who were pregnant. But all of this made it even more difficult to explain the 'The Special'. It was a source of great unease in the mind of every member of staff. Somehow or other, it figured in every nightmare.

6.

Poor Anna! She was puzzled by the ubiquity of sex. The whole hospital was like a tropical rain forest, alive with heat and weird noises. They had covered it during their training. The topic had been discussed quite reasonably and it had all made sense. That's all very well in the classroom. Here though, one could actually feel it.

The Director had told them that when a person becomes mentally ill, the first thing he loses is his ability to conform. He lets go of all morality. He no longer sees a reason for holding back, for not doing what he wants to do. In addition, he has quite likely been sexually repressed in some way, so when the crisis comes, he rebounds to the very opposite type of conduct. "Beside," he'd added, "when the sexes are fertile, the managers find it easier to keep them separated." He had looked around the trainee group and fixed each pair of eyes.

"I advise you, each and every one of you, to sort out your own problems before you ever go on the wards. Get the giggling over with. Flush away all erotic little whimsies you might have at the back of your head. For God's sake ..." he banged the desk and made everyone jump, "... I'm not just talking about dirty minds or furtive orgasms ..." He looked at them helplessly. Then he sagged, and his voice went flat. "Don't let it get at you."

They had not taken it in. During their midnight debates by the light of candles, they found they differed on what the experts had been trying to say.

"He might just be nuts himself," quipped one.

"He might just," said Anna, "have been warning us against that very idea. After all ..." she looked at the previous speaker, "isn't it a common feature of madness that the sick believe they are sane, and everyone else is mad?"

She saw him squirm, but she wanted to hit him almost. How dare he be so arrogant? "To nurse our patients well, we must not put ourselves in their shoes. If we start to understand them, then it might be too late."

They'd gone back to their own rooms then. They were all very subdued. Was she imagining it? Anna didn't know. But from that day on, her friends and fellow trainees had seemed to become more overtly sexual. As she passed along the corridors, she could hear male and female gasps coming from some of the rooms. From her own window, she spied on one couple, hiding in the angle behind the bicycle shed. She had watched the whole five-act opera from prelude to shattering finale. She knew quite well that she was a sight too unliberal for even her closest friends. Too pious. Too much the prude.

"It's not that!" she wanted to scream at them all. "I feel the same things that you do. Don't you think I yearn for a man pressing against me? Don't you believe that I want to stroke his fine chest and die with him between my legs?" She beat the walls of her room to the rhythm of the mattress next door. "You are playing with fire," she wailed. "You will get your fingers burned."

7.

"I wouldn't mind a bit of that," she heard a young porter mutter. She clouted his face and went to see his boss.

172

"Don't leer at me," she told one of the male visitors. "It wouldn't take much to keep you inside!" He had gone green and ran out of the building.

It was nearly time for her first turn of night-duty to end. She should write-up the Ward Report. She was new, of course, and perhaps went into rather more detail than was necessary. But she felt it only right to describe exactly what they got up to. The next evening, when she came on, the Day Sister drew her to one side.

"Are you all right, love?" she asked very softly, leaning back in her chair and looking up into her eyes.

"Yes," she said brightly and then gave a little laugh. "My internal clock is a bit knocked up by the changeover, but it usually adapts in a couple of days."

"That's fine then," the Sister laughed. "We've left you some Instant Coffee in the locker ... top quality."

"Ooo, that's unusually good of you."

"Marjorie died this morning."

"Oh dear. I'm sorry."

The sister tilted her head slightly on one side. "She was dead when we came on duty."

Anna's face went red and she primed her gun with denials.

"She was cold," said the sister. "Rigor mortis had set in. Luckily for you she was in a flat position or we'd still be waiting to send her down to the morgue."

Anna's mind was racing at full tilt, recklessly, like a child on a bicycle racing through a cemetery. "I didn't notice a thing."

"You put it in the report," pressed the Sister. "Isn't that your writing?" She held the book open and tapped sharply at the page. "Zero four thirty hours: Mrs Marjorie Smith waking other patients with her usual obscene chatter." The sister was calm again. And very quiet. "Judging by her rectal temperature, she died just after midnight."

Anna was mute. She made one or two clipped gestures, a bit like a duck in an animated cartoon. Her eyes were so blue by the dim lighting they looked as milky as cataracts.

"I want to help you, love. It's too late to replace you for tonight, but I'm off-duty at midday tomorrow. When you wake up, have a good hot shower and come and see me. I'll make you some breakfast." She took hold of her hand gently. "We've got to talk."

173

The young girl's eyes rested on the sister's stern but smiling face. "Are you a Lesbian?" she asked.

Like a rag doll, the sister's head fell. "We've got to talk, I said. Come about three o'clock."

## 8.

She changed the sheets of those who wet the bed. She gave out the medicines at eleven o'clock, and ten minutes later the Night Sister called in to help with the ones in the padded cells. All staff were forbidden to go in there alone. No matter what emergency they spied through the peep-hole, they had to call for help on the telephone. The patients were too demented, too violent and too strong.

Once the Night Sister had gone, she knew she was safe for at least three hours. She took off her nurse's hat and her starched cuffs and collar. She made some coffee, put her feet up, and started to read a small paper-back book. She would not go to sleep. She was a good nurse. She did everything by the book. She was fiercely rigid in her ways and knew that these sick people depended on her. No, she would not go to sleep.

Not if she could help it.

She thought about poor Marjorie's death. That was one hell of a shock. She was sad, angry and puzzled, all at the same time. Had she fallen asleep last night? Was that possible? She could swear not, but then ... would she know? Would she be able to tell. Whatever else, she mustn't fall into the same trap again. This time she would stroll through the ward every five to ten minutes. Perhaps every quarter of an hour. That was more sensible. They would all be asleep though. Except the one who thought she was a nun. Or the one who'd never slept in seventeen years.

It was warm in the ward. The hospital was so big that the maintenance men could not adjust the enormous boilers to small changes in temperature. By the time they had dropped it two degrees, the night might have turned cold again. It was safer to keep it warm. The patients were like babies. They were better when it was warm.

There was a noise in the corridor. Oh no, not the damned Night Sister coming back again. Trying to catch her out, eh?

She whisked on her hat, cuffs and collar, patted her apron and went to meet her with a flash-lamp. Show her a bit of pomp, the old bitch. Whistle her aboard like an admiral changing ships. Kiss her wrinkled old arse!

There was nobody there. She glanced into one of the peep-holes to see if there was any problem. How strange. A naked man. Perhaps they were full on the Men's side. No real harm done anyway, since he was securely locked up.

He lay in a patch of moonlight, one arm behind his head, and the other laid modestly over his groin. Or was it? She peered more closely. He was holding himself. The vile, sensuous sod was not just holding it, he was flaunting it. Wagging it at her now, he was, with a moonlit grin on his face.

She heard a noise again, turned her head slightly. A figure, a shadow, seemed to flirt in the darkness by her desk. She looked back into the padded cell. The man had gone. Poor Flora was curled up on the floor, moaning, sucking her thumb, her hair matted with shit.

9.

Anna knew at once that something was up. She could smell it on the fetid air. Something was afoot. Look, there was a mouse. Now how often were mice as cheeky as that? Hospital mice were less fearful, to be sure, but not usually given to standing on their hind legs and beckoning. It made her cross, that. She walked over intending to stamp it flat but she heard a noise again.

In the dim, shielded light by her desk, the young man was lying on the floor. His legs were open wide like a crocodile's slimy jaws. At the back of the throat, a nestful of furry, pink mice were dancing round a maypole.

She moved closer, slowly, like someone who walked in her sleep. She was close enough now to see it in all its Byzantine splendour. It jutted upward like an obelisk. It was Cleopatra's Needle come to life. He fondled it – as soft as a velvet lure – and he toyed with his testicles like golden guineas in a purse. The gland was a piece of pale blue porcelain and its opaline sheen seemed to steam. And the

176

smell! Oh the smell! It rolled down the slopes from the alpine goats and sent the perfumer reeling.

There were others in the semi-darkness. She could see their figures in the lamp's penumbra and all hard and upright like Pacific statues or the monoliths at Stonehenge. Men and women. God alone knew where they came from. Only He could explain how they had advanced thus far. They breathed in rhythm and gave out the same slight moan of a tribal chant. They sounded like people making love. They sounded like people being made love to.

The men were rampant and virile. Thin ones, broad ones, blonde ones and black ones.

The women were radiant and gasping, their mouths opening and closing like the lids of kettles on the boil.

A great heat came from their bodies as if a forest fire were licking the limbs of trees. She was aflame herself as she helped the young victim to tear off her clothes. He denuded her of every single garment – her slip, her pants, even her hair clips. She writhed on the waxed wooden floor like a scalded eel and her nails scratched the walnut like scrabbling claws. She felt him on her. She felt him in her. She felt herself melt like butter on toast and then she was being devoured.

He was killing her. He was tearing her open like a Roman priest and pawing through her entrails. Then came the eruption. Then came the great cataclysm. Mother Earth heaved as she brought forth the mountains, and the sky stormed through her tunnels as if she were a cosmic sponge.

At last she saw truth. At last she knew Jesus for what he was. The stone was rolled back. She saw the shroud bursting into rags and felt the deep, crimson pain as they hammered down the corona of nails. "Oh pardon me, God," she moaned, twisting jerkily to pull it deeper in. "It's my first time, you see." And that is where she died a little, impaled on her very own Christ. And after all these years, he had more than a passing likeness to that darling lad who once sold her chocolate at the village shop.

Oh look at him, Maggie. Did you ever see the like? Such a tiny bum, you're puzzled how his legs join on. And did you see how he dawdled outside, with his hands in his pockets, pulling his pants tighter across the front. Oh my God, Maggie, I'm feeling so giddy. I think I might faint and make a spectacle of myself. Say a prayer for me, Maggie. Don't tell our Mam. I'm going to swoon on that sack by his knees.


## 10.

She lay quietly in bed.

"She's not violent," said the Sister.

A doctor looked down at her, his blue eyes troubled like Cork harbour when a storm is due. "How are we feeling today?" he asked.

"Come a bit closer dear, and then I'll tell you."

He nodded calmly and made some notes. "She can have a go with Kevin, morning and evening. If she doesn't sleep, send in Peter to give her an injection." He looked at her like a vet estimating the weight of a dog. "She can go to the cinema once a week. That new boy, Jesus, can take her. The holes in His hands are healing nicely."

During the day, various people came to visit her. Her elder brother, the one that had played naughty games with her until their Mam had heard him grunting. A man came round with papers and books, and he smuggled in her dirty magazine. It was all soldiers, sailors and policemen. They had so much hair on their bodies. Wild men of Borneo.

"Do you want to see a priest?" they invited on Friday. She said "Yes, please," with relish. As she confessed, she tried to make him blush. She put her hand on his knee and fumbled for his rosary. But the foolish man just groaned his Latin as she did her penance all over him.

Then one day the Sister dropped by. "You never did come for breakfast," she chided with a lovely smile.

"What time is it?" asked Anna.

"September," she said, "and the menopause will be on us before we even know it."

Anna nodded. It all made good sense. "This is 'The Special', isn't it?" she spoke calmly.

The sister smiled and patted her hand. "That's right," she said. "'The Special' where we keep our own staff who've snapped under the strain. Every mental hospital has one, no matter what they say." She took the younger woman's hands in hers. "You're quite safe, my dear. You're among old colleagues." Her voice was low, like that of a German film star – Lillie Palmer perhaps, or maybe Marlene Dietrich. Her eyes were limpid. Her high cheekbones gave her the same exquisite shadows as the famous face on a photograph.

"You'll be able to meet them later. Sisters, nurses, even a doctor or two. But there's no rank now and no hierarchy. You're all treated alike – exactly the same – and they'll give you the best of everything."

"Men?" asked Anna in a whisper, as if the word might send the Gestapo clattering in.

"You're not separated here. They'll even bring young patients before they find them a permanent ward to settle in. You'll have first pick." She smiled and Anna noticed she had heavy lipstick on. "They never tell. Why should they? And even if they did, whoever would listen to them? They soon forget about it or else, my dear, they will dream about it forever."

She clutched her bosom as if a pain had gone through like an arrow. "You shall have all the men you want," she sighed. "My poor darling shall have her fill."

And what might that be, Anna wondered. What will be my fill?

The few family visits faded to none. "What's the point," her kin asked, "when she's lost her mind? It's not our Annie." Oh no, she thought, I haven't lost my mind and I was never your Annie. I'm just the one born between Jack and Maggie. "She doesn't even know us," they said, but she knew them inside out. She didn't speak. She had nothing to say. But had she spoken, it would have been their perfect ruin. And they'd stop her men. They'd punish her again by rationing out her men.

"Bye, bye love," they would say. "See you at Christmas." Bye-bye bloody blackbird, she thought. I'll never see you again. You'll never tell your children they had an Aunt called Anna who lost her mind in September and never found it again.

Time passed. They kept their promise about the men. They herded them in already wearing canvas shifts that were over-sewn and untearable. She ate them like oysters. She devoured them raw. The shy teenagers were best for they slid into her mouth, soft noses and all. If it was their first time, they wept. One or two said "Thanks," as they were led away. Her hair grew white from so much loving. She used so much of her magic on them, she shrivelled inside her skin. She watched it in the mirror, how her breasts sagged and her cheeks went hollow.

"You're getting old," said Sister when they wheeled her in.

"No," she answered sprily. "I'm getting more used to it."

They took her to the church to see the sister off in a carton coffin. "When it's my turn," she instructed, "don't forget to put enough stamps on."

She died at fifty-four, looking eighty. Nobody went to her funeral. By chance, she went in the same grave as the Sister who'd been her friend. They recorded it in a dossier, tied the dossier with string, and sent it down to the archives. This was the fancy name for miles of laundry baskets that stood end to end along the underground alleys that carried pipes and cables. A young porter lurked down there like a ferret. He used to curl up on a basket with a dirty book and give himself a little thrill.

Sometimes he couldn't manage it. At other times, a hot wind blew through the tunnel and stirred a hint of steam. It was like a soft morning in Ireland. "Honest to God," he told his mate. "It's like a girl wrapped her hands round my tool, and such words she whispers. I get twice as big, and hard as rock. Oh, God," he sighed, "it's like being shagged by an angel."

"Hush now," said his mate in dread.

The pipes gave an ecstatic groan, not at all like an angel.

---

```
A B R A C A D A B R A
A B R A C A D A B R
A B R A C A D A B
A B R A C A D A
A B R A C A D
A B R A C A
A B R A C
A B R A
A B R
A B
A
```

180

The God Abraxas appears on magical gems and rings to avert evil. He was mentioned by the Gnostic, Basilides, who taught at Alexandria in the 2nd century A.D. In 'Journal of the Plague Year', 1722, Daniel Defoe says that common people thought the disease must be caused by an evil spirit. To protect themselves from it, they wore a talisman: the word 'abracdabra' in a triangle. The true basis of the charm is the idea of 'gradual diminution' or 'whittling away to nothing'.

# The Wife's Mother

*Da-shi-zhi: a great and perfect being in Chinese Buddhism. With the power of love, she broke the laws of Karma and so liberated living things from the endless cycle of rebirth.*

## 1.

There were just the two women, one young, one older, and both were in pain.

It wasn't physical pain. Nor was it the same pain. It was something felt deep inside. With one, it was seated in the heart; with the other, it was rather in the stomach.

They weren't speaking much. What few words they did exchange were in a low voice, as if they were muddled or ashamed. They didn't touch each other, either. They didn't cuddle. But somehow or other you could tell they were close. They looked like refugees, hating this place and only coming out of urgent necessity. They were displaced persons who had nowhere else to go. There was something about the way they sat – not deep back, relaxed, like waiting for a bus ... but forward, on the edge of the seat, as if getting ready to run.

I said that they didn't speak much. That's quite true, but even so, they did say things.

"What time is it now?"

"There's always a smell, have you noticed?"

"I'd give my eye-teeth for a cup of tea."

"How much longer, do you suppose?"

Inane words. The quiet cluck of a tiny flock of hens keeping in contact. Nothing of any import. Most of the time they didn't even reply. One said something just for the sake

182

of saying something. They might have said more appropriate things, but these were precisely the things which were not being said.

They thought about them, to be sure. You could see that. During the long intervals of sniffing silence, you could feel the hum of their minds working. The younger woman's head was whirring like a modern clock with a new battery. The old woman's was just ticking slowly, steadily, like an antique mechanism in the turret of a historical building.

What one of them said had no bearing on what the other said. It was like a play from the sixties. Harold Pinter maybe, or even Samuel Beckett. There's no way you could have called it 'having a conversation' or 'a little chat'. There was no exchange of ideas. They made no real contact for the simple reason that nothing – nothing – went across the line that kept them apart. Mother and daughter with barbed wire between them and a Frontier Post where every little thing was checked.

"He asked me to wank him." The younger woman sounded numb, as if she were standing in the freezing cold, as on the days she took a spray of flowers for her dad's grave in the cemetery.

The older woman blinked several times, as though a mote of dust had got into her eye. She lifted her hand towards her chin, stopped, and let if fall again. "We're the only one's here, I think." Her voice was flat. Terribly flat. Weary, stale, flat and a wee bit tragic as if she were sorry for herself.

The daughter was off on a track of her own. "He actually asked me to toss him off."

Her mother sucked at her top lip. "Fancy!" she said, letting the mask slip. Then she stared in another direction hard, very hard, screwing up her eyes as if she were shooting table tennis balls off a jet of water at a fair.

"I think I'll just have to go and wash my hands," she muttered, easing herself to her feet. "Unless you want to come with me?"

She didn't wait for a reply. It was just one of those silly things one says which don't really mean anything. There were no signs so she set off down the corridor to the right. She hoped it would be easier than the maze at Hampton Court Palace.

The daughter didn't even notice that she'd gone. She had said she was coming with her. So she brought her along, in the same way one carries a house-key or a needle and thread. In case. That's it: just in case. After all, you never knew did you?

The older lady didn't find the female toilets, but she found a fire bucket just inside an Emergency Exit. "This is an emergency," she muttered, and was surprised when an orderly went past with some sheets, and never even noticed.

She didn't want to go straight back. It wasn't easy for them these days. She didn't understand which of them was to blame or, if both of them, to what extent. There was a rift between them. Oh yes, you could certainly say that! There was a rift and it never got mentioned by either.

She felt sorry for her now. Poor cow! That's why she was coming out with things that she shouldn't really talk about. It was all right for men to mention them, among themselves, because men – well – they were like that, weren't they? She knew what the words meant, or at least she had a good idea. She'd been married, don't forget. And she'd had a son called 'Our Robert'. So she wasn't as shocked as she made out to be. A woman of her age was supposed to be shocked. It was expected of her. Which is why she read certain newspapers, so she could be shocked some more.

Her mother had told her what her great-grandmother had said. It was a treasured piece of family wisdom. 'Things' got into men. It was best to let them out. This made it sound like tape-worms, or shrapnel, but "No", said her mother, "it's urges." Her ear, although very wide, had never quite caught the fine distinction between "It's urges" and "It surges". Therefore she had lived her life imagining that men got knocked over from time to time by great waves that started somewhere in their trousers.

It had remained a mystery – even with a husband and a son with a filthy mind. She gave credit where credit was due. She never spoke ill of the dead. But the life that she had lived had never been marked by wonders. She had never felt the earth quake, nor seen a mountain spew lava, nor yet hidden herself from a typhoon. To be perfectly honest – which one never is while there are other people around – she had never

184

actually seen a grown man without clothes on. It had all happened in the dark, if you know what I mean, with billowing sheets and night-shirts, like two ships from Nelson's fleet.

In the midst of all that, something had happened, but she couldn't for the life of her tell anyone what it was. He had lain on her, and bounced on her. She'd tried to explore him somewhat timidly and found only a snail and some slime. What with 'the birds and the bees', she had somehow got the idea that it was all to do with gardens. When the news announcers said that a girl had been raped, she always wondered who would want to rake her and why? She was shocked, though of course she did her best to conceal the fact.

"There's none so blind as them that won't look," she had chastised herself many times. But even when she found those sticky bits of cut-off shirt-lap under Robert's pillow, she'd just replaced them with slug poison.

When he'd first come out in acne, she'd sprayed him while he was asleep.

Anyway, if she didn't know everything about sex, she recognised which words referred to it, and she didn't like to hear those words coming out of the mouth of her daughter. When Robert announced he was "fucking off up town", she waited all night to fathom the mystery when he finally arrived home. She still felt it was something to do with drinking until you were sick!

All right! So she was behind the times! But it irked her to hear these things talked about as casually as cleaning your teeth or clipping your toe-nails. It seemed careless. No, much more than that – it seemed to be improper. It was a slap in your face when it came from your own daughter. Her own baby. Her own little girl. Hard to remember that she wasn't a girl any more. She hadn't been for a very long time. Not very practical, of course, but she could scarcely accept that she was now someone else's wife.

With all that that entailed! She nodded heavily.

Then quick as a flash, she just cleared it out of her mind. One flick from a feather duster and the piano looked like new again.

"I wouldn't say no to a cup of tea!" she muttered.

It was the first thing she said when she found her daughter again. "Aren't you thirsty, love?"

"I dare say they've got one of those slot machines," answered the girl. "It always tastes stewed to me."

"It's the same in the canteen," picked up the mother readily. "They seem to have this idea that if you pop twice as many tea-bags in then there's no need to wait. You know what I mean? It comes out strong enough to stand your spoon up in it, but it tastes like ... you know what!"

She had meant to say "cat-piss", or "witch-piss", which weren't really bad words. But it didn't seem right. Not here. But the girl hadn't heard anyway. So she might just as well have said it anyway. There were far more bitter things she wanted to mention. She could feel them trembling on the tip of her tongue. It was neither the time nor the place.

"Would you like half a chocolate biscuit?" she asked. That's another of those things that women keep in their handbags.

Time passed, but it was a long time passing. She thought of that song she used to like: "Where have all the flowers gone?" And she started to weep silently. God alone knew how she'd got herself into this mess. When you're still young yourself, you don't think, you don't imagine how one word leads to another. You just say things. You come right out with it. Kids are kids and you buy the bread. Then, little by little, age rises up the sides of the bath until you realise you're drowning in it. They just look at you. They have their own lives to live. And you can see it in their eyes – they're not much bothered about you.

Where did it go then? All that love? "When I grow up I'm going to marry you, mam." That's what Robert had said. How silly! How lovely! How could he forget? Now going by his slut wife, her with the foulest mouth, he was just a fucking machine. Sex was all he thought of, she accused, apart from watching telly, food, drink, and playing darts with his mates! Oh, how they change, don't they? And, oh, how badly we misjudge them.

A nurse came out of the Intensive Care Block. They both stared at her, their buttocks almost lifted from the seat. She smiled at them and nodded. She knew what they were waiting for but she wasn't the one who bore the news. She had a coffee break and she was going for a quick snack in the Houseman's bedroom.

They relaxed again. Well, to be precise, they retreated from the sudden 'red alert' to a 'steady orange' condition. They called back the missiles and defused the warheads. They both went "phew!" together.

"Last time I went in," murmured the daughter, "he asked me to toss him off." She shook her head as if this were some offensive memory from back in childhood. Robert had done that – made her play with him. Lots of her friends at school said that their brothers did the same, and worse. But her own husband? Martin? The man she'd loved and married?

The nurse had heard. She told the doctor. The nurse and doctor both understood. "Don't feel it's dirty," they tried to assure her. "What with all these tubes and electrodes and gadgets ... he can't make love to you. But he's trying to tell you he wants to."

"But, but.." she'd stammered. "Like that?"

"That's all he can offer."

She'd been outraged. "Offer? You call that an offer: asking me to play with his thing? That's not an offer. That's bloody childish. That's plain barmy. Little boys do that, not grown men. I didn't marry him to play mucky games!"

They'd looked at each other sadly. "You do realise that your husband may die. We're doing all we can to save his life but all the same ... he may die."

The nurse, who was married herself, patted her on the hand. "The thing is – he knows it."

She looked horrified. "You told him?"

The doctor shook his head. "He's not stupid even though his skull's fractured."

They took him for an operation then. It was the first of many that would have to follow, given that he hung on. They'd told her to think about it. She had thought about it. For almost five hours now she'd thought of nothing else. And still she could not reconcile herself. It was such a strange thing to propose. She'd never done it. He'd never asked her to do it. It was something she couldn't bear to think about ... men doing that. It made her feel lousy. It made her want to scratch. She shivered and tried to stare out of the window but she saw no further than her own weird nightmare reflected in the glass.

## 4.

The mother felt like a cheap dictionary with several pages missing. She understood nothing. She didn't even know why she'd come here. Her girl hadn't asked her to.

Not easy that. Not easy at all. So many years of being right, the source of all truth, and now doubted – except for things like chicken pox or how to make Lancashire Hot-pot. Not even a dictionary, you see – just an old crossword puzzle.

She sat there, feeling cold, feeling old, and scarcely hearing her daughter's voice. All the while she was carping at her in her mind. That silly hair-style. Those ridiculous clothes. What did she think she was? Had she ever looked in a mirror? Thinking it, but not saying it. Bitterly aware that her influence had dwindled. As it had from the very first day her little girl had met ... him!

Like most mothers, she'd usually been able to edge her daughter away from boys that seemed unlikely. Never so daft as to condemn them outright because that would only cause a rebellion. No, something more subtle and corrosive, like a telling remark here, and a wary question there. "He's got lovely shirts. I wonder if his mother chooses them?" Or a few days later – "Are you his only girl or ...?"

And her son too. Their Robert. The first thing he'd brought home she knew exactly what to do. "Can she cook as well?" "Her picture's been in the newspapers." Or best of all: "Someone saw your girl in the pub. Buying her vodka, he was!"

Mothers know how to damp down a lad's ardour. When you come across those magazines, hidden under the corner of the carpet – you start feeding him nettle soup, or give him a spoonful of brimstone and treacle. It's that bit harder with girls though. It goes a lot deeper with them. She'd been a girl herself once, so she ought to know. You can say what you like but it doesn't seem to make much difference in the end. They go and get stuck with something that should be locked up or shot.

You're not quite sure how or when it happened but suddenly it's all out of your hands. She comes home and tells you she's going to be married. You feel so hurt. You had the right to be consulted. It was your concern too. But evidently not. She mentions things casually as if you should have known – almost as if she believed she had told you. So convincing sometimes you wonder if perhaps she did, and that you'd forgotten. Now you know why she went to so many dances. You were dubious about how often she stayed at a friend's house, miles away and no telephone. Yours no longer. Given to someone else.

Now it's done. Whether you like him or not. Approve or not. And you don't like him. He's not like our kind of people. And you don't approve. But it's too late to do anything. You no longer have any hold over her. Other than sentiment. The fact that you are her mother. And once, when the strength of that was tested, she told you that he and her future baby would have to come first.

How do you explain it to the family? Grandma and grandad, aunts and uncles and cousins? Not to mention neighbours who ask their questions in a roundabout way but all the time seem to know more than you. "Useful to have a son-in-law in that line of work, I dare say?" But you had no idea what he did. You had only just found out he existed. You hadn't even got used to his name. "And how's your Martin getting on?" or "Does your Martin like his new job?" He wasn't their Martin. She'd never been able to warm to him. To think of him as one of the family. And the main reason for that was he wasn't interested. In his life there was no room for his wife's mother. That's what she was. The wife's mother. That's how he spoke of her. That's all the label she deserved in his eyes.

She grieved. Oh how she grieved. The hurt. The pain. Even, God forgive us, a screaming out for vengeance! The wife's mother indeed! To be brushed aside as nothing more than that. Nineteen years of loving and working just discounted. If I died, she thought, I'd be lucky if he found time to come to my funeral. And if he did, the wreath he'd bring would be small and cheap, and it would be labelled "To the wife's mother".

# 5.

She shivered with remembered anger. Caught her breath in a silent gasp. The fear had come back. The fear she'd felt when she first heard the news. She'd not exactly prayed for him to have an accident but it had been in her mind. Her very first thought had been – thank god, thank god, he deserves it! Sorry, god. Sorry. But I can't help feeling glad. My heart leaped when she told me. There was no one else to turn to she said. I've got her back, I thought. She's mine again. My little girl. We can start all over again and make it nice this time. But oh dear god – she hadn't really wished that on him, had she? Sorry. So sorry.

"Sorry to hear the terrible news about your Martin." And she had to nod. Put on a pretended grief that would conceal her shameful inward rejoicing. Not now though. Not any more. She'd been to see him. Her duty. As the wife's mother. And there had been nothing, not one word, that she could say. It was his eyes. He knew. "Not dead," they seemed to flash. "Not gone. Not rid of me."

Even now, she couldn't think of anything to say to her own daughter. Not that she seemed to notice. The girl only talked a little herself. The shock, the doctors said. She didn't want to listen. She had enough on her plate. When she did come out with something, like just now, it didn't always make sense. Almost as though she was rambling. So personal. God knows what else was going through her head. But even though the mother was troubled, she didn't dare to force a change of subject. So she just gave the little hand one more squeeze for comfort, and patted the fingers to some secret rhythm.

The daughter didn't notice her mother's distress. She was staring fixedly at the random pattern on the floor tiles. "He wants me to do that. He said so." Her breath shuddered and she gave a quick gasp. "Your hand," he kept telling me. "Use your hand." She choked. A little splutter. "Oh god, Mam! Oh Jesus!"

The other woman rubbed the hand harder, quite heedless of the chance mimicry. But she kept her head turned well away to conceal the fact that her face was wet. She'd be hard put to say who she was weeping for. Herself, the girl or him? Not that she'd ever been one to display her emotions. She

190

could usually cover things by giving the floor a good clean. Or if things weren't as bad as all that, then making a cup of tea. Not possible here. Neither course of action was available. The floor was spotless already. There was a drink dispenser they'd vowed never to touch again. So she gave her nose a good blow instead. Under the fuss she managed to dab her eyes.

They sat in silence. There were sounds of a sort. But they were hushed. Stifled. Rather like a cathedral or an art gallery. An occasional squeaking of a wheel. The ghostly rustling of starched aprons. Bottles of course. And tools being dropped into steel dishes, shaped like kidneys. The sort of noises in fact that, once you've been there, you always associate with a hospital.

Not to mention that oh so typical smell. Enough to make anyone afraid. What was it exactly? Ether? The older woman blinked in the gloom. No one likes coming to these places. Not even to visit. If there's the slightest chance of getting well, the patients can be relied upon to try. They want to get out of it. Go home. These places – full of death, dettol and discretion – but not a lot of dignity. Still, she thought, it comes to all of us.

"They wear crepe-soles, you know."

"What?" the younger woman blinked.

"When I had that job in the supermarket one of the girls had been half-way to being a nurse once. In training school they were all told about crepe soles."

"What are you on about, mam?"

"It's not just to be quiet. It's good for the arches and jolting the spine. The boss of the market said it was good too. On your feet all day, you see." She nodded with emphasis. "And it did work. Leastways, I got no back trouble."

"I'll have to get Martin some."

The older woman turned her head in dismay. Their eyes met bleakly. Their faces were like two wooden masks.

"Don't my darling."

The girl started sobbing.

"Don't love."

They clutched one another, their shoulders shaking, trying not to make a noise.

A nursing sister went by. She knew who they were. She knew better than to say anything.

# 6.

It was about five o'clock in the morning when they sent for them.

"You'd better come now," the young Houseman said. "I think he's fading away peacefully."

The mother stayed by the door while her daughter advanced on the snow-white bed like a nun nearing the Pope.

His eyes flicked to the wall-clock and noted the time. "So then," he murmured softly, "this is it." He gazed at her mutely.

"No," she said very softly. "It isn't right."

He was silent a moment. How do you tell a woman that it isn't just lust – that it isn't a question of "one more for the road"? It's important. That's all. It's a matter of life and death.

His eyes focussed on the figure by the door. "So your old lady's here too?" He grinned and held out his hand to her. "Come to gloat, my old love?"

When she bowed her head, he wrung her hand warmly. "It's nowt, ma. It was never owt. A game, that's all. A bit of argy-bargy for the sake of something to say. I didn't know how else to play it, you see?"

The older woman felt ashamed of all her past malice as she realised that she had already been forgiven. He was setting the record straight. He was getting ready.

It was obvious that he had – what did her husband used to call it? – a hard on. There was only a sheet covering him. This time she was not at all shocked. He was a man. Just a man. What else is there for it but to go out like a man should? She lifted her head and turned emphatically to her daughter.

"He has a right to have a child!" That was all she said.

"What?" gasped his wife.

"He's your man. You're his woman. The two of you are married and you have no right to refuse." She held her daughter close and squeezed her urgently. "We're going to be so lonely, you and me, love. Think. Think! Look at his face."

The girl moved her head around dumbly, looking at all the tubes, the mess of dangling bottles, the electric wires and machines.

192

"Bugger that!" snapped the mother. "I'll go outside and leave you alone. Do your best, sweetheart. He'll not be able to help much, but he doesn't give a damn if it hurts him."

Her son-in-law was gawping at her like an idiot ... and crying too. "I'm counting on you, Our Martin," she said, and closed the door behind her as she went to sit outside.

The morning shift was coming on duty. The night staff brought the day staff up to date, and then the nurses started doing the rounds with the washing trolley. One of them came towards her, only nineteen or so, and smiling as she had been taught.

"Leave it off, love," said the mother. "He's dying. My daughter's with him."

The smile gave way to a look of concern. Nurses' faces can change as slick as lantern slides. She just patted the woman's hand and she reached out to open the door.

"I'd give five pounds for a cup of tea," sighed the old lady.

The young girl hesitated, weighing up the rights and wrongs, and the chances of sister catching her, and what sister might say. "Back in a jiffy," she whispered and skipped off.

As she sat there, sipping her cup of tea as if it were pure bliss, she heard their noises from inside. She was whimpering. He was grunting. Now and then a bottle fell, or one of the machines started to beep before someone turned it off.

There was a bright golden light shining under the door. It stretched across the fitted carpet like an angelic finger.

"What on earth ...?" mused a passing porter.

"Part of his treatment," shushed the mother.

Then there were cries, or rather the tiny screams, of a dying rapture and things floating round the room.

7.

What can I tell you? The staff found him in a hell of a mess. He'd had a seizure of some sort, and all the gadgets were unplugged or on the floor. Incredibly though, he was a little better and, as the hours went by, the progress went on. There was no miracle, you realise – or nothing that could ever be called such. There was no sudden cure at all ... he just got steadily better. No-one could explain it so no-one did explain it.

"Oh it happens that way sometimes," they said with nods of their heads. "It's what we call a case of spontaneous remission."

The family doctor made no comment at all on the timing of her pregnancy and delivered a beautiful baby girl.

"We'll call her Elizabeth," said Martin. "After your Mam."

That, and the fact that they all lived happily ever after is as much as I'm allowed to tell you.

You will just have to fill in the rest for yourselves.

# Apocalypse

*"Enuma Elish": actually this means "When the heavens above", and they are the opening words of a Creation Story. They describe how Marduk became the supreme God of Babylon.*

### 1.

"She's so young," said the new attendant.

"She's an eighteen year old blasphemy," replied the Training Officer. It was a shock to hear him use such a word.

The girl sat with open legs in the middle of the padded floor as she stabbed herself with a scrubbing-brush for floors and howled with glee.

"It must be agony," said the trainee. She was only young herself and she winced each time the brush went in.

The Officer shrugged. "It's the agony that gives her the thrill."

"Can't you stop her?"

He looked at her dryly. "Care to suggest *how*?"

"Take it off her."

The officer made a tut-tut noise and shook his head patiently and sadly. "She'd kill you."

The new attendant inspected her more carefully. "But she's only a slip of a thing."

"To be sure. But she's mad. You're not."

The younger one blinked, still unhappy. "Couldn't we rush her? Half a dozen of us."

There was a moment's silence. When the Officer spoke, his voice was flat, matter of fact, and toneless. "Have you see her nails?"

"They're broken."

"They're filthy. First, there's shit under them. She eats it, you know. Second, when she's not ramming that scrubbing-brush up her, she plays with the sores inside her cunt. You can see the state of it, can't you? She doesn't bleed much any more. That's pus."

The new attendant choked and hid her face against wall. The Officer felt sorry. But it was no use trying to let them down gently. You'd got to banish the image of Florence Nightingale as quickly as possible. So the first visit was here. The second was to the Autopsy Room.

He stared at the demented woman inside the room with the padded walls. He knew she was aware of him. He knew she was putting on a display. And instead of being attracted – who could be attracted by that? – he was revolted. But that was enough for her. Any emotion would do the trick. He'd noticed that. He'd noticed each time he'd come here. If you showed any revulsion, she soaked it up and started to writhe in orgasm.

"That brush," he murmured, more for the sake of something to say. "It was always used for scrubbing the ward floor. Can you imagine? God knows how many different kinds of infection she's given herself." He pursed his lips and sniffed. "Even to this very day, we don't know how she got hold of it. We can only assume ... we can only guess ... that someone gave it to her."

The new girl turned round and stared at him.

"But – that's like helping her to commit suicide!"

He shook his head. "No. It's not suicide unless it's done wilfully. She has no mind. At least, that's what the padre tells me. According to him, this is closer to murder." He watched her face undergo many changes as all this penetrated her brain. It was sad to see all her illusions die.

"After what I've now told you..." he asked, "would you still take your chance and go in?"

He was content when she shrank away from him, away from the door too, and shivered. He just took her arm and they walked together toward one of the locked doors that led, eventually, to the world outside.

"What we wonder ...," he began. Her eyes turned toward him. "We have no way of checking, of course. But there's a question that we'd like to answer."

197

They both stopped. Dark shapes reflected in the glass-like sheen of the polished lino.

"She knows we're there, you see. However silently we creep up on her, she grins straight at us."

"So?" said the girl?

"Well – does she go on doing it – that – when nobody's there?" He paused and stared at her with sad, aging eyes. "If not, then what the hell does she do?"

## 2.

They went to the men's wing, one day later. She needed a little bit of getting ready. He had to find out how much she knew, and how much she didn't know.

"It's a boy this time. Name of Andrew." Again he tried to sound matter of fact. "He seeks sexual relief something like twenty times a day."

She looked horrified.

"Except when it rains," he continued. "When it rains, he clings to the bars of one of the windows and stares outside without moving."

The girl swallowed and licked her lips. "Is that possible? What I mean to say is: is the body capable? Can a man do that without ... er ... ?"

"Without collapsing or blowing a fuse?" he finished her statement for her. "That's a very outdated point of view," he told her gently. "In the old days when they knew even less than us about insanity, they noticed that decency was the first thing to be eclipsed. So they just inferred that the sexual activity was the cause. Nowadays, we try to view it as a result."

"But surely – it's so abnormal ...?"

"And so it would be, as far as most people are concerned. We could satisfy our hungers more simply, more delicately. But these are not ordinary minds. Something has happened to them. The only thing we can honestly say about them is – they seem to be disordered – or, not the same as ours. "

They approached a bed with cot-sides. It was evident that Andrew was blind. The Training Officer showed her the chart, attached to the foot of the bed. All that it said was "Epilepsy". The ink was faded.

"That's not a mental illness," she remarked.

"His only living relation was a grandmother, crippled with arthritis. This is where the council sent him."

The boy threw back his sheets to show his erection. "Touch me," he shouted to nobody in particular. He thrust it through the sides of his cot. "Touch me," he begged again.

"Fuck off!" screamed the schizo in the next bed. "He's doing it again!" he wailed. "Sister, sister, I'm going to hit it with a hammer!"

"Touch me," begged the boy.

Nobody else took any notice. One old man shuffled past and raised an imaginary gun. "Pop," he said, giggling quietly. "One more clay pipe and the gold watch is mine."

Andrew began to rub himself furiously.

"He's blind," she murmured.

"Yes."

"But you said that when it rains – he stares out of the window?"

The Training Officer gave a slight shrug. "It's the best way of describing it. I don't know if he likes the sound or whether it reminds him of something. All I can say is: he seems to be fascinated by it."

"Has he always been mad?" asked the girl.

"No," said the officer. "Only for the last eight years."

"Eight years? My God, how long has he been here then?"

He stared at her sadly. "Fourteen years. Since he was seven, in fact. Before that he was on the children's ward."

She stared at him in horror. "Do you mean that – being here? Are you telling me that we – made him mad?"

"Something did!" and he bit his lip. To say more would have been unethical. It would be held against him. It might even lead to his removal.

Almost as soon as the thought shot through his head, he realised what a weird thought it was to have there in the first place. But there had been others like it. Recently they had been getting more frequent. The vague feeling that somewhere behind the scenes, a hostile power was preparing to bring him down. He had begun being careful as regards his colleagues, some of whom had been his friends for more than thirty years.

By rights, he supposed, he ought to have reported to the doctor on duty. Maybe he was doing too much, needed a

199

rest – or maybe he was having a close encounter with paranoia? He thought not. Oh they'd been forever rebuked not to concoct their own diagnoses – they were nurses, and in charge, but they were not doctors! But after such long service – call him arrogant if you want – he actually knew more than most of the medical staff. Sometimes, they actually wrote down what he suggested to them. His diagnosis, his treatment, and his success.

He shook himself and looked at his young trainee again. She was obviously deeply concerned for their young Andrew.

"Do you realise," he asked softly, "that he doesn't know what a girl is?"

She held her hand to her mouth.

"He's never seen one, never heard them mentioned. No one has told him anything. All the poor sod knows is that doing that is the closest he gets to happiness."

She swallowed and took a deep breath. "Does no-one ever ... You know?"

"Lend him a hand?" He smiled ever so slightly. "Why do you ask?"

"Because he was asking for it. 'Touch me,' he said. 'Please touch me.'" She licked her lips, slightly red in the face and stammering a little. "Well, I mean, how could he possibly know about that ... unless someone ... had ... touched him?"

His head was tilted back. He looked down at her like a sergeant in the Guards, wearing a peak-cap. "Clever girl", he muttered, so softly that she almost didn't hear.

3.

It was not too strange, having only the one trainee. They'd been short of staff for donkey's years, as fewer folk applied. The causes were obvious – poor pay, lengthy training, and tough work. It's a wonder they ever got anybody but, to their constant surprise, they did. They had lowered their standards, of course. They were willing to take anybody, if not as a nurse then as a ward orderly or an attendant. There were some parts of the clinic where physical strength was the prime consideration.

As long as there was someone to teach, he felt that little bit more secure. At times, he was tempted to give someone a bad mark and fail them – just to make them repeat the course again. But no. He hadn't done it. He had never quite sunk that low. But he had been tempted.

In better days, things would have been very much different. If things had gone as the investors had planned, this girl would have gone to lunch with fellow students on the same course. The canteen would have been filled. But only a third of the servery was used. There were empty tables everywhere. If someone dropped a fork the noise echoed for minutes afterward.

In his own day, the boys and girls had flirted at coffee breaks. Everyone had a special person in his heart and they tried to get together on days off. There'd been little caresses when they passed one another, and the occasional noise of kerfuffle in a linen cupboard. It couldn't be very pleasant for her, having no-one to talk to but him.

In one way, he would like to be rid of her too – except that he wasn't too keen on mixing with his peers just now. There was that suspicion, remember, that someone among them was planning his downfall. That being so, he found it helpful to be with her. It attracted no comment. They just assumed he was being kind.

He could rule her life, if he wanted. He realised that. He could make her miserable, her could make her crack, or he could have her eating out of his hand. Yes, and he could corrupt her too, if that should be his fancy.

He shuddered and wondered again about his health.

But how do I know that they are right and, therefore, that I am wrong? He wondered about that very seriously. The doctors decided who was sick, but it was the law which decided who was insane. And the law was part of the system of state rule. The communists used to have quite a different view of mental health – as do the Chinese today. How very strange that was. A people who prided themselves on being one of the oldest and finest cultures in the world, had also invented 'The Death of a Thousand Cuts'. Were they all that different from the Juju men of Africa?

Ah, belief, he thought! What is true for one man is nonsense for another. The food we possess, and which the lands of famine need, is actually the cause of a million deaths. He'd seen films of Nazi deeds in the land of Beethoven, Schiller and Goethe. How like the one unto the other. Could it be the same wickedness abroad? Was the same evil once more marching through Europe?

That frightened him. That made him sick in the stomach. The Huns had come from Asia in the fourth century and ravaged Europe. How long before we saw the rebirth of the Teutonic dream of glory? And were we any better? Was anyone in Europe or America any nobler? He thought of the four star restaurants, at four star prices, where savages dine and die a little. An American senator had suggested that they distribute free credit cards throughout the blighted lands of Africa! It was one of the ideas which helped him get elected!

"Come with me," he ordered her abruptly. She didn't raise any objection. She left her jam pudding and dabbed at her lips. The legs of her chair screeched on the tiles.

He led her to a lift. It too was lockable.

4.

On the top floor, he led her toward the private suite where they housed their most important client.

"Good morning," said the old man with hair and beard so white he might have been a Father Christmas. "I am that I am."

The Training Officer hissed at her out of the corner of his mouth. "This is God."

The girl was quick and talented. She bowed and looked as humble as possible. She was not at all upset that God was positioned, without any visible means of support, midway between floor and ceiling. Perhaps he did yoga? Maybe He was partial to films written by Clive Barker? There He was anyway. One couldn't pretend not to have noticed. This was no flimsy or feeble phenomenon that one could easily ignore.

"I am about to speak," announced God. "You may lie flat, if you wish, or... " he searched his long memory, "you may rend your robe, if it puts you more at ease."

"Thank you, Almighty Father, but I'm quite happy just as I am."

"A teensy weensy sprinkle of sackcloth and ashes?" He suggested. "Very simple to arrange."

"It is already greater honour than I deserve, simply to be in your effulgent presence."

God beamed on her. "Charming," He smiled, and gave her a gracious pat on her head.

After that, He seemed to fall into a state of bliss and smiled at everything around Him. An archangel stepped out from behind God's back and whispered urgently into His ear.

"Thank you, Michael!" He snapped with some acerbity. "We are not yet senile!"

The archangel, a soul of tact, silently withdrew.

"It's bad enough handling one, you know. But when the four of them get together ... oy, oy oy!"

"I thought he was your official messenger?" said the young girl. "A sort of divine dog's-body?"

The Training Officer was aghast. "Do not speak unless you are spoken to," he hissed.

"Thank you, thank you," God waved his hand wearily. "If she offends me once more, I shall turn her into a pillar of salt or ... a burning bush." He paused pensively. "I've a feeling I've already done that? I mustn't repeat myself or else I shall become boring."

God pulled himself together and eased his robes. "Michael has his uses, of course. When he forgets himself, or oversteps the limit, I pull out his remex. It takes him a month or two to grow a new one."

"What is a remex?" asked the girl, displaying a morbid streak.

"The primary quill in his wings." God chuckled quietly for He had no evil in Him. "It makes him fly in ever decreasing circles, don't you know. Over the years I've gathered quite a heap. Would you like one for writing a sacred book?"

"I'm not writing a Sacred Book."

"Oh! That's strange. Every one else is." He reached behind. "Would you care for a Swedish bed-quilt? We make them by hand and the Tog value is so high, they can't even measure it."

The girl was shaking her head and on the point of saying "No, thank-you," when she realised that God had already moved on. He was still talking about Michael, of course.

"He's never been the same since he heard the legend about his driving the devil out of heaven. Oh I wish I knew how that one started! What's more, if ever I found out who slipped him the news ...!" He spat in disgust, and the floor exploded like an incipient Etna.

"Then," He went on, "there was that business with the Nun who dreamed she had been pierced by his golden lance! I sent out a general alert that time. I had squads of seraphs haul him in front of me. 'Where have you been?' I demanded, in my best Mount Sinai voice. 'Oh,' he replied serenely, 'just poking about'."

The Training Officer held back a titter.

"What's so funny?" demanded God.

"I've got hay-fever," replied the man.

"Perhaps," offered the girl, "you're allergic to feathers."

"Ah," thundered God pointedly. "I plucked both his remiges that time! He was grounded for fifty years."

Plainly, the Almighty was still not too happy with His pesky angel. "Humph!" He coughed with a slight pout. "Now he has his own fan-club, don't you know? I warned him what Freud would say."

"I was always given to understand," said the girl with due deference, "that Angels were sex-less."

"Devils aren't," snapped the Ancient of Days. "And they are supposed to be fallen angels! Did you suppose that they grew the extra bits magically ... on the way down? And another thing ..." he rambled a bit when he was angry. "You must also know of the Book of Enoch. It mentions how the sons of God lusted after the daughters of the earth. It says they gave birth to giants." He smiled smugly. "Our mutual friend, Michael, is supposed to have swept them into hell and turned them into demons and devils. I don't quite see how you can suppose that angels are therefore sex-less."

## 5.

"Speaking of which," the girl butted in.

"Speaking of what?" asked God with heavy suspicion. He had to be extremely careful. What with Jews praying that the Arabs might die, Arabs praying that the Jews might disappear, and everyone else wishing the USA might just evaporate ...

"What is this USA?" He had once asked of Michael. The archangel, feathers still ruffled from the loss of his remiges, had handed the Almighty a dollar. "What's this?" asked God, holding it with a pair of sugar-tongs, "a membership card for the O.T.O.?" He flushed it down the celestial sewers and straight into the face of the Emperor Vespasian.

He looked again at the girl's sparkling eyes. "Don't tell me that you too are smitten by Michael?"

The girl shrugged and raised her eyebrows. "He's rather cute," she admitted.

"Oh my God," groaned God. "Please be practical. Have you thought what it's like to have babies that are covered in fluff?" He shook His head from side to side in sheer vexation.

"So it is wrong to have sexual thoughts?"

"Did I say that?" God held his hands out to an unseen audience. "When did I say that? What kind of God do you think I am, huh? I'm not just Almighty – I also know everything. Am I some sort of nit-wit then who makes sex just for it not to be used?" He slapped his own forehead in futility. "Is this the Logic I hear so much about?"

"You made sex," she recited from her catechism days, "in order that the human race would multiply."

"How very kind of you to tell me! Do you think that people hated babies so much that I had to offer them a bribe to get pregnant? My dear child – my very dear child – when you think of Michael ... preening away at his feathers ... is it babies you have in mind? I promise you my lass, no payola was needed."

"Then what is the pleasure for?"

God blinked at her in some surprise. "You're a persistent little person, aren't you? But, good for you. You have put your finger on it. What is the pleasure for? What was my reason for making it so nice?" He inclined His holy head and added *sotto voce*, "It was all over and done with before clergymen were invented, by the way. If they don't like it: tough luck, is what I say."

He arranged his clothes and adopted what might be called 'a proper teaching posture'. God is a stickler for rules, and when he wants you to understand something, he doesn't just say it, he causes it to become so. The Mafia borrowed it from Him.

"There is matter and there is anti-matter," He said. "There is night and there is day." So far, so good. The young girl had been able to take it in.

"There is life and there is death," He went on. "There is Good and there is Evil. There is order and there is chaos. And in all cases, the one is the necessary outcome of the other." He smiled at her as she lost the thread.

"In the Great Games, during a race, coming in First is not the direct cause of someone else coming in Second. The one thing is not the reason why the other thing is so. Try to understand me, little one. Most of these things are due simply to the system of laws with which I invested the universe."

He was getting into his stride now, and she was too over-awed to interrupt.

"When I made the waters of life, I foresaw, but did not create, the prospect of atomic bombs. When your fathers erect a dam between two mountains, they do not even ask if that was why I made the river. They stop the flow. They halt time. They also bring into being the faint chance of its bursting. They blame Me, of course, for the great calamity which ensues. My fault, as usual."

He mused for a moment, pulling at his beard, like Rasputin in a certain photograph.

"I gave monkeys speech and made the possibility of man. I also gave you the power of creation and hoped you were tall enough to bear the responsibility. You make your own successors and you are cruel to them. You take the spark of magic I gave and you shape it for your amusement. I give you lungs – it is you who give yourselves cancer. I make ecstasy possible, it is you who use it to go mad. There are no freaks of nature. You, you – you give birth to monsters – you offer the milk of your soul for stray demons to lap."

6.

"I am not mad," the girl said to herself.

"I am not mad," said the Training Officer, using his left hand to cross the fingers of the other hand.

"You are not mad," God told them. "But you will be, when you feel the eternal void crackling round your heads." He touched them both lightly, and they felt a new kind of beauty flowing into their hearts.

"How did the devil come into being?" God asked. "By

pride, as theology says? He was originally an angel. Some say he was originally a rival God. But whichever of us created the world – the Devil or I – which one put the seed of rebellion in the other, and why? Did we have need of an enemy? Or was it an inevitable outcome – the summons back to chaos?"

His eyes fell for a moment. "I have read the Bible, you know. I have also skipped through the Koran, the Analects of Confucius, the Rig-Veda, the Tripitaka, the Granth, the Book of Mormon – and sometimes the Daily Mirror. I wrote none of them," he added sadly. "I merely looked at what I had done and I was pleased. I was happy with my handiwork. I considered it all well done and I permitted myself a quiet smile."

"All that," he continued, "in only six days. According to tradition, I rested on the seventh. When, then, was the devil made? While I slept, perhaps? He was dreamed up by Adam and Eve who wanted to be God too." He sighed heavily. "Oh I never banished them from the Garden of Eden, you know. That hackneyed old story was put about by their family. I wanted to keep them but ... they broke out. They escaped."

He leaned slightly to His right and spoke over his shoulder. "When was that, Michael?"

"It was seven minutes past seven," came the cold civil reply. "On the first Sabbath. They found out what they were not ready to know." The voice of the archangel paused a moment as if he had a struggle to say it. "They hid in the shadow, under my wings."

God shook his head and moaned. "I would have given them Will when the time was ripe. Instead of which ..." his voice trailed off.

Michael's head popped up, over God's right shoulder. "They nicked it."

7.

God gave the Training Officer one of his sullen stares. "Could you have done better?" He asked with a slight touch of contempt.

The man's eyes tried to look humble, but he couldn't

quite hide that little green glint. God caught a glimpse of it. God drew Himself up. "All right," He said with greater dignity than General de Gaulle. "I'll step down."

"Oh, you mustn't do that!"

"I'll take a sabbatical then."

"Where would you go?"

"Too far to be any trouble." God grinned. "Don't you worry, my son. If I give you the Golden Chariot, I don't intend to be a back-seat driver!"

"But who – who – would be your substitute?"

"You, of course. Though I don't like the word substitute – shall we say 'understudy'? Now, now, now, don't sulk! I've been an understudy myself countless times. I once took the part of a cat, in the stage musical. Nobody ever guessed. I once became a bull, just like Zeus, but to save the life of a foolish matador. I've been King for a day, and once – just to teach myself a lesson in humility – I worked as a civil servant in the French Prefecture at Mâçon. "

"Shall I be able to do all the things that You can do?"

"Well, you can't change from man to woman and back."

"I wasn't thinking of that."

"And I won't let you make more than one visitation per week, earth time."

"I had no intention."

"Then what were you thinking of?" God looked at him for a moment and smiled. "Ah," he sighed. "You want to make all men love each other and bring about universal peace!" He shook his head and his hair shimmered with eternal hi-lights. "I have never been able to bring that about myself."

It seemed for a moment that the Almighty was lost in thought. Here and there all through the cosmos there was an outburst of subdued mutterings as God's words were made into realities. "I wish you well," He said eventually, and dusk turned into dawn.

"I wish you very well. I would not for the life of me wish to discourage you. But take a tip from someone older, and don't get mixed up in religion!"

Angels in white carried God on their wings. It was visiting day and his mother had baked Him a cake. They glided along the empty corridors as if they were Renaissance Popes riding on a sea of fluffy ostrich feathers. He elevated His hands and sent invisible rays of pure God-Power into all the cells and wards and treatment rooms.

The young girl stopped trying to kill herself with the scrubbing brush. It seemed as if something scampered away from her and hid itself inside the shielded light-bulb. The girl herself began singing.

The young man stopped the endless sexual game. Once again, it seemed that something darted across his blankets and coiled itself up inside an ancient slipper. The boy himself smiled and said "Hello," in all directions.

Every patient turned to his neighbours, even those who had never uttered a word since they were born. They fell to discussing the nature of truth.

The doctors withdrew. The nurses stepped back. They were frightened. They were struck with awe. One or two of them decided it was the last straw and sat down on the floor. The thing from the light-bulb took shelter in them at once. The thing from the ragged slipper glided unnoticed up a doctor's rectum. And there were others, hundreds of others: an animal here, an insect there, along with scissors and hot coals. They all sought out their new quarters.

"And the first shall be last," mused God, causing rain in the Sahara. "And the last shall be first!"

The young trainee stared at the Training Officer as he floated in thin air and radiated shimmering beams of light. It was like the Bernini sculpture in St Peter's, as she floated upward into His arms. "Let there be light!" He commanded.

"My name is Lucy," she replied.

And in that loving, God shut the mouths of all Freedom Fighters. He struck all bigots dumb and took away the tongues of every radical politician He could find. Priests fell silent. Freemasons bulged at the eyes. Occult orders burned the documents attesting to their authentic origins and superb lineage.

"These are your parameters," said God. After all, He was the first scientist. "There shall be silence everywhere. He who hates or harms his neighbour, shall have no neighbours. Tongues are finished. Noses are in. Every seventh day, the whales will give a concert."

His voice lifted. It grew dark over Geneva. He raised his clenched fist. Flies throughout the world fell flat on their backs.

"No one shall ever speak the truth again. I forbid it."

A thousand hostile creeds crumbled into sand.

"You may only *be* truth. You may only *live* truth. And to that end you must direct your will."

And then, true to his own decree, God shut up.

Death died. The old life ended. The epoch of love began, and the world hit on a new way of showing the date. That is why, on the seventh day of the seventh month, they blow the Ram's horn and start the Jubilee – spot on the seventh hour.

# Blessed Molly

*Vagabond: a homeless wanderer who is
often without money or other means of
support. Nomad: a person who moves his
home to pursue his livelihood or follow his
flocks to new pasture.*

*1.*

Not far from the centre of any great city, there is the 'hot
quarter' or the 'red-light district'. Have you never wondered
why they develop at those particular spots? In London, for
example, the name of the district is Soho. Ask anyone. They
will speak of the exotic eating places first and pretend that
these are the most important charm. Then they'll tell you
about the sleazy cinemas, the girls, and the vice trade. Of
course, you can pick up girls in several other places too:
Earl's Court, for example, or King's Cross. But the hub of
the wheel, so to speak, is definitely that one square mile
called Soho.

If you visit Paris, then you'll find several areas, just as in
London, but the most famous of all lies in the shadow of
that imposing basilica called 'Le Sacré Coeur'. The district
itself is called Pigalle. Here there are the famous theatres: Le
Moulin Rouge, Le Lido and so on. Here are the same sleazy
cinemas, the same video shops, and the same women. But
there is another trap for tourists – there are more drag
queens about. So before you make a deal, check their
inventory. If you renegue on a harlot then all hell will be let
loose.

Now it seems to be quite the same wherever one goes –
Hamburg, Rome, Madrid, or even Zurich. I say "even
Zurich" because the Swiss are not very much into sex. I

think it's the altitude. They are not very much into anything, as far as one can see, apart from themselves, and jewellery. The two things go together quite nicely. On the streets of the cities, even in the red-light district, there are so many diamonds on display you'd think it was Christmas! And you can watch the Swiss men looking, always looking, and finally deciding that it's cheaper to do it yourself.

The facts about these special districts are very simple. You know that ghost stories or folk-tales linger for centuries? For example, an English scholar called T.C. Lethbridge went to search for a legendary giant said to be close to an Iron Age camp at Wandlebury, near to Cambridge. To his surprise, he unearthed a set of three hill carvings ... one of them was a Sun God some 120 feet high! It has been dated to 200 B.C. Well, all the red-light districts seem to date back to inns where travellers used to stop for rest and amusement. Isn't that odd? The girls have continued the same trade for centuries, even though travel has speeded up and there is no need for stop-over points.

There are usually ghost stories too. Whores often lured their clients to a place of theft and death. That and the fact that the women themselves always stood a greater chance of being murdered by sheer sexual ferocity. You'll often find a church dedicated to Mary Magdalen, or else everyone knows that there are the remains of a graveyard. At any rate, I comfort myself that this is why my youngest son used to think that a brothel was a kind of spicy soup. He learned better as he got older, but can still be quite excited by the word 'Mulligatawny'. I tried to explain that this was actually a soup, and the Tamil name meant 'fire water'. But I don't think he believed me and he did some odd experiments of the 'Jekyll and Hyde' variety.

In many ways, of course, red-light districts are essential. Old men go there to ward off senility. Young men go there to lose their cherry and find some courage. The 'in-crowd' goes there too – it's so naughty and daring! But then of course, they are all quite lonely too. We all have dreams, you see, but we seldom work-out correctly what would satisfy them. When they don't believe in anything, they turn everything into a spree. Clearly, if they were not starving, they would not go to such great lengths to seek joy. So you see, despite the facade, they are all lonely at heart. You must have noticed how they always cough before they speak. There are balls of furry fear in their throat. They wipe their nose frequently too, as if the truth gave them hay-fever.

In a factory where dyeing and spinning are done, women can observe colour even in a single fibre. To you and me these little tufts of fluff would all be white. "Oh no," they say. "That one's rose, this one's duck-egg blue, and that one hasn't taken up the dye." It's quite amazing. They say that it's just the same with 'noses' – those people whose delicate sense of smell can pick out the separate components of exquisite perfumes.

## 2.

I mention all this because it is exactly like that with 'the girls' of a red-light district as regards 'men'. One glance at anything in trousers and they can tell what he wants and whether he's dangerous. They make mistakes, of course. But then, so do most film-stars vis-à-vis their choice of husbands! But it does make one wonder rather if these red-light areas haven't built up some sort of special power or magnetic aura. I mean to say – centuries of sex without love ... it must have *some* effect.

Men are a bit silly, you know. When they get the hunger, they only need to feed it once a night. On the age-old principle of "they're no different from me", every one of them believes that a woman feels just the same as he does. So if he finds her sexy, she must want to be crushed. This is why most men make love as if they were ploughing a rocky field.

On exactly the same grounds, and any tart will confirm it, many clients believe that a woman can make love only once a night. As a result, they expect to pay her a whole night's wage, i.e., one seventh of a weekly salary. Now if you were a Jezebel, would you tell the truth? Not on your life! You'd just make sure they enjoyed it and act out the myth. That's how you get your 'regulars' – the clients who seek you out specially. It's a bit awkward if they see you saying farewell to another man, but you can always explain that he only wanted a 'quickie'.

Now daft sods like that are called 'oncers', in the

language of bawds. Quite similar in a way are the 'nevers', that is to say, what you and I might call 'virgins'. Although, when you get down to brass tacks, it's extremely unusual to relate the word virgin to a boy. I suppose that's because male virginity had no political value – and no bearing on who was the father of some important baby. A question of heritage and land, rather than the hymen. Strictly speaking, a male can be a virgin only in the sense that he has not yet entered a woman. If we are talking about a boy who is gay, then I suppose the point can be stretched to say he has not been entered either.

But he might have been having orgasms for years! But then too, so might a girl, I dare say. There's the familiar method of tickling the clitoris, though it often causes tennis elbow. Then there's a little known type of dildo, or imitation dick, which works on the principle of a balloon. In a state of total collapse, it is 'threaded' past the hymen, then inflated, and then agitated by means of a thin stick. I think it is called a 'lollipop'.

Anyway, the word virgin does seem odd when used to describe men. The ladies refer to them as 'nevers'. A Never can be very good money, even better than a Oncer. If he's youngish, he is usually brought along by an elder brother, or by a gang of friends. Very often, it is a birthday present, and they ask you to lay-on the works: champagne, some chocolate biscuits and all the rest! Well, for a booking of that quality, he mustn't catch you at it on your bit of street. That would break his little heart. He has stars in his eyes usually, and you try not to piss on them.

With a Never, you too have got to play the little innocent. So you take off your war-paint, and pretend to be knitting socks for refugees, all alone in your prim, modest room. Well, I mean to say, it takes time to hide the whips and the handcuffs and the nun's costume! And time is money. If they want you to play Snow White for a Sleeping Prince, it's best not to have the Seven Dwarves under the bed. Therefore it is pricey. Also it is rather sweet and most of the girls like doing it.

Oncers and Nevers apart, most of your clients are 'gloves'. That is to say, they are not remotely interested in your name or your personality. They just want to use you and then forget. They want to borrow your body for thirty minutes. You are an accessory, like free air at a garage. You are just an aid for tossing off and they chuck you in the pedal-bin straight after. That's why you ask for your money first.

It doesn't actually do a whole lot of good for your ego, you realise. It isn't easy, is what I mean. When all's said and done, you're a woman – even if you've gone commercial. But their attitude is: I've got some hot sperm burning a hole in my scrotum and you'll do as a fire bucket. My God! Whoever called it 'Love for Sale'? Love doesn't enter into it. As far as love is concerned, they might just as well use a recently strangled ferret, a pound of warm liver, or a hole drilled in a tree.

### 3.

You've all heard of the clubs in Port Said, where women let themselves get shagged by a donkey. Anyone who has passed through the Suez Canal knows about it. Especially the soldiers. But how many know about that place in Paris where you can watch a man fucking a piglet?

Yes. I agree! It makes me feel sick too. Not my cup of tea, I tell you frankly. Nor yours either, I suppose. But we live in a strange world, in which strange things go on. That particular show is one of the most popular in Paris. The crowds come in droves. In the tourist season, you have to book a month in advance or buy tickets on the black market. Stranger still, there is a list as long as your arm of candidates ready to perform the active role on stage! Quite disgusting.

In Hamburg of course, it is a kind of sexual circus act which draws in the crowds. The man and woman, both naked, dangle by their hooked knees from two trapezes. There is a full build-up with a roll of drums, a spotlight and a Master of Ceremonies. He explains in lurid detail the unbearable agony that would follow a bad aim. "One, Two, Three", he counts, and everyone holds his breath. Then they set them swinging from opposite corners of the theatre roof. They hurtle together like a couple of clock pendulums (or is it penduli?) and – with any luck – she is impaled on his throbbing prick.

216

On average it takes a whole minute before the applause breaks out. Men and women in the audience are too stunned, too absorbed. They think what might have been. It takes time to gasp, ooff, and then to scream "encore". The couple do their best – the show must go on. But hanging from hooks is not the same as lying on a mattress. You don't have the solid basis from which to make your thrusts and parries, if you follow. So they writhe together for a few seconds, like a pair of frying snakes. Then they burst a hidden pouch of spurious semen which wangs its contents over the entire audience. Very few people notice that it is cold.

Money for old rope, as they say.

Other places, other customs, and different prices. When you really get down to it, everything depends on what you are looking for, doesn't it? Whatever it is, they can cater for you. Relief? Company? One hour of oblivion? You're men, mere amateurs. They're women, the experts.

You should see their elegant flats – and how much they look like gypsy caravans. Lots of red, plenty of mirrors, and tassels everywhere. I knew one chap who described them as tumours stitched all over with sequins. Each girl adds her own little touches. These are often based on a favourite film. Or else they involve dolls from childhood and photos of her dad, her husband, or even her child.

However well she does it – no matter how pleased you are – you cannot really forget that you have only hired her and that she belongs, body and soul, to someone else.

Long, red nails like a vixen. Huge eyes, accented to look like an infant animal. Long legs like an Amazon gold medallist. Breasts as full as ripe melons. And a face like that of a pork butcher wondering how much he dare ask for his sausages.

No. There's nothing wrong with sex. Not when it's natural and dew-fresh. To run through the midnight grass with bare feet – oh, that's a pleasure. To roll down the sides of the mountain locked in an embrace. That is our privilege, our right and often our ruin. Just as microbes have adapted so that they can use us as their prey – so other entities are parasitic on our negative emotions. Quite obviously, I am not against sex. I'm all for it. As King Lear says: "Let copulation thrive!" But there are unnatural things that we

217

can do, and after aeons of doing them, you can understand that the glory of sex turns sour. Debauchery is like tainted food. It causes the stomach to digest itself and the brain to welcome blight.

### 4.

She was very young. The girls found her wandering the streets. At first they thought she was illicit competition and they forced her to move on. Then they thought she might be a lesbian looking for their services. It took time for it to dawn on them that she was just lost and desperate. That very night, when the music stopped and the lights went out, she had decided to jump off a bridge. She wasn't lying either. When it comes to suicide, the eyes do not lie. So they took her to a cafe. They wrote down the names of hostels, the address of some nuns who helped girls like her, and even suggested that she go to the police. Anything – anything was better than that.

"Can't I be one of you?" she asked.

It was the one question they had all dreaded hearing. New recruits, brought in by 'The Man', are made to feel at home, in a cordial, sporty way. They are hardened already. The pain has been long forgotten. But new girls – new in the sense that they had never done it before – were like reliving it all over again. It was a universal grief along all the streets.

Now the girls are better than any pimp or manager at noticing talent. They can see at a glance whether someone's got it or not. They know if she should be a waitress, a maid, a schoolgirl or a 'Mae West' type. They know if she can 'peel', or be a stripper. They can tell if she should just check the hats at the entrance or keep the toilets clean. In other terms, if men want gold, they are the geologists who can say where they should dig.

But they have hearts too. After all the things they have done in their lives, they don't think twice about it. But there's something about a new girl, just the right age, that rips your heart out. If it was what she really wanted, then they would have to help her do it. But there wasn't one of them who didn't wonder whether they could – just for once – make a fairy-tale come true. Hell was all around. They had

had enough of it. Just for once in their lives, they wanted some puffy clouds and a cherub or two. Like the inmates of a death camp ... if one got away it was a triumph.

They hid her. In spite of the dangers, they smuggled her off the streets and out of sight. The sisterhood knew, but there wasn't one of them who would tell the pimps. If anyone saw her, by accident, then one of them would say she was her sister and the rest would back her up. They'd wink heavily, letting The Man know that he mustn't give the show away. That would do the trick. It was one of the holds that The Man held over them – the threat to expose everything to their family.

If the police took an interest, they would lie about her age and give a display of nervous strain. The cops were rarely a problem. They did what they had to do but only when someone higher up reminded them to do it. Beside which, very few of them held a grudge against the girls. It was The Men they wanted to get their hands on. One way or another, there was strength in numbers, and so they would keep the pimps quiet and the cops calm.

In the meantime, they would try to work something out. The last thing they wanted was to teach her their trade. Somehow or other, she was their joint symbol who embodied all their dashed hopes and bankrupt lives. They would collect money every week and all of them would donate something. She would go to a school. She would train for something else. She would dress like a nice girl and speak like a lady.

They even prayed for her. Oh yes, hookers do pray, and I have no evidence to suggest that they are not heard. They didn't go to the church of St Mary Magdalen though. They'd stand out a bit too much. They went to the huge cathedral where they were unseen among the steady flow of Americans and Japanese.

Only when they could, of course. Round about midday.

## 5.

The boy's mates all called him Bath. It was a nickname and a friendly one. His real name was Matthew which had always been shortened to Matt. Then, by a sort of poetic back formation, it changed into bath-mat. Finally, in that secret society sort of way that boys, and men, cultivate, they dropped the original Matt and simply called him Bath. It's what boys do. It's all part of the mystic *esprit de corps* and horse-play. It was one of the few ways that you could get into a gang. If you didn't get the right nickname then you weren't one of the lads. It was as simple as that. So, in fact, he was very happy to be called Bath, though it got on his nerves when people asked why. "There is no why," he snorted. "That's how it is, that's all!"

Ah well, you know what lads are. Or maybe you don't? Just take my word for it: they knew that he hadn't lost his cherry yet. They did not use the word virgin except to describe the girl they were in love with from a distance. Not one of them knew, nor ever found out, why she was that much more desirable if she were a virgin. Perhaps she would not see just how clumsy they were? Or perhaps she could not compare one with others?

But as regards a male, each one could remember – vividly – the stage when they hadn't yet made it. When you're very young, you're just eager to know more and to be pointed in the right direction. Then when you're a little older, you smarten up. You spray your shirt with beer mixed with dad's after-shave. After that though – you hide it. You feign indifference and put on a show of not being all that interested. But rather than be thought queer, you might even hint that you had a nasty accident with your bike once.

So nobody picked on him or made him feel ridiculous. He was just the last one, that's all. There has to a last one. Every gang has a 'first'. Just to prove that he'd done it, he usually does it where the rest can see. They can't see it all, of course. That would have put him off. But he made sure they saw her knickers and his tool. From that moment on he was the King, the Champion, the local Hero. He ruled by his smile. His smile said it all.

Then a weird thing happened. At the moment of supreme triumph, when the gang would have eaten out of his hand, he appeared to lose interest. Impressing them and giving a boost to his own reputation seemed much less important now. Among the girls his eye lit upon one who was somehow special. No-one else could see it. She could be the plainest. They always thought she was the daftest. But she would beat them. She would win. Within no time at all, she had him living with her. That finished it for them. Whether he got married or whether he came back – that was it! He had sacrificed his status. He was no longer the cock of the midden.

Well, as I say, one by one they screwed up their courage and sallied forth to lose their cherries. Only Bath hadn't yet made it.

"Do you want to make it?" they asked him.

"I suppose so."

"Is that all? You only suppose so?"

"Well then, yes. Of course I do." He grinned bashfully and there was a sort of shame in his eyes. "Yes," he repeated. "I wish to God I dared."

"With a girl?" asked Ralph, whose father had been a commando just to disguise a slight delicate trait.

"Even with your grandmother," he replied.

They would never abandon Bath. Even if he turned out to be, you know, queer – they wouldn't let him down. He was one of their lot. He could count on them. No question of that. But that wasn't why they were grilling him. He was the last. He was the only one who hadn't breached the barrel and drunk the healing draught. It was a matter of gang pride and they all owed it to him to help. He could be their mascot, if that's how he was made. But they wanted, for his own sake, to give that rousing cheer and wave his underpants out of a bus window. After all, he'd cheered each of them along.

"Is it the priest?" asked another lad, who confessed the most lurid things every Friday night.

"Are you deformed?" asked someone else, much more down to earth.

"Do you ...? Are you ...? Have you ...?" Tried a third in a warped voice.

"I'm just too fucking shy," he said.

They didn't let on how relieved they felt.

They all shut up and began a 'group ponder'. Despite the boasting and the blather, they were all still a bit shy too. According to the latest wisdom on the streets, guys who were shy ran the serious risk of ending up impotent. Like the holy name of God, that's a word one never pronounces. Therefore, none of them every dwelt on the subject. So much so that they weren't quite sure what it meant. Neil had heard in history that King Harold's army was impotent before the Norman long-bow. It would puzzle him all his life and make him think of quills and quivers!

Men are very gullible like that.

## 6.

When they arrived at the red-light district, there was a lot of nervous laughter, of course. But there wasn't one of them who didn't feel his backbone curling like a question mark and an unsettling sensation of congestion inside his underpants.

The girls did their thing though. They sidled close and under their breath they hinted at lewd things. One didn't know how to react. One couldn't be sure that one had heard them right. They retreated into a hamburger bar with red faces and shaking hands. They just ordered cold drinks and started jabbering all at the same time.

"Hello, boys!"

It was the kind of voice that has wrecked ships and brought down drunken Rugby players. A sort of scarlet velvet, tightly stretched, with peekaboo slits in.

She looked at them, all gawping and dumb. She eased her coat back and let them have it from both barrels. They could not have been more paralysed if she had been Terminator 8!

"You're pooling your pocket money, right?" She batted her long eyelashes and made a wind of change sweep through the open necks of their shirts. "Which of you is the lucky one tonight?"

Six fingers pointed. Bath was just about ready to accept the electric chair.

"How old are you?" she asked with great gentility.

"Tw.." he began and stopped. "Niii.." he stopped again. He looked at his pals like a fish short of water.

"Eighteen," they said in unison, all standing slightly to one side and nodding like car salesmen.

The lady – she was every inch a lady – in her high-heeled shoes, her net stockings, and her sequin dress – the lady regarded him very knowingly. She slid her arm around his waist and let her fingers rest, ever so gently, on his buttock – the left one, to be precise.

"You're very big for your age, sport. I bet you're an amateur boxer, aren't you?"

Bath found that his tongue had swollen as if stung by a bee or rendered useless by an Amazonian dart loaded with curare. He couldn't formulate words or construe any grammar while the lady's fingers did – er – what the lady's fingers were doing.

"You're real hunky," she told him. Did that mean he had a disease? "I want you to let your friends go home. I want you to saunter slowly round this block four times."

"How much do we owe you?" asked Ralph, taking out a squashed bundle of notes.

She smiled at them sweetly and gave them free tickets for the porno cinema. "Be sure and sit together," she warned, "The aisles are swarming with rats."

After they had gone, she patted his arm in a motherly fashion. "Are you a nice boy?" she asked him seriously. "I don't mean this, tonight. Things like this are only natural after all. I mean – do you hurt people? Do you mean what you say? Have you got a heart?"

He stared at her in some confusion. "Do you mean, have I got a disease?"

She laughed loudly and gave him a hug. "Don't you look at me that way, boy. I'm not the one. I'll tell you true though, I wouldn't have minded one little bit. No sir, not one little bit. You're a gorgeous fellah, d'you know that?"

He blinked at her, wondering if she was pulling his leg. "Do you mean that?" he asked simply.

"I not only mean it, honey, it's also true." She gave him a pat on his bottom so that he laughed too.

"You give it five minutes, honey. Then you go out and start walking, like I said. Anybody try to chat you up, you say 'No way', and walk on by." She cuddled him close. It was quite a thrill. But something about her manner spoke of love – real love.

"What is it?" he stammered, his heart beating like a rabbit's.

"I may be a bitch," she grinned, "but first and foremost, I'm a witch. And you, my lad, are going to see some real magic."

"What?" he gasped, believing her.

"Your most secret dream – come true."

The message travelled across town in two shakes of a lamb's tale. They must have done it with drums! It's a sneaky world down there. They are furtive about what they do and how they do it, but they're more efficient at it than the police! The plan was clear. The girl was to be got ready. She was to be sent off in a taxi. An ideal birthday gift had been found.

7.

She thought she was being given a trial – being sent on to the streets for her first job. She was terrified. They'd told her the formula of words to use. It sounded crazy to her. But they promised it was a code of the trade, a kind of in-talk known only to the ladies of the streets.

It had been raining heavily, but now it was just the finest of slight drizzle. More like a low cloud, really. Or a sea-mist rising across the mouth of the harbour. Men did look at her, of course. It was the district for looking. One asked her for a light – but that was the wrong signal. They'd told her, that would be a policeman in disguise.

Then she saw him. Young like herself. Tall. And staring at her gormlessly. They'd said that it was up to her to make the first approach. One mustn't ever leave it to the client, they said. He may be shy and it's up to you to help him.

"Hello, Bath." she said.

It was what they'd told her to say. She was repeating the lines that they'd taught her. They'd also warned her that he might not reply. What they hadn't warned her about was his face – his handsome face.

"Why do they call you Bath?" she asked. That was the second thing she'd been told to ask. After that, she was on her own.

But that question was all that the lad needed. He was familiar with the lie of the land and could find his tongue to explain the mystery of his name. She laughed and told him it was ridiculous. He laughed and told her she was beautiful.

All unaware, they walked away from the tourist streets into alleys and shadows where few people lurk at night. She told him that she wasn't a prostitute yet – just a trainee. They told each other everything. All that they knew. They

stopped behind a broad tree in a tiny square, in the shadows of a glaring street lamp. Very delicately he kissed her. Even more delicately, she touched him – there, and felt the vibrant trembling of his soul.

They didn't know that this was making love. Not this mutual doting quest or this consent to expire. They didn't know either that two tramps were sprawling on a bench, a man and a woman, their heads touching as they occasionally drank from a bottle. Normally they wouldn't have made a comment. That sort of thing no longer held any interest for them. Surviving was far more pressing than the begetting of life.

"Are you seeing what I'm seeing?" he asked her hoarsely. He hadn't spoken all day. Neither had she. One of these days, she told him once, we'll just forget how. We'll have to make do with signals. That's when they'll take us away. But she was rigid. She was staring at the huge shadow thrown by the tree.

"I don't know what you're seeing, do I?" she hissed quite logically. "But what the hell is in that bottle?"

They sat up straight then. They ignored the near naked couple who were having it off against the tree – him making noises like a broken bellows and her going "Oh, ah, oo, oh!" as if she were being tattooed. They'd seen that often enough. Nobody ever worried about them, and they in their turn never took any notice. This time though, it was different. It was like the rain had turned to gold. Drops, flakes, discs, palettes of gold – all gliding down side to side like leaves in a lullaby.

And the youngsters were up to their knees in gold. His little arse was gold. Her breasts were gold. And hidden wings were swirling up the gold. The whole scene was something happening in a glass dome that made a snowstorm when turned in the hands.

"I love you," they heard one of them gasp. "And I love you," the other gasped back. Impossible to tell which was which. And the birds sang.

"I swear to God, the birds are singing," sighed the old man.

"Damn me if you ain't right," replied the old lady.

And for the first time in seven years, they held hands.

There is no point in spoiling it all by telling you the

details of the rest of their life. They were young, so they lived long, and they never forgot their friends. They often visited them and they all went to a local restaurant once a year. She brought her first baby for them to look at, and every one of them cuddled it and cried. She was their darling, their mascot, their good-luck charm. He was proof that knights in shining armour do exist, even if they are shy.

The friendship went on, even during the years after the 'girls' lost their charms and they left the red-light district to be barmaids or office cleaners. One even became a nun, in an order that ate well and had comfy beds. Another had her throat cut by a john who was ashamed after he had fucked her. "I love you and I hate you," they heard him scream. The same old conflict caused not by Christ, but the friends of Christ.

They lived happily ever after – isn't that how it goes? Well it'll do, anyway. That couple of old tramps, they often went back to the park and slept beneath that tree. Even when he died of cold and she watched them take him away, she wiped her eyes, and drank from her bottle.

"Mine eyes have seen the glory of the coming of the Lord," she piped like a dusty flute. It was all she could think of to turn it into a funeral. But she was never cold again. For the rest of her days, she wondered what was special about her that she'd been allowed to see that invisible, mystic beauty. After that, they called her Blessed Molly, though nobody knew why.

---

*The Nightingales are singing near*
*The convent of the Sacred Heart ...*
T.S.Eliot, Sweeney Among the Nightingales

# Adieu

They say that a book should speak for itself. If it has been well written, there is no need for an epilogue. But here, at the end, it might be nice to speak direct: me to you. If you're happy in life, I'm glad. If you're miserable, I am sorry. Maybe you took a wrong turning? Perhaps you got on the wrong train? If your eyes are bleak, then I wrote this book for you.

I believe in the existence of evil. I know too that there are people, individuals and groups, who worship that evil. They are dangerous because they like to play on your fear. I am trying to teach you to be less afraid. Do-gooders should watch out. The subject has too strong a hold on them. They stray too close. Their fanatic faith makes them easy to trap. They set off meaning to root out evil, but so many do not come home. God does not help fools, any more than the Devil deals in justice.

Not enough policemen believe in evil, and far too many Social Workers do. In the Church of England, and elsewhere, the question of a personal devil is left to you to decide. It's as if they thought he was elected, and you could vote whichever way you want. I admire sincerity. I respect faith. But neither bring you the power or defence. I once met Jesus in a mental hospital. To play safe, should I have knelt before him? I met the Devil too. Should I have refused to treat him? I have also met priests, and would-be priests, who behave like butlers or secretaries ... the ones who are prouder and grander than the boss.

Indeed, one of the points of these stories is: some of your nicest neighbours might worship Satan. Their targets are rarely glamorous. After all, in the eyes of God, the Prince of Wales is just as worthy as one of the homeless souls in the city centre. He just makes it more obvious. As do journalists, of course, who love to accuse others of things they have done themselves.

I know of Satanists who go to church every Sunday, just to put others off the scent. They are not afraid. They do not tremble at the altar and gladly cross themselves. Holy Water does not scald them either. Don't you know? They use pages from the Bible as toilet paper! They can manipulate disgust. Which is why it pays not to be namby-pamby!

The church once taught that the Earth was the centre of the universe. Is the church so right about everything else? Take care. Priests have sent more souls to mental hospital than psychiatrists were able to cope with. In spite of that, I do believe in God and a life beyond this. I'm not asking you to join me. I've told you what I know. It is possible that my knowledge will help you. Spitting on it would only make you feel good for a moment or two. Right now you are the Judge, so let tell you about Magic. It is the ability to exert your divine Will. Just find out where it is kept.